MW01055210

RARÁMURI SOULS

Smithsonian Series in Ethnographic Inquiry
Ivan Karp and William L. Merrill, Series Editors

Ethnography as fieldwork, analysis, and literary form is the distinguishing feature of modern anthropology. Guided by the assumption that anthropological theory and ethnography are inextricably linked, this series is devoted to exploring the ethnographic enterprise.

ADVISORY BOARD

Richard Bauman *(Indiana University)*, Gerald Berreman *(University of California, Berkeley)*, James Boon *(Princeton University)*, Stephen Gudeman *(University of Minnesota)*, Shirley Lindenbaum *(New School for Social Research)*, George Marcus *(Rice University)*, David Parkin *(University of London)*, Roy Rappaport *(University of Michigan)*, Renato Rosaldo *(Stanford University)*, Annette Weiner *(New York University)*, Norman Whitten *(University of Illinois)*, and Eric Wolf *(City University of New York)*

RARÁMURI SOULS

*Knowledge and Social Process
in Northern Mexico*

William L. Merrill

Smithsonian Institution Press
Washington, D.C.   London

© 1988 Smithsonian Institution
All rights reserved
Printed in the United States of America

Edited by Michelle K. Smith
Designed by Linda McKnight

LIBRARY OF CONGRESS CATALOGING-IN-PUBLICATION DATA

Merrill, William L.
  Rarámuri souls
  (Smithsonian series in ethnographic inquiry)
  Bibliography: p.
  Includes index.
  1. Tarahumara Indians—Religion and mythology.
2. Tarahumara Indians—Social life and customs.
3. Indians of Mexico—Chihuahua—Religion and
mythology.
  I. Title. II. Series.
  F1221.T25.147 1988   299'.78   87–62623
  ISBN 087474-684-1
British Library Cataloguing-in-Publication Data is
available.

∞The paper used in this publication meets the
minimum requirements of the American National
Standard for Permanence of Paper for Printed
Library Materials Z39.48-1984.

Frontispiece: The Rarámuri homeland.
After Pennington 1983: 277.

All photographs were taken by the author except where
noted in the caption.

For Cecilia

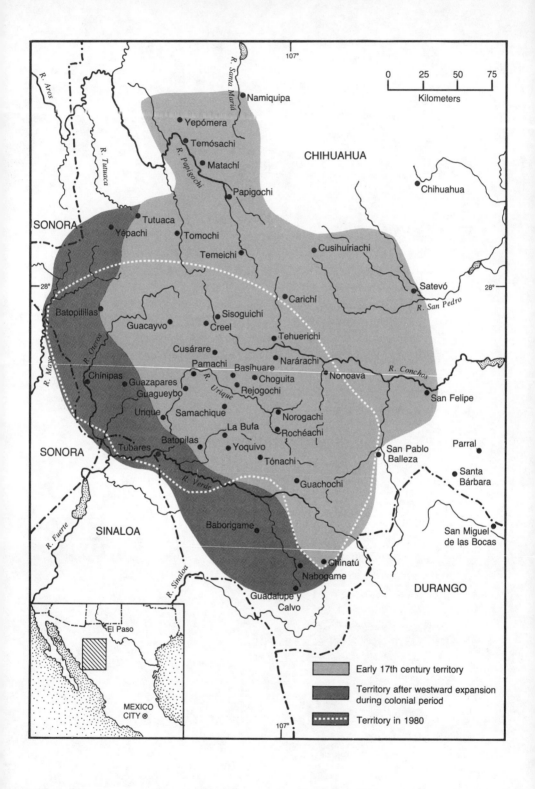

0	25	50	75

Kilometers

R. Aros

R. Santa María

107°

• Namiquipa

CHIHUAHUA

• Yepómera

• Temósachi

R. Papigochi

• Matachí

• Chihuahua

• Papigochi

R. Tutuaca

SONORA

• Tutuaca

Yépachi •

• Tomochi

• Cusihuíriachi

Temeichi •

• Satevó

28°   28°

R. San Pedro

• Carichí

• Batopilillas

• Sisoguichi

R. Oteros

Guacayvo •   • Creel

• Tehuerichi

• Cusárare

• Narárachi

R. Conchos

Pamachi •   Basíhuare

• Chinipas   • Nonoavá

Choguita

R. Urique

• Guazapares   • Rejogochi

R. Mayo

Guagueybo •   • San Felipe

• Urique   • Samachique   • Norogachi

La Bufa •   • Rochéachi

SONORA   • Batopilas   • Parral

Tubares •   • Yoquivo   San Pablo

• Tónachi   Balleza •   • Santa

R. Verde   Bárbara

• Guachochi

SINALOA   San Miguel

• Baborigame   de las Bocas

R. Fuerte

R. Sinaloa   • Chinatú

Nabogame •   DURANGO

Guadalupe y •
Calvo

El Paso

MEXICO
CITY ⊙

■ Early 17th century territory

■ Territory after westward expansion
during colonial period

⋯⋯⋯ Territory in 1980

107°

CONTENTS

LIST OF
ILLUSTRATIONS

RARÁMURI
ORTHOGRAPHY

The Rarámuri speak three distinct dialects, distinguished from one another on the basis of phonology, syntax, and vocabulary. Miller (1983:table 8) designates these dialects as Western, Eastern, and Southern. Miller's Eastern Rarámuri is labelled by Burgess (1984) as the Central Dialect and is the dialect spoken by the Rarámuri among whom I lived.

The phonemes of Eastern, or Central, Rarámuri are as follows (Pennington 1983:276):

voiceless stops and affricate:	*p, t, č* (represented here as *ch*), *k*, and *ʾ* (glottal stop)
voiced stops:	*b, g*
voiceless fricatives:	*s, h*
nasals:	*m, n*
liquids:	*r* (flap), *l*
semi-vowels:	*w, y*
vowels:	*i, e, a, o, u*

The values of the vowels are very close to those in Spanish. Stress is phonemic. For more detailed discussions of Rarámuri phonology, see Brambila ([1980]), Lionett (1972), and Burgess (1984).

RARÁMURI
KNOWLEDGE

Evil, for them, is not sin. To the Tarahumara, there is no sin: evil is loss of consciousness. The high philosophical problems are more important to the Tarahumara than the precepts of our Western morality.

For the Tarahumara are obsessed with philosophy; and they are obsessed to the point of a kind of physiological magic; with them there is no such thing as a wasted gesture, a gesture that does not have an immediate philosophical meaning. The Tarahumara become philosophers in exactly the way a small child grows up and becomes a man; they are philosophers by birth.

Antonin Artaud, avant garde French writer and dramaturgist, composed this glowing testimony in 1936, following a month's stay among the Rarámuri, or Tarahumara, as he and other outsiders have known them (1976: 10–11; cf. Schneider 1984).[1] For Artaud, his journey from Paris to the Rarámuri's remote mountain homeland in northern Mexico was a pilgrimage. He came in search of the primeval principles of the cosmos with which Western society had lost contact, believing that the Indians of Mexico, especially less assimilated groups like the Rarámuri, could provide him access.

The Rarámuri did not disappoint him. They allowed Artaud to participate in their peyote ceremony and, by his account, revealed to him their esoteric knowledge of the universe. He portrayed their lives as pervaded by philosophy. From his perspective, philosophy in general and Rarámuri philosophy specifically did not exist exclusively in the form of thoughts and words but was immanent in the world, embedded in objects and nonverbal acts. Thus, he argued, the two-pointed, sometimes white, sometimes red headbands of the Rarámuri revealed "that *within* the Tarahumara race the

I

Male and Female principles of Nature exist simultaneously, and that the Tarahumara have the benefit of their combined forces. In short," he continued, "they wear their philosophy on their heads. . . ." With their philosophy so objectively present, Artaud could dismiss the claim of many Rarámuri "that this arrangement is the result of chance, and that they use the headband simply to hold their hair in place" (1976: 8, 11; original emphasis).

As this example suggests, many of Artaud's interpretations of the Rarámuri are suspect, but it must be remembered that his intentions were primarily artistic, not ethnographic (Schneider 1984; Hayman 1977). His essays provide some interesting observations on Rarámuri life at the time of his visit, but his insights into the culture are colored by his efforts to achieve personal enlightenment and confirmation of his own elaborate conception of the universe. His portrayal of the Rarámuri as philosophers should be regarded in this light, as partly a reflection of what they said and did and partly a product of his theory of philosophy and the universe, which demanded that they be. At the same time, by attributing to the Rarámuri a devotion to philosophical rather than material concerns, Artaud hoped to challenge the equation of material poverty with lack of civilization that the Mexican government was using to justify its efforts to assimilate the Rarámuri and other Native groups.

While his desire to defend the Rarámuri's interests is laudable, Artaud's assessment of their philosophical inclinations contrasts dramatically with the conclusions of many anthropologists who have investigated this area of Rarámuri life. Undoubtedly the most radical stance on these issues was taken by Robert Zingg, who in 1930 and 1931 undertook nine months of fieldwork among the Rarámuri in cooperation with Wendell Bennett (Bennett and Zingg 1935). About the same time as Artaud was praising the Rarámuri as philosophers, Zingg (1937) characterized them as "Philistines," an eminently practical people with a materialistic but realistic orientation to a fairly inhospitable natural environment. Such an orientation, he suggested, obviated the development of the "higher interests" of mankind, like art, music, and literature. Their indigenous religion was remarkable only in its "unrelieved drabness" (1942: 88) and was accompanied by a mysticism "so crude as to be scarcely rationalized into simple intelligibility" and by dreams that were "crass, material, and commonplace" (1937: 16). For Zingg, even their personalities were "wooden," and he found no "evidence of tenderness, affection, or caressing" (1937: 14–15). Only through drinking and participation in the colorful ceremonies introduced by Catholic missionaries were they able, he felt, to escape the dreary world provided by their culture.

when, as in the Rarámuri case, intellectual activities have few centralized or institutionalized dimensions, often taking place in private. In the absence of readily accessible data and objective criteria for evaluation, whether Rarámuri theoretical knowledge should be characterized as simple or complex and the Rarámuri as philosophically inclined or not becomes largely a matter of personal perspective. In contrast, the extent of individual variation associated with this knowledge can be established more objectively, and here the findings of more recent studies confirm the conclusions of earlier work. Pastron (1977: 36), for example, reports the existence of a "relatively uniform and consistent corpus of notions and ideas" about witchcraft and shamanism but also areas of "substantial disagreement or controversy." I encountered essentially the same pattern in my research on Rarámuri theoretical knowledge.

EXPLORING RARÁMURI KNOWLEDGE

My interest in northern Mexico began in the summer of 1974. I had just completed my first year of graduate school in anthropology at the University of Michigan and was spending the summer in Mexico studying Spanish in anticipation of beginning research in South America the following year. I had enrolled in a language school in Cuernavaca where, as part of the course of instruction, students were encouraged to read extensively in Spanish about topics of personal interest to them. Scanning the shelves of the school's small library, I came across a copy of *Los Indios de México*, written by the Mexican journalist Fernando Benítez (1967). I took the first volume of the set to a corner of the school's garden and, surrounded by manicured lawns and flowering hibiscus, jacarandas, and colorines, I read for the first time about the rugged, arid north and the people who lived there.

When I returned to Ann Arbor in the fall, I reviewed the literature on northern Mexico and found that I was becoming increasingly intrigued by the area and particularly by the Rarámuri people. The Rarámuri held a number of attractions for me. For several years, I had been investigating the use of psychotropic plants by Native Americans, and the Rarámuri were one of the few American Indian groups to use peyote outside the context of the Native American Church. They also retained the Rarámuri language as their primary mode of communication, an important consideration since I was interested in investigating world view and religion through an indigenous language. In addition, the standard anthropological classification of culture areas included northern Mexico as part of North America, which had been of greater interest to me than either Mesoamerica or South America. Finally, the Rarámuri homeland is mountainous, straddling the continental divide of the Sierra Madre chain. The six years since I had left my home in the southern Appalachians of North Carolina and particularly my year in Michigan had left me yearning for uplifted terrain. Like Lévi-Strauss (1972: 333), "I prefer the mountains to the sea. . . ."

The following summer, my wife Cecilia Troop and I made a brief tour of Rarámuri country to talk with local people about the prospect of doing fieldwork and to determine if we liked the area enough to live there two years. On the whole their reactions and our impressions were positive, so in 1977 we returned to begin my doctoral dissertation research. To find a suitable location for research, we asked several other researchers, government officials, and Jesuit missionaries for their advice, which they freely gave, and we eventually settled on the Rarámuri community of Rejogochi.

Rejogochi sits along a small creek in the transitional zone between the uplands of Chihuahua's Sierra Madre and the deep canyons to the west, about fifty kilometers south of the railhead of Creel. Rev. Luis G. Verplancken, S. J., suggested this community as appropriate for our work, kindly introduced us to the residents, and assisted us in almost every other way imaginable. We were initially attracted to Rejogochi because an abandoned adobe house was available there, built several years before by workmen while constructing a Jesuit school for Rarámuri children. The house was in an advanced state of disrepair, with no roof or door and its mud walls eroding away under the assault of the Sierra's elements. In fact, when we arrived, it was being used as a pig pen. But it was the only potential residence in the area and, with considerable work, could be made habitable. After receiving permission from the residents of Rejogochi to use the house and conduct a research project there, we began settling in.

Almost all my firsthand knowledge of the Rarámuri comes from Rejogochi and nearby communities. I lived in Rejogochi for twenty-four months between 1977 and 1979 and for an additional seven months between 1981 and 1987. Cecilia joined me for all but five months of this period. Our son Benjamin was with us for two months in 1984, as was, in a sense, our daughter Luisa, who was born in 1984 soon after we left Rejogochi.

The research I intended to undertake for my dissertation was a study of Rarámuri world view and the way in which they dealt with logical problems like contradiction and paradox. A more immediate goal was to find a topic that would be appropriate for a *festschrift* being organized back in Ann Arbor for Professor Volney Jones, an ethnobotanist with whom I had worked closely

Figure 1. The Rejogochi valley. View looking north. A rancho fiesta sponsored by fourteen neighboring households on Día San Juan (June 24, 1981) to cure their maize fields and to celebrate the beginning of the summer rains. The woman waving the white banner accepts responsibility to sponsor the next year's fiesta from the current sponsor, who kneels before the crosses. To symbolize the transfer of responsibility, this year's sponsor later gives her successor the basket behind her containing traditional ritual foods. A matachine dancer, accompanied by violins and guitar, performs beside the women.

for several years. I learned almost immediately upon arriving in Rejogochi that, as other researchers had reported, the Rarámuri consume with gusto and great frequency intoxicating beverages that they prepare from maize and other plants. While most of Rarámuri culture was not yet available to us, Cecilia and I were beginning to be invited to drinking parties. By discovering how the people in Rejogochi explain the phenomenon of inebriation, I reasoned, I could produce an ethnobotanical study that simultaneously would get my research on Rarámuri world view under way.

Given the central place of drinking in Rarámuri life, I assumed that they must have developed an elaborate theory to explain the inebriation process. My initial attempts to elicit such a theory, however, proved fruitless because I phrased my questions in such a way that the focus was on the

Figure 2. A Rejogochi homestead. June 1981. The two houses are occupied by one family on the edge of its maize field. When the owner was troubled by dreaming of his dead mother the family abandoned the stone house on top of the hill, moving to the log cabin on the right. A goat corral and elevated chicken coop stand in front of the cabin. The owner built the house on the left when the local communally owned sawmill distributed surplus lumber. The wooden structure near the walls of the stone house is used by a neighboring household for storing their maize.

effect of alcoholic beverages on the body. Finally I happened to ask someone, "What do our souls do when we drink?" and I received the immediate response, "They go over there." After posing the same question to a number of other people, I concluded that the Rarámuri consider inebriation to result from the departure of their souls during drinking (Merrill 1978). In the process, I began to suspect that the concept of the soul was basic to Rarámuri world view, so I decided to investigate it more thoroughly.

I soon determined that I would learn nothing about souls by listening to conversations since the Rarámuri seldom say anything about souls in public. Like most explanatory knowledge among the Rarámuri, the concept of soul is not esoteric or secret, but it is transmitted in detail almost exclusively within households as elders attempt to respond to the questions of their younger relatives. Kennedy seems to have encountered a similar pattern among the Rarámuri with whom he worked. In the passage quoted earlier, Rodrigo of Uarárari told Kennedy that he knew nothing about theological or other theoretical matters because neither his parents nor grandparents had instructed him; in other words, he had no other access to such information.

The concept of soul is seldom mentioned in public partly because as basic explanatory information it is rarely appropriate to do so. The Rarámuri say, for example, "I got drunk yesterday," not "I got drunk yesterday because my principal soul found the smell of the beer I drank offensive and temporarily left my body." The statement without explanatory elaboration is sufficient, just as in American society "I got drunk at the party" does not require "because the alcohol I consumed interfered with my synaptic processes." In addition, the Rarámuri consider all knowledge about the universe to have been established at the beginning of the world and passed directly from God to the first Rarámuri people. People are reluctant to convey this knowledge publicly for fear they will be accused of distorting received wisdom or of setting themselves up as spokesmen for the others, which could be a serious breach in this egalitarian society.

By bringing up the topic when people were together, usually during drinking parties, I was able to generate some public discussions of the concept of soul, but the information I received was not entirely satisfactory. Typically I would be sitting with a group of men sharing beer during a break from work on some project. I would ask a question directed to no one in particular, one man would respond, and all the other men would agree with him. Later, after the group had dispersed to continue work, several different men would call me aside and point out that what I had been told earlier (to which they had agreed) was wrong. They would offer to provide me with the correct information but at another time because the topic was too important to discuss while drinking. I naively would arrive at their homes in the following days expecting Rarámuri world view to be revealed to me. Usually I would be told nothing unless I happened to find the person alone and even then the information tended to be brief and fragmented.

The Rarámuri display a unanimity of opinion in public that obscures the diversity of ideas they hold privately. Such public agreement despite private disagreement derives not from social pressure for ideological conformity but from the conviction that people should be allowed to think what they want and therefore should not be openly challenged in their thinking by others. They also feel it is important to create and perpetuate an image of social harmony and to refrain from performing actions, such as disputing the ideas of others, that would lead to interpersonal conflicts. Of course, individuals do sometimes argue violently but almost exclusively when they are intoxicated and usually about personal concerns such as the failure to fulfill one's social obligations. In more sober circumstances and on less volatile topics such as the concept of soul, the Rarámuri create a facade of public consensus that veils the extent of their privately held differences of opinion not only from outsiders but from themselves as well.

Eventually I resolved the problem of learning about the concept of soul by scheduling private interviews in my home. These interviews grew out of Rarámuri language lessons that Cecilia and I were receiving from a Rarámuri man, whom I will call Cornelio Rowhárare.[2] Cornelio was then about twenty-seven years old and had learned Spanish as a boy in a government school. Initially we would insert a question or two about souls or other matters between paradigm exercises but, after three months, instruction in the Rarámuri language was supplanted almost completely by discussions of Rarámuri culture. At the same time, Cecilia and I participated in the community's activities and talked informally with most of the other local people, recording in the process information on many different aspects of Rarámuri life.

Over the first year I began to notice considerable individual variation within the community on various topics I was investigating. To pursue the problem of intracultural diversity more systematically, I initiated formal interviews with a second man, Mariano Sikóchi. He was about twenty years older than Cornelio, and, as a doctor, musician, and official in the local Rarámuri political organization, he assumed a more active role in community affairs than did the younger man. In addition, although he spoke a smattering of Spanish, he was for all intents a monolingual speaker of Rarámuri.

The interviews with Cornelio extended over eighteen months. We met on an average of three days a week with each interview lasting two to three hours. Interviews with Mariano were comparable in frequency and duration but occurred over an eight-month period. These interviews tended to be open-ended discussions in which I would raise an issue and the man would respond, usually at length. When he indicated he had nothing more to say about the topic, I posed another question and the process was repeated. To ensure that I collected comparable data from Cornelio and Mariano, I asked them the same questions and reviewed the interviews with each so that issues raised by one were addressed by the other. The major differences between the two sets of interviews were in the languages spoken and the recording techniques. The interviews with Cornelio were conducted in both Rarámuri and Spanish, and I noted down the gist of what was said, occasionally asking him to repeat a statement to record it verbatim. The interviews with Mariano were conducted entirely in Rarámuri and were recorded on tape for transcription.

Through these interviews, I was able to collect very detailed expressions of Rarámuri world view as well as to determine the specific areas within the Rarámuri concept of soul on which these two men tended to agree or disagree.

I also was able to document the processes by which they worked out their ideas. On the other hand, the information I collected during these sessions obviously was affected by the interviews taking place in my house and being structured by my questions. I also paid each man for his time. This interview context probably encouraged Cornelio and Mariano to systematize their ideas more than they otherwise would have and probably led them to conceive and express completely new ideas in response to questions that the Rarámuri never ask one another. Topics also were juxtaposed that in ordinary life are kept separate.

To control for the potential bias of these formal interviews and to determine the extent of individual variation within the larger community, I attempted to cover the principal issues relating to the concept of soul with many other people. Most of these discussions were informal and took place outside my home, during drinking parties and casual visits and while walking to the local church in Basíhuare or other destinations. They were conducted almost exclusively with men because the Rarámuri frown on conversations between unrelated members of the opposite sex. Cecilia, however, was able to collect information from women on a variety of topics. In all we worked with around thirty men and ten women of the sixty adult members of the community.

When I began analyzing the information I had collected, I discovered, as presumably most anthropologists do, that what appeared to be variation in the early stages of investigation turned out to be fragments of a larger and essentially coherent picture. Nonetheless, I also began to realize that some of the individual variation I had encountered represented an undeniable if disconcerting feature of Rarámuri theoretical knowledge. Its prominence precluded my simply ignoring it, and my attempts to explain it away were unsuccessful, so I began to think about the implications of this variation for my understanding of the Rarámuri. Doing so forced me to reconsider how the study of knowledge in societies like the Rarámuri's should be approached and, of equal importance, how that knowledge should be represented in ethnographic writing.

VARIATION, REPRESENTATION, AND
THE REPRODUCTION OF KNOWLEDGE

The manner in which knowledge is to be investigated and represented is determined ultimately by how it is conceived. Until recently, anthropologists who studied theoretical knowledge tended to regard it as static, internally consistent sets of ideas that could be understood apart from the activities of everyday life. Their accounts focused on the content of this knowledge, often emphasizing the logical and semantic relations among ideas. The connections between knowledge and social process seldom were examined, and the "messier" aspects of knowledge—variation, ambiguity, contradiction—tended to be ignored.

Reservations about the legitimacy of this approach have been voiced periodically for decades, Paul Radin's *Primitive Man as Philosopher*, published in 1927, providing one of the most cogent if indirect early critiques. Since the 1970s, however, dissatisfaction with its inadequacies has become widespread, leading anthropologists from diverse perspectives to concur in rejecting it. Their concerns are both methodological and theoretical. In an evaluation of "relativist" studies of belief, for example, Sperber identifies a major methodological flaw: "All native utterances get distilled together; their quintessence is then displayed as an homogeneous world-view where, indeed, no epistemological differentiation of beliefs occurs. This, however, is a fact of ethnography, not of culture" (1982: 165).

For the most part, recent critiques have been directed less toward this approach to the study and representation of knowledge specifically than toward the conception of culture (often equated with knowledge) that underlies it, the view that culture is a finished product to be discovered and delineated (Dougherty and Fernandez 1981, 1982; Ortner 1984). In considering recent trends in symbolic and cognitive anthropology, Dougherty and Fernandez (1981, 1982) conclude that these two perspectives are converging in the development of a radically different concept of culture, one in which culture is regarded as a process that guides and gives meaning to social interaction while simultaneously emerging from it. In this view, culture must be studied in social context, partly because it is inextricably linked to social action and partly because it is interpreted, manipulated, and applied in distinct ways in different contexts by the members of society.

This perspective bears affinities to conceptions being developed outside symbolic and cognitive anthropology, particularly in the more practice-oriented approaches of scholars such as the British social theorist Anthony Giddens (1976, 1979, 1984) and the French sociologist Pierre Bourdieu (1977; cf. Ortner 1984, Karp 1986). Giddens and Bourdieu share the view that culture and society do not exist independently of the individuals through whose actions they are constituted. This processual notion of culture engenders an alternative view of knowledge as a dynamic historical formation that must be studied not in the abstract but as it is linked to concrete social practices. This conception of knowledge is clearly superior to the earlier, more static and reified view and is especially appropriate to the study of Rarámuri theoretical knowledge. In Rarámuri society, this knowledge is not compartmentalized from the rest of life, there are no specialists who dedicate themselves to elaborating and systematizing it, and no formal educational institutions exist to perpetuate it. Its transmission is informal, and like the knowledge itself, part of the flow of everyday life.

When knowledge is seen as a process embedded in social life, individual variation is no longer a troubling anomaly. Many anthropologists justify ignoring variation because it tends to be associated with minor details, but in my view the significance lies not in the content of the variation but in the phenomenon of variation itself. Variation testifies to the dynamism of culture and knowledge and directly reflects the social processes of which they are a part. Moreover, as the African philosopher Paulin Hountondji (1983: 60; cf. Kenny 1985) has complained, anthropologists who eliminate ideological variation from their ethnographic accounts in effect deny the members of the societies they describe the right to a diversity of opinion. Ironically, some anthropologists hesitate to report variation for fear that doing so might suggest that the members of small-scale societies lack coherence in their thought or are irrational. The members of these societies are thereby placed in what might be called a "small-scale" paradox: if they are ideologically homogeneous, their supposed "primitive" status is confirmed, but if they display a diversity of opinion, they are seen as deficient thinkers.

Although variation should be examined in any account of knowledge, it is particularly relevant to a description of Rarámuri theoretical knowledge. Presenting only those ideas upon which the Rarámuri agree would impoverish the account as would confining the description to basic assumptions upon which consensus can be presumed. In addition, theoretical knowledge is by its nature speculative and individual variation is intrinsic to it. Failing to acknowledge the existence of the variation would preclude an accurate portrayal of the knowledge. Variation in Rarámuri knowledge also needs to be addressed because some writers have interpreted it as evidence that the Rarámuri are not interested in theoretical matters. An alternative interpretation is that the Rarámuri hold different ideas on a subject because they are indeed thinking about it. From this perspective, variance indicates only the absence of a mechanism to insure standardization of different people's ideas.

My goal in the following pages is to explore Rarámuri culture and society by way of their own understandings of themselves and their world. I adopt this approach out of the conviction that a consideration of human agency must constitute a central element of social and cultural analysis. Determining the nature of such agency requires as a first step comprehending the models of the world in terms of which the members of a society operate, what Hallowell called their "culturally constituted behavioral environment" (1955: 86–89). My intention, however, is not to isolate sets of ideas and trace their connections to generalized examples of behavior. Instead, I try to arrive at a more realistic portrayal of the relationship between knowledge and practice by examining Rarámuri knowledge as it appears in the contexts of everyday life.

I focus on the Rarámuri's concept of soul because this concept is a basic component of the intellectual framework within which they understand their universe. It defines the essence of human existence on the biological, spiritual, and social planes and the nature of the articulation of the individual with the moral and natural worlds. At the same time, it is directly involved in motivating and justifying a number of practical actions related to fundamental existential concerns, particularly health and death. As such the concept of soul is closely tied to the roles and activities of the principal ritual specialists within Rarámuri society, but it is neither appropriated by them as a body of esoteric knowledge nor dependent solely upon them for its elaboration and perpetuation. Rather it is part of the commonsense understandings of the members of the society at large, who rely on it in the conduct of their daily lives.

The concept of soul also provides an excellent avenue for investigating how variation in the basic knowledge of the members of a society should be understood theoretically and represented ethnographically. Much of the variation associated with the concept of soul is so-called "random" or "idiosyncratic" variation because it cannot be correlated with factors like gender, degree of acculturation, or the role structure of society (Burton and Kirk 1979: 842; Pollnac 1975: 89). Most studies of intracultural diversity disregard this kind of variation and also tend to ignore areas of knowledge on which the members of the society generally agree. Variation and consensus must be considered together, however, because they are products of the same processes, namely those by which knowledge is produced and reproduced within the society.

Here I examine the variation and consensus in the Rarámuri's ideas about souls not as an end in itself but as a way of developing a general model of the reproduction of knowledge that can be applied to all societies. I isolate the basic conditions and principles in terms of which the reproduction of knowledge must take place, emphasizing that different kinds of knowledge require different kinds of practices to be reproduced. I also argue that the reproduction of knowledge can be understood only by considering both its relationship to social practices and general social processes *and* the logical relations among the ideas of which it is composed. This perspective reconciles some of the differences between more practice-oriented scholars, who emphasize the external relations of knowledge, and more mentalist anthropologists, who tend to ignore external factors in favor of the internal relations among ideas. It also incorporates the reproduction of knowledge into the more encompassing processes of the production and reproduction of social life as a whole.

Before beginning the discussion, I must emphasize that my description of the Rarámuri and their knowledge applies primarily to the Rarámuri of the Rejogochi area. I have attempted to indicate where the beliefs and practices reported for other Rarámuri communities differ significantly from those I encountered in Rejogochi, but I have not addressed the issue of regional variation systematically. Because the topics on which I focus have not been investigated in most other Rarámuri communities, the degree to which my account is applicable to the Rarámuri as a whole remains to be determined.

THE
RARÁMURI

The Rarámuri live in northwestern Mexico some 450 kilometers south-southwest of El Paso, Texas, and 1,100 kilometers northwest of Mexico City. Their rugged homeland of mountains and canyons covers approximately thirty-five thousand square kilometers along either side of the continental divide of the Sierra Madre in the southwestern corner of the state of Chihuahua.[1] Two major river systems drain this region. The Río Conchos flows almost due east out of Rarámuri country, dropping gently down from the Sierra and then through foothills and plains before abruptly turning north and then slightly east again, crossing the Chihuahuan Desert to link up with the Río Grande. On the western side of the divide the rivers are more dramatic. The Río Fuerte and its constituent streams churn and tumble through the mountains, excavating spectacular canyons in the western slope before emptying into the Gulf of California in northern Sinaloa. It is along these streams and their tributaries that most Rarámuri make their homes, for it is here that they find arable land.

Rarámuri country is characterized by extremes in altitude, climate, and vegetation (Bye 1976; González Rodríguez 1982; Pennington 1963; Schmidt 1973). The highest peaks in the Sierra Tarahumara, as this section of the Sierra Madre is known, rise to about three thousand meters above sea level while the canyons drop precipitously to around three hundred meters. The altitude of most of the upland area, where the largest numbers of Rarámuri reside, averages two thousand meters and is covered by extensive forests of pine and oak. Here the summers are cool and the winters mild, but snowfalls are not uncommon, and the temperatures at the higher elevations are the coldest in the Mexican Republic. The canyon floors by contrast are semi-

17

tropical, with summer days often uncomfortably hot and the indigenous thorn forest embellished by introduced citrus, avocado, and mango trees. Many Rarámuri who live near these canyons practice a form of transhumance, farming the canyon tops for most of the year and then descending into the canyons to pass the winters with their herds of sheep and goats. In the Batopilas canyon they also cultivate a winter crop of maize (Robert Bye 1986: personal communication).

REJOGOCHI, 1987

The Rarámuri community of Rejogochi, where I have conducted most of my research, lies at an altitude of approximately nineteen hundred meters in the transitional zone between the uplands and canyons. Rejogochi is not a compact village but rather a collection of homesteads scattered for about five kilometers along either side of a small creek that flows in a southwesterly direction until it empties into the Río Urique ten kilometers below Rejogochi. Between 1977 and 1987, its permanent residents numbered about 150 people, organized into around twenty-five households. An additional hundred Rarámuri lived in ranchos within a five kilometer radius of Rejogochi.

Rejogochi's climate is warmer than that of most upland communities and better suited to raising maize, the mainstay of the Rarámuri. The area is free of frost between mid-April and mid-October, leaving ample time for the local varieties of maize to mature, but the major climatological concern for the people of Rejogochi is whether there will be sufficient moisture to sustain their crops. Rejogochi receives most of its precipitation in two periods, from late June to October and from December to March. Because they plant in April and May before the summer rains begin, winter precipitation in the form of rain and snow is as crucial to the success of their maize as that of the summer, but precipitation in neither period is entirely reliable. In the winter of 1977–78, for example, precipitation was scant and the summer rains began quite late, in mid-July. As a result, much of the maize produced few or no ears despite considerable rain in July and August. In 1984 the maize crop suffered because the summer rains were unusually heavy.

Maize is the principal component of the Rejogochi diet, followed by beans, with squash, potatoes, and chiles of secondary importance. Complementing these domesticated plants are a variety of weedy and wild food plants, which the Rarámuri collect on the valley floor and adjacent hillsides (see Bennett and Zingg 1935, Pennington 1963, Bye 1976, and Bye 1979b for details of Rarámuri plant use). They also eat small rodents, birds, snakes, lizards, fish, several kinds of insect larvae, and deer, but these wild animals are far less significant in the Rejogochi economy than are domesticated animals. The Rarámuri of Rejogochi keep cattle, goats, sheep, horses, burros, chickens, turkeys, pigs, and dogs. Of these, cattle, goats, and sheep are the most important. Cattle are used in plowing, and people occasionally drink cow's milk or convert it into cheese. Together with goats and sheep, they also provide hides, fibers, and meat, although the Rarámuri seldom slaughter them except during religious fiestas. The major contribution of these animals to local subsistence is manure, which the Rarámuri use to fertilize their fields. The Rarámuri erect their corrals on fallow land so that the livestock deposit manure directly on the plots that need to be fertilized. When the area within a corral is covered with manure, the corral is shifted to an adjacent spot, and the fertilization process continues.

Some families in Rejogochi own no livestock while others have forty or more head of cattle and over a hundred sheep and goats. Poorer families

Figure 3. Hoeing maize. June 1981. Rejogochi men weed and hill maize during a drinking party, each man hoeing two rows at a time. During breaks, the workers drink maize beer provided by the owners of the field and then adjourn to drink at the hosts' home until the afternoon.

Figure 4. Plowing maize. Rejogochi, June 1981. View looking south. A man weeds his maize fields with a yoke of oxen borrowed from a relative. His stepson (in white hat) follows, hoeing the furrows into hills around the plants.

borrow livestock from the more prosperous, but the animals are seldom available for the lengths of time required to fertilize entire fields. The result is considerable differences in the quantities of maize harvested by different households. In 1978 I calculated the average maize harvest per household per year in Rejogochi at approximately six hundred kilograms, but the harvests of individual households varied from a high of around thirteen hundred kilograms to a low of one hundred kilograms. Obviously people who harvest only one hundred kilograms of maize a year will exhaust their supplies long before the year is out, but even families whose production falls around the average frequently run out of maize before the next year's harvest.

People compensate for dwindling or exhausted maize supplies in several ways. One of the most important is to increase their exploitation of non-domesticated resources, particularly wild and weedy plants. Another is to visit more frequently in the homes of people known to have adequate food supplies, for Rarámuri etiquette requires people to provide food for everyone who comes to their home, assuming they have the means to do so. Destitute

Figure 5. Shelling maize. Rejogochi, February 1979. A man, his two daughters, and young brother-in-law shell maize onto a commercial blanket to make beer. His wife molds clay into a censer, surrounded by a metate and mano for grinding the clay and a wooden bowl for mixing it with water from the plastic container. A chicken coop rests on stilts behind her. Photograph by Cecilia Troop.

individuals may work for the members of more prosperous households in exchange for food, sometimes even moving in with their benefactors. The Rarámuri call these people *piónike*, derived from the Spanish *peón*, but they regard this relationship not as one of master and servant but as one of mutual assistance that can be terminated by the peons. People who need maize also buy from other Rarámuri or local Mestizos. The majority of Mestizos around Rejogochi operate small stores and extend credit for maize and other items to their Rarámuri customers against future harvests or other anticipated income. As Kennedy (1978: 30) points out, this arrangement exposes the Rarámuri to exploitation, and in my experience the Mestizos in the Rejogochi area do take advantage of the opportunity.

Whether or not their maize supplies are low, the people of Rejogochi also buy processed foods like wheat flour and instant tortilla mix and a variety of other goods ranging from soap and cloth to candy and soft drinks, assuming they have money or good credit. The men earn money by working on road

Figure 6. Grinding maize. September 1977. A Rejogochi woman grinds parched maize kernels with water into a wooden tray to make kiorí, *a basic item in Rarámuri diet. Gourd dippers, a plastic bowl, and discarded cans are among her utensils. She works in the shade of a lean-to next to her maize storehouse. Clothing, a ball of brown wool, and dried plants hang above her.*

construction crews and in the sawmill owned by the local *ejido,* a communal economic unit established in many areas of Mexico as part of the agrarian reform program of the Mexican Revolution. They also fell trees to sell to the sawmill or to a wood products company that has a purchasing station in the Mestizo settlement of Creel, forty kilometers to the north. Both men and women may sell some of their crops and domesticated animals or perform odd jobs for Mestizos, like chopping firewood (men) or tending their herds (men and women). They usually do wage labor temporarily, working only as long as required to obtain the amount of money they need. In addition, the *ejido* distributes its profits (most of which come from its sawmill operation) among its members at intervals during the year, sometimes in the form of cash and sometimes as maize or beans.

The Rarámuri reckon descent bilaterally, and the basic social and residential unit is the nuclear family (Kennedy 1978: 157–80). Unless separated by marital difficulties, married couples live together year-round. They usually

live with their unmarried children, although some parents send their children
to stay with other relatives, particularly those with no children, to help with
chores or to relieve some of the pressure on their own resources. After marriage, a new couple typically lives with the parents of one spouse or moves
between natal households for a few years, until they can build a house and
set up a separate household.[2] Elderly people who have difficulty performing
heavy chores like grinding maize and hauling firewood often move in with
their married children or grandchildren. Thus, a household may contain all
or only some of the members of a nuclear family who may or may not be
joined by the parents, siblings, or other relatives of either spouse and the
spouses and offspring of married children.

All but a few households in Rejogochi shift residence during the year.
Several families come to Rejogochi only to farm plots of land they have inherited there, maintaining their principal residence elsewhere. About half
the permanent residents of Rejogochi also move during the growing season
to cultivate land in different locations, a few in different parts of the Rejogochi
valley but most in other places. In addition, in late fall or early winter many
residents move to rockshelters or houses that serve them as winter quarters.
Again around half of Rejogochi households move to winter homes that they
do not use at any other time of the year. These two groups of households
overlap but do not completely coincide.

Most of these winter residences are located on the forested mountainsides
above the Rejogochi valley, where they are closer to firewood, better shielded
from the wind, and warmed earlier by the morning sun. In many cases,
people have a clear view of their valley homes from these sites, and return
to the valley floor often to visit or drink with other people, to graze their
flocks of sheep and goats, or to complete miscellaneous tasks. Social relations
are not significantly disrupted by this change in residence. The residence
shifts that occur during the growing season, in contrast, tend to move people
in and out of several local interaction networks.

The principal context within which the members of different households
interact is the drinking get-together. The Rarámuri prepare alcoholic beverages from a variety of substances, most importantly maize kernels, and
few weeks pass in Rejogochi without at least one drinking party. Most parties
are sponsored by individual households, but neighboring households sometimes pool resources or at least try to coordinate their drinking. A household
usually prepares beer to encourage the assistance of neighbors in a work
project or ritual and to compensate them for their help. The guests in turn
attend the parties because they enjoy them and, more importantly, because

they feel obligated to do so. The members of the community are linked to one another not so much by bonds of kinship as by relations of obligation that have been established through their mutual assistance over years or in many cases generations.

Attendance at these drinking parties almost without exception is by invitation, and different households invite different but overlapping groups of individuals to drink with them. The connections among the members of various households that emerge from their attendance at drinking parties constitutes what Kennedy (1963, 1970a, 1978) has called the "tesguino network," *tesgüino* being the Spanish term for the Rarámuri's maize beer. Since each household tends to invite not only close neighbors but the residents of nearby ranchos who in turn invite to their own parties people from the ranchos beyond, the tesguino network links households for great distances across the region.

The diffuse organization of the tesguino network contrasts with the more center-oriented pueblo organization established across Rarámuri country by Catholic missionaries in the colonial period. In the pueblo organization, people are linked to one another only because they share an affiliation with the pueblo. The people of Rejogochi belong to the pueblo of Basíhuare, the center of which is the Mestizo settlement of Basíhuare, located about ten kilometers to the north. Rarámuri from as far away as fifteen kilometers gather at the church in Basíhuare to conduct business, adjudicate disputes, and perform ceremonies of the Catholic ritual calendar. Although several hundred people participate in the larger pueblo ceremonies like Easter, never do all the residents of the pueblo assemble in Basíhuare at once. In fact, those who live in more distant ranchos go to Basíhuare much less often than to adjacent pueblo centers like Cusárare, Choguita, and Raramuchi, which are located closer to them.

The affairs of the pueblo are directed by a set of Rarámuri officials chosen by the men of the pueblo. The leader of this organization is the *siríame* (governor), who supervises major pueblo events like ceremonies and footraces and represents the Rarámuri in dealings with outsiders. He also serves as the chief justice of the pueblo and the principal guardian of the community's moral values. The governor is assisted by a *teniénte* (lieutenant governor) and *alakánte* (mayor), who serve as his principal advisors and fulfill his duties in his absence.

The other pueblo officials all rank below the governor, lieutenant, and mayor. Principal of these are the *mayóli* (majors), the *alawási* (sheriffs), and *kapitáne* (captains). The four *mayóli* arrange marriages, perform marriage

Figure 7. Basíhuare. June 1981. Mestizo homes flank the two long buildings and basketball court of the government boarding school. The church, to the right of center, is partially hidden by trees. The stone and plaster building on the hillside serves as the local jail and office for the Basíhuare section president.

ceremonies (although their services are not required), and resolve disagreements between spouses. They also oversee the activities of the *tenánche*, four women who sweep the church and offer incense during religious observances. In the past, the two *alawási* administered public lashings to thieves and other offenders sentenced to this punishment by the *siríame*. This practice was discouraged by the Mexican government and no longer exists. Today the *alawási* do little more than keep dogs away from food offerings and dance spaces during ceremonies and distribute the wooden canes which the major pueblo officials hold as symbols of their authority. The four *kapitáne* are the police and messengers of the pueblo. They also are entrusted with caring for people during drinking parties to ensure no harm comes to them while they are drunk and in particular to intervene in fights before someone is injured. Five to ten *sontárasi* (soldiers), most in their late teens or early twenties, assist the *kapitáne*.

The other officials in the Basíhuare pueblo organization perform religious rather than political functions. I have mentioned the *tenánche*, who clean the

Figure 8. The Basíhuare church. April 1987. The pueblo officials lead the first Easter procession early Maundy Thursday morning. Members of the Easter sodality known as Pharisees, with plumed hats and wooden swords, follow the opposite sodality, the Soldiers, to the church door while the Soldiers' flagbearer waits in the churchyard with his red banner. The monuments to the left of the door mark the graves of two Mestizo men, sons of Basíhuare's first non-Indian settlers.

church and perform ritual duties throughout the year. The male counterparts of the *tenánche* are the *méstro* (teachers), who number from three to five. The *méstro* ring the church bell to call people together for church services and recite prayers during the services the Rarámuri perform when a priest is not present to celebrate Mass. Another position of considerable importance in the pueblo ritual organization is that of *chapió*. Usually there are four *chapió*, and they are in charge of the dancers known in Spanish as *matachines*, whose performances are a necessary component of several major pueblo fiestas.

Since the turn of the century, when the first Mestizos settled in the area, the residents of Rejogochi have become increasingly involved in the pluralistic society of the region. A 1983 census of the Basíhuare school district lists 101 Mestizos and 509 Rarámuri living within its boundaries (Secretaría de Educación Pública 1983). This ratio of Mestizos to Rarámuri is the same as that found in the voting membership of the Basíhuare *ejido*, which consists of all heads of households within the *ejido* (45 Mestizos to 206 Rarámuri). Most of the local Mestizo men over thirty-five years of age speak Rarámuri quite well, but hardly any of the Mestizo women and younger men know more than a few words and phrases. The situation among the Rarámuri with respect to Spanish is comparable but somewhat reversed. The majority of younger Rarámuri men and some younger women learned Spanish in nearby elementary schools sponsored by the Mexican government and the Jesuit mission. Older Rarámuri men generally have a very limited command of Spanish while older women tend to be monolingual Rarámuri speakers.

Although the linguistic barriers between the two groups have been partially breached, relations between them are superficial and each maintains an unfavorable stereotype of the other. Mestizos view the Rarámuri as dirty, undisciplined, of inferior intelligence, and childlike, who in their poverty and ignorance should be pitied or despised. The Rarámuri portray the Mestizos as immoral and unscrupulous people who attempt to seduce or rape Rarámuri women and to cheat the Rarámuri in economic transactions. Mestizos consider themselves civilized, the Rarámuri uncivilized, while the Rarámuri believe that the Mestizos are the children of the Devil and the Rarámuri are the children of God. Close friendships seldom develop between Rarámuri and Mestizos, and intermarriage is disapproved by both.

Indians and Mestizos tend to live apart—the Mestizos concentrated along the major roads, the Rarámuri in side valleys—and to maintain largely separate social networks. Interactions between members of the two groups are primarily between men and most are of an economic nature, involving Rarámuri working for Mestizos or purchasing items in their stores and Mestizos buying livestock and horticultural products from Rarámuri. Politics also brings the two groups together, but these interactions also are predominantly between the men of each group since women are largely excluded from political matters.

While Mestizos cannot serve as officials in the Rarámuri's pueblo political organization, they share membership with them in the *ejido* as well as the national political system. The *ejido* operates a sawmill and controls local lumbering activities, as well as holding ultimate title to all the land within its boundaries. Because the business of the *ejido* requires literacy and some familiarity with the workings of the state and national economy, Mestizos tend to control its affairs. The national government is represented locally by the "section president," the "section" being a subdivision of the *municipio*, in this case, the Municipio of Guachochi, which in turn is a unit of the state of Chihuahua. The section president issues permits for the sale of cattle, records all births and deaths of which he is informed, and collects a minimal tax each year from the section residents. In addition, individuals who seriously

Figure 9. Appointing the Pharisees. Basíhuare, February 1979. Rarámuri and Mestizo men listen at the pueblo officials' patio near the church as Basíhuare's Rarámuri governor delivers a sermon to the four men chosen to lead the Pharisees in the Easter season. The governor stands in front of the officials' bench holding his cane of office, the Mestizo section president of Basíhuare and two other Rarámuri officials to his left. Photograph by Cecilia Troop.

injure or murder someone or commit grand larceny usually are turned over to the section president to be jailed. Section presidents tend to be Mestizos but occasionally a Rarámuri man holds the office.

Unlike many other communities in the region, Basíhuare is relatively accessible from the outside world. The main road between the major Mestizo towns of Creel and Guachochi transects the Basíhuare *ejido* from north to south and a secondary road connecting the smaller settlements of Cusárare, Norogachi, and Rochéachi passes along its eastern edge. Logging roads, most of them impassable in the rainy season, venture into many of the valleys where the Rarámuri have their homes and fields. Foreign tourists, usually guests at motels in and around Creel and mostly Americans, come to Basíhuare almost every week and descend in droves at Christmas and Easter to watch the Rarámuri's elaborate celebrations of these religious holidays.

The road through Basíhuare roughly follows the route of a mule track laid down in the early 1900s between the booming silver mines in the Batopilas canyon and the newly established railhead at Creel. The deep gorges of the Río Urique south and west of Basíhuare had until this time discouraged travel through the area. In 1907 a suspension bridge spanned a narrow section of the canyon to open the most direct north-south route between the mines and the railroad (Shepherd 1938, 1966: plate opposite p. 17). In the same year, a stone house and barn were built in Basíhuare, one of several "stations" along the mule track designed to supply the muleteers and their animals with food and shelter and to protect from bandits the ingots of silver and gold they carried. The mining company hired a Mestizo man to operate the station. He and his family became the first non-Indians to settle permanently in Basíhuare.

Before the construction of this road, Basíhuare was among the most

Figure 10. The mule station in Basíhuare. Corpus Christi, June 1981. Built in 1907, the now-abandoned mule station provides shelter for the sponsors of many Basíhuare pueblo fiestas. Matachine dancers perform before wooden crosses and a table on which food offerings are placed. A gourd rattle for the tutubúri ritual rests on the table and a white banner, symbolic of fiesta sponsorship, leans against it. The matachines' two "directors" (chapió), with arms folded, stand behind them next to seated musicians. Other men chat in small groups while the women distribute food on the porch.

isolated areas in all of Rarámuri country. There were no mines in the immediate vicinity to attract settlers or development, the absence of roads pre
cluded commercial exploitation of the abundant forests, and the rugged terrain
offered little to Mestizo farmers. Catholic priests, who began proselytizing
the Rarámuri in the late sixteenth century, did not arrive in Basíhuare until
the nineteenth, only about three decades before their mission system collapsed. Throughout the colonial period, Basíhuare remained just beyond the
control of the church and state, apparently becoming a refuge for non-Christian Indians and fugitives from Catholic missions and Spanish justice.

Several writers have traced the course of Rarámuri history of the past
four centuries, focusing on the most significant events in the region (Spicer
1962; Pennington 1963; Fried 1969; Kennedy 1978; Deimel 1980; González
Rodríguez 1982). To understand the current situation in Basíhuare, it is crucial to understand how these events, many of which have taken place far
from Basíhuare, have impinged on the history of Basíhuare specifically. The
events that have had the most impact on Basíhuare have been associated with
the exploitation of the region's natural resources, the expansion of the Catholic
mission system, and the Rarámuri's resistance to the incursions of outsiders.
In the historical sketch that follows, I examine these three areas to determine
why Basíhuare remained outside direct Spanish and Mexican control for over
two centuries and what the local historical circumstances were out of which
the contemporary society and culture of Basíhuare emerged.

BASÍHUARE IN RARÁMURI HISTORY

Sixteenth and Seventeenth Centuries

Today the Rarámuri live mostly in the uplands and canyons of southwestern
Chihuahua, but at the time of Spanish contact they occupied a much larger
area, approximately forty-five thousand square kilometers, that extended
north and east into the foothills, plains, and basin and range country (Pennington 1963: 1–13, map 1). They lived along the valleys of the Fuerte and
the upper Conchos, as they do today, but also farther north on the upper
reaches of the Río Yaqui, known locally as the Papigochi, and farther east
on the various tributaries of the middle Conchos. Despite local environmental
differences, their adaptation was essentially the same across the region, based
on subsistence agriculture supplemented by hunting and gathering. Agricultural activities focused on the floodplains of the area, where the soft earth

was easily worked with digging sticks and flood deposition maintained the fertility of the soil. In steeper areas to the west, slash-and-burn plots and terraced fields possibly augmented their narrow floodplain lands (Pennington 1963: 47–49).

In the four hundred years since contact, the Rarámuri have been forced to the south and west, displacing or assimilating the original Indian residents. These people and the members of other neighboring Indian groups shared with the Rarámuri a rancheria settlement pattern and like them spoke languages of the Uto-Aztecan family. Some, like the Yaqui, Mayo, Pima, Guarijío, and Tepehuan, have survived until today, while others like the Concho, Tubar, Témori, Chínipa, and Guazapar have disappeared (Miller 1983; Pennington 1963: 1–13). The early historical documents report trade and intermarriage among these groups, particularly along their common borders (Font 1611; Guadalajara and Tardá 1857: 281–82). Hostilities involving up to several hundred warriors also were recorded but the lines of battle did not invariably coincide with those of ethnicity (Font, in González Rodríguez 1982: 156; Contreras 1638: 284v).

Miller (1983: 118, 123) interprets the diversity of Uto-Aztecan languages in northwest Mexico as suggesting that the speakers of these languages have occupied this area for several thousand years. The meager archaeological evidence indicates that the prehistoric inhabitants of the area gradually shifted from being nonsedentary hunters and gatherers to becoming semisedentary farmers of maize, beans, and squash. They continued to rely heavily on wild plants and animals, however, and the use of wild plant fibers to produce various items, including fine textiles, is striking throughout the archaeological record (Zingg 1940; O'Neale 1948; Ascher and Clune 1960; Clune 1960; Green 1971; Di Peso 1979). At contact the more easterly Rarámuri were located near what presumably formed a major trade route between central Mexico, Casas Grandes, and the American Southwest (Di Peso 1979; cf. Minnis 1984). The role of the Rarámuri's ancestors or predecessors in this trade network has not been determined, but evidence of their involvement has been discovered by Zingg (1940: 5–6, 35), who recovered exotic shell and Casas Grandes–style pottery from a rockshelter in the Sierra south of Casas Grandes, in the center of contemporary Rarámuri territory.

European settlement in what is now the state of Chihuahua began in the 1560s with the establishment of a Franciscan mission in the San Bartolomé Valley and the discovery of silver at Santa Bárbara, both located to the southeast of aboriginal Rarámuri territory in an area occupied by Tepehuan and perhaps Concho Indians (West 1949: 10–12; Gerhard 1982: 236–38, 241;

González Rodríguez 1982: 34). In the subsequent half-century, the impact of these settlers on the local Indian populations was minimal, for their mining and agricultural operations were small and restricted to a few localities (Pennington 1963: 13–14). In 1631, however, major silver deposits were discovered at Parral, also southeast of Rarámuri country. Within three years, hundreds of fortune seekers, laborers, farmers, and ranchers had converged on the area (West 1949: 13; Gerhard 1982: 218).

Rarámuri and other Native people were drawn to Parral to work and trade, and expeditions from Parral entered Rarámuri country to barter for maize (Contreras 1638: 234v; West 1949: 68–69). The amount of food and supplies required to provision the mines soon surpassed what was available locally, and Spanish agricultural enterprises expanded into the areas occupied by the Rarámuri. Spanish grain farmers appropriated the stream valleys suitable for irrigation, and stockmen turned their livestock out to graze in direct competition with the herds that the Indians were beginning to build. Complaints frequently appear in the colonial record of Spanish livestock destroying Indian fields, a problem that together with the loss of water rights to the Spanish led to the displacement of many Rarámuri (West 1949: 10–14, 57–76; Pennington 1963: 18; Sheridan and Naylor 1979: 88).

At the same time, Catholic priests of the Society of Jesus initiated formal missionary activities among the Rarámuri. In the first decade of the seventeenth century, Jesuits completed several expeditions into Rarámuri country, entering from both Sinaloa on the southwest and the Parral area on the southeast (González Rodríguez 1982: 39, 150–62). These contacts led some Rarámuri to leave their homes to relocate in mission settlements established for them and the Tepehuan to the south and east of their traditional territory (Tardá 1674; Dunne 1948). In 1639, the Tarahumara Mission was created as an independent unit separate from the Tepehuan Mission, and the first mission pueblos were established within aboriginal Rarámuri country (Dunne 1948: 45).

A cornerstone of the colonial mission system among the Rarámuri and other Native people was the program of *reducción*, in which the missionaries attempted to congregate or "reduce" the Indians into concentrated settlements (Salmón 1977; Spicer 1962). Reduction seems to have succeeded in only a few Rarámuri missions. The key to its success was the establishment of the missions as self-sufficient units, but several factors conspired to prevent this from happening. Raiding by hostile Indians, particularly the Tobosos and their allies, and the devastation of drought and other natural disasters caused the failure of the crops of many missions, especially in the early seventeenth century (Pascual 1651). Mission crops also suffered because the Indians often were taken out of the missions to work on Spanish farms and had insufficient time to tend the missions' fields or to complete projects, like irrigation works, that would have enhanced productivity. In addition, in many missions, particularly those in mountainous areas, arable lands were insufficient to support concentrated settlements. In some cases, the Indians dispersed to farms during the growing season and congregated in the mission centers during the winter (Andonaegui 1744). In most missions, however, they appear to have remained at their farms for most of the year.

As early as 1645, some Indians began deserting the missions (Dunne 1948: 50–51). They were motivated to do so in part to avoid starvation but primarily because of mistreatment by missionaries or Spanish settlers and by their desire to escape forced labor and acculturation. By the last decade of the seventeenth century, many Indians also recognized a connection between living in the concentrated settlements and the likelihood of dying in one of the epidemics of smallpox, measles, or other European diseases that successively devastated the Indian population throughout the mission period (Gerhard 1982: 183, 188; Neumann, in Sheridan and Naylor 1979: 46; cf. Neumann 1969).

Most Rarámuri entered the Spanish colonial economy as unskilled and often seasonal workers. There are reports of Rarámuri slaves working in the mines of Parral (West 1949: 52), and the Indians in the missions were subject to labor drafts, particularly under the system known as *repartamiento* (Sheridan and Naylor 1979: 88–89, 95–100; cf. Andonaegui 1744). However, throughout northern New Spain, free labor was more important than forced labor. Unlike in central Mexico, Indians in the north were relatively few in number, widely dispersed, and often violently resistant to Spanish attempts to expropriate their labor. There was, as a consequence, a local labor shortage. Moreover, the predominant form of mineral extraction in the north was vein mining, which required skilled labor. The Spanish imported experienced mine workers from the south: Tarascans, Mexicans (that is, Aztecs and other Nahuatl-speakers) as well as Mestizos, Mulattos, and Africans (West 1949: 5, 48). Because of extensive intermixing of these various ethnic groups, by the early nineteenth century mixed-race individuals were more populous than either Indians or Spanish in Nueva Vizcaya, the colonial province of which Chihuahua was a part (Gerhard 1982: 172).

The local Indians who worked in Spanish mines, farms, and ranches came both from the missions and from areas yet to be missionized and included both Christians and non-Christians. They were employed in larger numbers in Spanish agricultural activities than in the mines, and, although some lived permanently on the farms and ranches, most worked only when an intensive labor input was required, as at planting and harvesting. For the rest of the year they tended their own fields and herds or sought work in other enterprises (Ratkay 1683: 21–22; Dunne 1948: 53; Pennington 1963: 20, 23).

To some degree, the Rarámuri participated willingly in both the missions and the dominant regional economy, and over the centuries hundreds if not thousands of Rarámuri have been assimilated into local Mestizo society. Yet, the history of their contact with outsiders also is replete with examples of their resistance to domination and the pressures of acculturation. From the early colonial period, they have adopted superficial submission, avoidance, deceit, and other forms of passive resistance in their dealings with outsiders, but they also have occasionally resorted to violence (Salmón 1977).

In 1616, less than a decade after the first Rarámuri entered a Jesuit mission, some Rarámuri joined the Tepehuan in what Spicer (1962: 28) has described as "one of the three bloodiest and most destructive Indian attempts to throw off Spanish control in northwestern New Spain," the other two being the Pueblo Revolt of 1680 and the Yaqui Revolt of 1740. The rest of the seventeenth century was punctuated by minor uprisings and four major revolts led by the Rarámuri in 1648–50, 1652–53, 1690–91, and 1696–98 (Pascual 1651; Neumann 1969; Sheridan and Naylor 1979). Several factors seem to have contributed to Rarámuri discontent: mistreatment by missionaries and Spanish settlers, including enslavement and temporary forced labor; displacement from their lands by Spanish farmers and livestock; and dismay at the enormous loss of life from epidemics that they eventually concluded had been brought by the invaders (Neumann 1969; Spicer 1962: 29ff.).

These revolts stalled the expansion of the Jesuit mission system and disrupted the Spanish economy, but only temporarily. The negative impact was much greater on the Rarámuri than on the Europeans. In the course of the revolts, the Spanish destroyed crops and houses, killed many people, enslaved a great deal more, and relocated entire villages. The Basíhuare area was far removed from the centers of rebellion and conflict, the majority of which were located in the more northern Rarámuri region around the Río Papigochi. However, rebels fleeing Spanish retribution and forced return to the Jesuit missions joined communities of non-Christian Indians west and south of the Papigochi (Neumann 1969; Fernández de Cordova 1704; Sheridan and Naylor 1979: 65). Basíhuare may have been one of these refuge areas.

Eighteenth Century

By the early eighteenth century, the complex of Spanish mines, farms, and ranches had spread over much of central Chihuahua, following a series of spectacular silver strikes at Cusihuíriachic and Chihuahua and more modest finds at a number of other sites. Large Spanish farms were established in the fertile Papigochi Valley, one of the most densely occupied Rarámuri areas. The same pattern was repeated around mining centers in the more westerly canyons, in particular Urique and Batopilas, which flourished in the first half of the eighteenth century (Gerhard 1982).

The mission system prospered during this period (Dunne 1948; Burrus 1963). Using their first missions in the eastern portion of Rarámuri country as staging points, the Jesuits expanded first north and then west into the heart of Rarámuri territory. Jesuits from Sinaloa also were making inroads into Rarámuri communities in the west (Ortiz Zapata 1857). This expansion was possible in large part because the Rarámuri never staged another large-scale revolt after the turn of the eighteenth century, although their violence against the Spanish and their successors did not cease entirely. The Jesuit Ignacio Xavier de Estrada, writing in 1730 from the Rarámuri mission of Temeichi, mentions "Indian uprisings" having occurred in 1701.[3] In 1703, there was another revolt, this time involving Rarámuri living in the western canyon area near Guazapares and Batopilillas, a major refuge for rebels in the seventeenth century revolts (González Rodríguez 1982: 40). Most Rarámuri aggression during the eighteenth century, however, took the form of small-scale raids against Spanish settlements in the style of and often in conjunction with the Apache.

Although the Apache were listed among the Rarámuri's allies in the revolts of the 1690s, the Rarámuri seem to have operated on their own in the early eighteenth century (Sheridan and Naylor 1979: 67; Mirafuentes Galván 1975: 46). By mid-century, however, many Rarámuri were joining Apache bands or aiding Apache forays into Spanish settlements (Braun 1764: 17; Lizassoain 1763: 6v–8; Bargas 1762). The Spanish especially feared this alliance because, as local residents, the Rarámuri were able to guide the Apaches directly to the wealthier or more vulnerable settlements and then out of the area safely (San Vincente 1773).

It is difficult to determine how many Rarámuri actually engaged in raids against the Spanish and the areas from which they came. Those most involved appear to have lived in the more eastern areas of Rarámuri country, near the major Spanish settlements of central Chihuahua and northern Durango (Queipo de Llanos 1773). In any case, the impact of this violence spread far beyond the centers of conflict because Indian fugitives often fled deep into the Sierra Madre, "stirring up the gentiles [non-Christian Indians] who live innocently in their canyons," as one contemporary official portrayed it (Ugarte y Loyola 1788).[4]

By the mid-eighteenth century the Jesuit mission system was converging on Basíhuare from all sides. Churches had been or would soon be built in the nearby Rarámuri communities of Samachique and Cusárare, and the conversion of Basíhuare appears to have been imminent. But in 1767, before they reached Basíhuare, the Jesuits were expelled from New Spain by the Bourbon King of Spain, Charles III (Dunne 1937; Florescano and Gil Sánchez 1976: 492–93).

After the Jesuits' expulsion, responsibility for their Rarámuri missions was divided among secular clergy of the bishopric of Durango and Franciscan missionaries of the Colegio Apostólico de Propaganda Fide de Nuestra Señora de Guadalupe de Zacatecas (Revilla Gigedo 1966: 42–50). The mission system they inherited was in disarray primarily because the Spanish colonial government had confiscated the missions' property. Between 1767 and 1772, the Jesuits' Chihuahuan missions lost over fifteen thousand head of livestock as well as large quantities of wheat and maize (Benedict 1972: 30, table 2). Government representatives quickly recognized the unjust harm they had caused the Indians in these missions and proposed to return the animals or compensate the Indians for their losses, but by the time measures were actually taken, the mission economy had been destroyed and most of the Indians completely alienated. The loss of their herds appears to have encouraged many Rarámuri to seek redress through raiding (Carrillo 1773; Campo 1773; Nava 1794; Parrilla 1794; Revilla Gigedo 1966: 47–48; Alcocer 1958: 159–60; Benedict 1972).

Nineteenth Century

By the end of the eighteenth century, silver mining in northern New Spain was in major decline. Many mines had flooded or the veins that could be worked by the technology of the day had been exhausted (Gerhard 1982: 30). The colonial political structure also was beginning to falter. The need to defend against the continuous raiding by Apaches and other Native groups became a major preoccupation of the civil and military officials and disrupted the economy of the north (Croix 1857; Rubio Mañé 1959; Porras Muñoz

1980: 400–411). In addition, in the early nineteenth century small local uprisings and large pitched battles between standing armies brought Mexico independence from Spain in 1821 (Almada 1955; Navarro García 1965; Lister and Lister 1966).

Despite these disruptions, the Franciscans reestablished many of the old Jesuit missions and began a program of mission expansion (Alcocer 1958; Revilla Gigedo 1966; Arlegui 1851). It apparently was during this period that a church was built in Basíhuare. I have found no information in the historical records on the founding of the Basíhuare mission, but the following indirect evidence suggests that it was established sometime between 1828 and 1859.

That Basíhuare was not founded by Jesuit missionaries in the seventeenth or eighteenth centuries is indicated by its absence from all lists of the Jesuit missions, including that of Tamarón y Romeral (1937), produced in 1765 and the most exhaustive compilation of the Jesuit missions and *visitas* immediately prior to their expulsion in 1767.[5] On the other hand, its establishment clearly predates the return of the Jesuits in 1900 because it is identified as a *visita* of the neighboring mission of Cusárare in a survey of the missions completed soon after their arrival (Ocampo 1966: 355). In addition, the church in Basíhuare is in the colonial style, and local residents report that their elders told them that it was there long before the Jesuits arrived in the twentieth century.

Cusárare was founded as a Jesuit mission in about 1744, closed in 1767 when the Jesuits were expelled, and reestablished by the Franciscans no later than 1791 (Escalona 1744; Tristán 1791; Revilla Gigedo 1966: 46). Originally it was a *visita* of Sisoguichi and later Guacayvo, first appearing as a separate mission in 1828 under the control of the Franciscan missionaries of the Provincia de Zacatecas, shortly after responsibility for the Rarámuri missions had been transferred to them from the Colegio Apostólico (Arlegui 1851: 458–60). In his 1834 overview of Chihuahua, Escudero (1834: 74, 179) designates Cusárare as a pueblo and mission. In 1854 it is listed as one of ten remaining Franciscan missions among the Rarámuri of the Sierra (Provincia de Zacatecas 1854). Since Basíhuare probably was established as a *visita* of Cusárare rather than as an independent mission, its founding presumably took place during the period when a missionary was assigned to live in Cusárare, apparently between 1828 and 1859.

In 1856, the Mexican government legislated the dissolution of properties owned communally by civil and ecclesiastical corporations. The intent was to break up the vast holdings of the Catholic church, but the result in the Sierra was to make lands controlled by the Rarámuri available to non-Indians.

As a consequence, Mestizos displaced Rarámuri from many of the best farming lands (Almada 1955: 247–48). The movement of non-Indians into the Sierra was stimulated by the discovery of several new mines and the reopening of others as well as expanded stockraising and, in the last decades of the century, major lumbering activities (Ramírez 1884; Champion 1962; Wasserman 1973; Carr 1973; Lartigue 1983). The Rarámuri in several areas met these encroachments with violence, revolting in 1876 in Nonoava, in 1895 near Guadalupe y Calvo, and in 1898 at Chinatú. At the same time, other Rarámuri retreated to less accessible areas (González Rodríguez 1982: 60; Almada 1955: 359).

The Franciscan missions among the Rarámuri were secularized in 1859, as a consequence of a law that dissolved all religious orders in Mexico and nationalized their property (Silva Herzog 1984: 80–84; Esparza Sánchez 1974: 93). These missions were transferred to the secular clergy of the bishopric of Durango and then in 1891 to the newly formed bishopric of Chihuahua (Ocampo 1966: 11; Almada 1968: 368). There is no indication that any priest ministered to Basíhuare during this period. In the last decade of the nineteenth century, Lumholtz (1902, I: 202) reports that only one Catholic priest actually resided in the Rarámuri country and mentions but one more who lived in a Mestizo town nearby and made annual visits to some Rarámuri settlements to perform baptisms and marriages. Between 1895 and 1900, a group of missionaries known as "Josefinos" attempted to revitalize the mission system under the bishop of Chihuahua, but were unsuccessful. They may have visited Basíhuare, however, because one of their centers was the pueblo of Cusárare, located less than twenty kilometers to the north (Piñán 1900; Ocampo 1966: 11, 354).

In the 1840s American troops occupied Chihuahua, and French troops invaded the state in the 1860s (Almada 1955; Lister and Lister 1966). The Apaches, joined for a time by other groups like the Comanches, also continued their raids into northern Mexico throughout the nineteenth century and into the twentieth, but the defeat in the 1880s of the Chiricahua Apache bands led by Victoria, Juh, and Geronimo ended the major threat (Lister and Lister 1966). The relationship between the Rarámuri and Apaches seems to have shifted by this time. Although some Rarámuri presumably continued to aid the Apaches, they increasingly became their adversaries rather than allies. Bourke (1891: 471), the chronicler of General Crook's various campaigns against the Indians, wrote that in the Apache wars of the second half of the nineteenth century the Mexican army relied on the Rarámuri, "who alone would stand up and fight with the fierce Chiricahuas, or could trail them through the mountains." Two Rarámuri scouts are credited with having killed Victorio in 1880 (Lister and Lister 1966: 164). The numerous stories the Rarámuri now tell about Apache atrocities and Rarámuri victories presumably come from this period.

In the late nineteenth century the mining industry enjoyed a brief boom, stimulated by Porfirio Diaz's politics of progress, which attracted the application of new technology and large investments of foreign capital (Wasserman 1973). By 1884, twenty-two mining companies controlled by American interests were in operation in the state of Chihuahua (Ramírez 1884: 380). By 1907, this number had increased to sixty-nine (Wasserman 1973: 298–99). In the Batopilas mining district alone, over fourteen hundred mines had been identified, of which seventy-two were highly productive (Ramírez 1884: 386–87). The remote settlement of Batopilas became a bustling town of several thousand, centered around the mining activities of the Batopilas Mining Company, which was managed locally by Alexander "Boss" Shepherd, a former governor of the District of Columbia (Ramírez 1884: 380–88; Aldasoro 1941: 19; Shepherd 1938).

At the same time, the first large-scale exploitation of the extensive pine forests of Chihuahua's Sierra Madre began, stimulated primarily by developments in the United States. In the second half of the nineteenth century, the forestry industry in the United States had overexploited forests from the Appalachians to the Pacific Northwest. To meet the continuing demand for lumber and other wood products, American capitalists turned to nearby Chihuahua. Several lumbering companies were formed, most of which were controlled by Americans and other foreigners with the support and in some cases the capital of powerful Mexicans. To facilitate the removal of lumber and minerals to markets outside the Sierra, a railroad was constructed, from which a network of roads led to interior forests and mines. Initially, lumbering activities were in the upper Papigochi valley and adjacent areas, and then as the railroad entered the Sierra to the west, to either side of its track. Only the disruptions accompanying the Mexican Revolution prevented the wholesale destruction of these forests (Lartigue 1983; Lister and Lister 1966: 298).

Basíhuare was not affected by this forestry boom because of its distance from the railroad and the absence of an adequate road system into the area. I also have discovered no evidence that mining had any direct influence on the area before 1900. Batopilas, the closest major mining center, is located over a hundred tortuous kilometers from Basíhuare with two major canyons between. The principal trails out of Batopilas prior to the twentieth century led southwest to Sinaloa or east through Tónachi to Parral and Chihuahua, passing nowhere near Basíhuare (Anonymous 1754; Ministro de Fomento 1890). When the mines reopened in the late nineteenth century, the Rarámuri from Basíhuare apparently did not work in them. In fact, few Rarámuri did, most of the Indian mine workers being Yaquis and Mayos from Sinaloa and Sonora (Brodie 1905).

Twentieth Century

In the first two decades of the twentieth century, the mining industry in Chihuahua collapsed, due to conflicts associated with the Mexican Revolution and a severe drop in the price of metals on the the world market (Champion 1955: 562). As in the previous century, the major mines shut down, and workers in both the mines and secondary enterprises were forced to move from the area or to take up other activities, typically farming. Unemployed miners did not establish farms or ranches in the Basíhuare area, however, because its arable land is scattered and poor.

The most significant effect of the mines in the early twentieth century was the construction of the road through Basíhuare connecting Batopilas with the railroad station of Creel. When the road was finished, the first non-Indian settlers moved in to operate the mule station established in Basíhuare, and their descendants now represent the principal Mestizo element in the local population. Some local Indians began to work for these Mestizos, caring for their livestock, cultivating their fields, and serving as assistants to muleteers. A few Rarámuri men from other areas—Samachique, Nárárachi, Guagueybo—moved into Basíhuare to work and most remained, marrying local women. The Mestizos opened a store, providing the Rarámuri of Basíhuare with their first easy access to manufactured goods, albeit at elevated prices. After the collapse of the mines, these Mestizos remained behind to farm and to operate the store. Some also became muleteers, providing the link between the remnant population in Batopilas and the outside world.

The social and political turmoil that characterized much of the nineteenth century continued into the first decades of the twentieth. Local revolts led up to the Mexican Revolution, which raged from 1910 until 1920. As the home territory of Francisco Villa, the state of Chihuahua was a major battleground, and several battles and skirmishes were fought in Rarámuri country (Almada 1955; González Rodríguez 1982; Lister and Lister 1966). No study has been made of the Rarámuri in the revolution, but their role as combatants clearly was of less consequence than that of neighboring groups like the Yaqui and Mayo (Spicer 1980: 227–35; Crumrine 1983: 274). A few Rarámuri served as scouts (Thord-Gray 1960), but most appear to have remained neutral and thus vulnerable. People in the Basíhuare area still tell stories of soldiers commandeering livestock and maize and of families abandoning their farms when troops set up camps nearby. During this period, some Rarámuri fled from adjacent pueblos to lands near Basíhuare to escape the violence.

Despite the conflicts that have raged around them, the violence that the Rarámuri have directed toward outsiders throughout the twentieth century has been infrequent, short-lived, and quite localized, for example, the small uprising in 1918 near Batopilas (Boudreau 1986, 1975: 49–51) or the conspiracy to kill or drive out all non-Indians from the Tehuerichi area that was rumored to have occurred around 1969 (Lartigue 1983: 96). Rarámuri discontent during the twentieth century, regardless if it found violent expression, has been directly linked to the dramatic increase in the number of non-Indians in the Sierra.

At the turn of the century, the number of non-Indians in the area was only slightly greater than the Indian population, but by 1940 non-Indians outnumbered Indians approximately three to one and by 1980 by about six to one (Plancarte 1954; Secretaría de Programación y Presupuesto 1983). Throughout the twentieth century, the Indian population has remained relatively stable. The non-Indian population has increased so rapidly because of high birth and infant survival rates and some assimilation of Indians into the Mestizo culture. Large numbers of non-Indians also have arrived from outside the Sierra, attracted as in previous centuries by employment opportunities in lumbering, mining, and farming.

The major effect of these demographic changes has been the displacement of many Rarámuri into areas that are at best marginal for maize agriculture. Few Rarámuri subsistence farmers are able to grow enough maize to last from one harvest to the next. They must supplement their agricultural incomes by working for non-Indians both in the Sierra and outside. The 1980 census indicates that of 56,400 speakers of Rarámuri in Chihuahua, over 16,000 live outside the Sierra (Secretaría de Programación y Presupuesto 1983).[6] Most of these emigrants are located in urban or agricultural centers to the east where they work at menial jobs or beg to survive, many on a permanent basis.

In the 1940s, gold and silver were discovered twenty kilometers upstream from Batopilas at La Bufa, and the mule track through Basíhuare was upgraded to handle the trucks that carried the metals to Creel (Aldasoro 1941: 19). Rarámuri and Mestizo men from the Basíhuare area found temporary employment on the road construction crews, but none seem to have worked in the mines. The basis of the local economy remained subsistence agriculture. However, when lumbering activities were resumed on a large scale in the 1940s and 1950s, the roads built for mining activities were the base for a requisite network of logging roads.

In this second major epoch of Chihuahua's lumbering history, the Mexican government has carefully monitored forestry activities to preserve the forests as a renewable resource, and the major companies involved have tended to be controlled by Mexican rather than foreign business interests. In the 1950s, the Instituto Nacional Indigenista, an agency of the Mexican government comparable to the U.S. Bureau of Indian Affairs, began a program to bring large sections of the Sierra under the control of local *ejidos*. The goal of the Instituto's program was to ensure that the residents of these areas of the Sierra, which included many Rarámuri and other Indians but just as many Mestizos, would have more say in the exploitation of their forests and a larger share in the profits (Champion 1962; Lartigue 1983).

In the 1950s, the first sawmill opened in the Basíhuare area, operated by a private Mexican company. At the same time, the *ejido* of Basíhuare was reactivated to represent the local people in negotiations with the lumbering companies, for although it had been officially established in the 1930s (Diario Oficial 1930), it had never actually functioned. In the early 1960s, the *ejido* acquired a loan from the Banco Nacional de Crédito Ejidal to build its own sawmill, which has processed much of the lumber cut in the area since. As is the case in most of the *ejidos* in the Rarámuri area, the administration of the Basíhuare *ejido* and its enterprises, including the sawmill, tends to be controlled by the local Mestizos, with the Rarámuri working in subordinate positions for the minimum wage. The Rarámuri cut most of the trees and perform the manual labor at the sawmill, while the Mestizos supervise the operation of the sawmill and haul the lumber out in trucks that they or the *ejido* own. Because there is never sufficient labor demand at the sawmill to engage all the members of the *ejido* at any one time, they rotate every few weeks to give everyone the opportunity to work.

Lumbering, like the other forms of wage labor available to them, remains for the Rarámuri as well as many Mestizos a temporary supplement to their subsistence agricultural activities. The large profits for local people that many anticipated have never materialized, in part because of mismanagement, in part because the market and thus the prices for lumber are controlled by business interests outside the Sierra. As Lartigue (1983) points out, the forestry industry in the region, rather than transforming the local economy and society, has tended to reinforce entrenched patterns of poverty, exploitation, and domination.

The Jesuits returned to Chihuahua and the Rarámuri missions in 1900 (Ocampo 1966). The reestablishment of the mission system was interrupted during the Mexican Revolution—in 1914, for example, Francisco Villa deported all foreign Jesuits to the United States—and during the Calles persecution of the clergy between 1925 and 1929 (Ocampo 1966: 95, 177ff.). In the years since, a resident missionary has never been assigned to Basíhuare and, because of a shortage of missionaries and the difficulties of travel, it was not visited by Catholic priests on anything resembling a regular basis until the 1950s.

Around 1950, the Jesuits inaugurated a program to enhance communication within the mission system and to facilitate the conversion of the "gentile" Rarámuri who lived within the boundaries of the mission but remained unaffiliated with the Catholic church (Vicariato Apostólico de Tarahumara 1980: 6). In addition to acquiring shortwave radios and pick-up trucks, they began building airstrips in inaccessible regions, one of which was located near gentile communities in a remote area of the Basíhuare *ejido*. Their efforts to incorporate the members of these communities into the church seem to have had an impact, for while local baptized Rarámuri still often refer to these people as "gentiles" they claim that everyone has now been baptized. Equally important in the integration of these gentiles, however, has been their extensive intermarriage with baptized Rarámuri, a practice that appears to have been under way for at least several generations.

In the 1970s and 1980s the relationship between the Catholic church and the Basíhuare community remained essentially the same as in previous decades. Basíhuare falls within the jurisdiction of the Creel parish and is administered as a *visita* by a priest who lives in Creel, assisted on occasion by nuns from a Jesuit clinic there. They come to Basíhuare for major church holidays and some Sundays to perform Mass, but local Rarámuri officials known as *méstro* (from the Spanish *maestro*, "teacher") lead the services most of the year. The Rarámuri of Basíhuare receive no formal instruction in doctrine, do not participate in confession, and rarely take communion. Only a few local Indian people have been married by priests but all have had their children baptized by them. The recent emphasis of the Jesuit mission program in Basíhuare has been less on strictly religious concerns than on the provision of social services through a school established in Rejogochi and the health clinic in Creel.

THE EMERGENCE OF CONTEMPORARY RARÁMURI CULTURE

The arrival of Europeans in their territory exposed the Rarámuri to new forms of social and political organization, the beliefs and practices of a highly structured, proselytizing world religion, a variety of technological innovations, and the violence, discrimination, and exploitation that so often are the lot of subordinate groups in colonial systems. Their interaction with outsiders has resulted in a number of changes in their indigenous way of life, but the Rarámuri of the sixteenth century would have little difficulty recognizing their descendants of the twentieth. The Rarámuri language remains the first language of most people today and for some is the only language spoken. Contemporary patterns of settlement, subsistence, and social interaction also bear close similarities to the indigenous formations out of which they developed. The areas of their culture that have been most dramatically affected are those of technology, political organization, and religion.

In the realm of technology, the introduction of the metal axe allowed a greater reliance on wood as a raw material and, together with the Old World plow, facilitated the clearing and cultivation of fields. The Rarámuri also integrated sheep and chickens very soon after contact (Guadalajara and Tardá 1857; Ratkay 1683: 20–21) as well as cattle, goats, horses, mules, and donkeys but apparently more gradually. These Old World animals provided the Rarámuri with basic raw materials like wool and hides as well as a new source of meat, which had previously come entirely from wild animals. Early reports document the Rarámuri's great desire for wool, which they quickly adopted for weaving, eventually ceasing to use native plant fibers (Contreras 1638; Zingg 1940). Sheep, goats, and cattle were particularly important as sources of manure, and cattle served as draught animals. With a ready supply of manure, the Rarámuri were no longer dependent on flooding or burning vegetation to maintain soil fertility, and they also were able to begin cultivating lands located off the floodplains.[7] Because the amount of arable land in any given area increased, settlement could become more concentrated, and because cultivation was more efficient, more land could be cultivated. Perhaps the most significant implication of the availability of these new lands was that they took the place of the floodplains appropriated by Spanish farmers.

While the introduction of Old World domesticated animals may have enabled the Rarámuri to become more sedentary in the long term, at the same time it seems to have increased seasonal mobility. Sheep and goats do not endure the cold Sierra winters well and die from exposure if they are not sheltered (see Neumann 1682; Escalona 1744). The Rarámuri in many areas began moving with their flocks to winter quarters, often rockshelters located in protected spots or, in the more westerly areas, at lower elevations in the canyons. Before European contact the Rarámuri in at least some areas probably migrated in winter, but the acquisition of livestock provided another incentive to do so.

The integration of these new domesticated animals also had an impact on social relations. Sheep and goats, for example, need to graze several hours daily and must be herded year-round. The addition of this major task to the existing chores would have required considerable adjustment in household work schedules. Responsibility for the flocks seems to have fallen primarily to women and children because their tasks included activities like plant gathering, which are compatible with the animals' needs, while the men's work cultivating crops and hunting could not be done with livestock around.

From the time these animals were introduced, they appear to have been owned by individuals rather than communally, with variation in the number of animals owned. The result is not only differential access to resources but, because of the important role these animals played in plowing and fertilizing the fields, differential access to the means of production. The potential for the emergence of marked status differences in such a situation is obvious, but a number of mechanisms exist to maintain relative equality. These include the practice of poorer families working temporarily for the members of more prosperous households or borrowing animals from them, the redistribution of food through sponsorship of fiestas by wealthier individuals, and the general etiquette of food sharing.

The Spanish also engendered important changes in the political sphere of Rarámuri life. Cultural contact inevitably creates a need for cultural brokers, and some Rarámuri men emerged very early as mediators between their people and the Spanish, particularly in trade. Two seventeenth-century Jesuit reports (Pascual 1651; Tardá and Guadalaxara 1676: 377v) identify such men as political leaders. Of more significance, however, was the political organization imposed by the Spanish colonial government and Catholic missionaries on the mission pueblos.

Initially the appointed Rarámuri officials served primarily to enforce the policies of their priests, but gradually their responsibilities were expanded. Near the end of the seventeenth century, for example, the Spanish transferred the punishment of Indian criminals to the local pueblo officials, having concluded that the whippings and other punishments the Indians received from the missionaries and Spaniards were a major cause of revolts (Spicer 1962: 332). Eventually these pueblo political organizations emerged as critical components in the multicultural colonial and postcolonial society of the area, providing a more complex, centralized structure than existed aboriginally for organizing the internal affairs of local communities and dealing with outsiders. Today this set of officials is duplicated in all the Rarámuri pueblos in much the same form as described above for Basíhuare (Aguirre Beltrán 1953: 69–93).

Since the time of their arrival, the most persistent concern of outsiders with respect to the Rarámuri has been their conversion to Christianity. Contemporary Rarámuri religion and cosmology reflect the influence of Catholicism, but the missionaries have had more impact on ritual than on religious belief itself (Fried 1977: 268; Bennett and Zingg 1935). Early colonial documents suggest that the Rarámuri considered many Christian rituals to have a material efficacy, especially in preventing and alleviating illness (e. g., Font 1611). Today elements taken from Christian rituals, like the use of the crucifix and ritual gestures in the form of a cross, are prominent in Rarámuri curing rituals. The Rarámuri also adopted the major fiesta days of the Catholic calendar and incorporated several rituals derived ultimately from European folk Catholicism. Most important of these introduced rituals are the colorful pageantry of the Easter season and the dances performed by the flamboyantly costumed matachines.

Christian theology has had considerably less influence on Rarámuri thought. Throughout the colonial period, missionaries lamented that few Rarámuri were well instructed in Catholic doctrine. In 1683 from the mission of Carichí, one complained that

> all the Indians are utterly incapable of receiving the blessed Eucharist, for the reason that they do not sufficiently grasp the idea of God, concealed in the Host. The sacrament of the Eucharist is not administered in any of these Tarahumara [Rarámuri] missions—not even to the dying (Ratkay 1683: 36).

Over a half-century later, another Jesuit reported from the same mission that "they cannot even cite the catechism" (Fernández de Abee, in Sheridan and Naylor 1979: 80). The Rarámuri superficially identified Christian deities with their indigenous gods—for example, linking God to a paternal deity associated with the sun and the Virgin Mary to a maternal deity associated with the moon—but little more.

The influence of Catholic ideas on the Rarámuri concept of soul follows this pattern. The concept of soul obviously is an important component of

Christian theology, but the ideas that constitute the contemporary Rarámuri concept of soul bear little resemblance to Catholic notions, and the way they use these ideas in explanations is, as will be seen, vastly different. In any case, there is no doubt that a concept of soul is indigenous to the Rarámuri. In a 1611 report, Font (1611; cf. González Rodríguez 1982: 159) writes, "They say that when someone dies, that the soul does not die but goes to the wilds where a fiend seizes bad people and allows the good to pass to better lands. The Tepehuan have believed the same, but neither one nor the other know how to explain more about this than what is said here." Similarly, in 1683, another Jesuit missionary, describing the Rarámuri's "religion in former times," wrote, "They believed that after death the soul went to a paradise, which they called *osomaehiqui*; there, they said, the souls sported and danced" (Ratkay 1683: 41).[8]

As Sheridan and Naylor (1979: 3–4) point out, Rarámuri culture change has been predominantly of the type Spicer (1961: 530) calls "incorporative." For the most part, the Rarámuri have adopted elements of non-Indian culture that reinforced their indigenous lifestyle while rejecting those that did not. Of course, the integration of introduced elements required some modification in aboriginal patterns, but overall the pre-existing order experienced little disruption.

To understand why the Rarámuri's incorporation of foreign cultural elements has taken the form that it has, we must comprehend the context of contact, particularly the relations of power and control between the engaged societies. The Rarámuri were first and most extensively exposed to European culture in the Jesuit missions. The priests designed their mission programs to give themselves a measure of control over the Indians' lives rivaled only by that found in prisons. In such a situation, the form of acculturation that would seem most likely to result is complete assimilation. Because the Jesuits' program of reduction rarely succeeded, however, most Rarámuri missions fell in line with a pattern that characterized much of northern New Spain, what Gerhard (1982: 27–29) has called the "empty-core pattern." Here the mission pueblos became essentially ceremonial centers with few or no permanent residents other than the priests and their assistants. The majority of Indians maintained or returned to their aboriginal pattern of living next to their fields in dispersed rancherias, congregating in the pueblo centers only to conduct business and religious ceremonies.

A major consequence of this pattern was that the Jesuits never established firm control over more than a few Rarámuri at a time, even when the missions were flourishing. Among other things, the missionaries had to rely on Native officials to administer the missions and on Native catechists to convey the Catholic doctrine both in the mission centers and to the widely dispersed mission populations. Even though most Jesuits seem to have learned the Rarámuri language, they could not have completely censored the transformations of the Christian message that resulted. They also were unable to ensure that their converts' enthusiasm for Christianity was equal to that for other elements introduced by the missions. As one dismayed missionary wrote in 1683,

> they are so excessively fond of beef that if it were possible—by some
> dreadful metamorphosis, that is—they would often change themselves
> into cattle. When they see a steer afar off, they dash out of their huts,
> leaving everything else, and rush toward it, shouting for joy and clapping
> their hands. They butcher the animal, skin it, and smear their faces and
> bodies with the blood, so that they look like monsters. Then they tear
> out the viscera, roast them a little over a fire, and when they are half-
> cooked devour them, yelling all the while. Often, on hearing the uproar,
> I would say to myself, "O unhappy wretches, in your love of cow's flesh,
> you run swiftly to nourish your bodies with a little food. But how slowly
> you move when you come to worship God, and how you drag your feet!
> Oh, first seek the food which will illumine your souls with heavenly light,
> and after that look for nourishment to sustain your mortal parts!"
> Indeed, I often said these things to them, but they fell in vain upon deaf
> ears; the Indians would break out into roars of laughter (Ratkay 1683:
> 32–33).

The Rarámuri's selective integration of Spanish elements into their preexisting cultural framework appears to have been completed before the Jesuits were expelled in 1767 (Champion 1962: 20, 429–30) and accomplished primarily in the missions themselves. Except for the few non-Christian Rarámuri who worked in Spanish mines and farms, only the Indians closely associated with the missions would have been exposed to the foreign culture to the extent required to integrate elements from it, to learn animal husbandry, for example, or details of Catholic ritual and belief. These mission Indians likely were responsible for diffusing this new culture to the Rarámuri who remained outside the missions.

The Rarámuri who deserted the mission pueblos accepted much of what the missionaries had to offer, including portions of their religion. One missionary's description of the activities of these people, whom the priests called "apostates," illustrates the extent of this acceptance:

. . . they withdraw from the pueblos to mountains and gorges, where
they practice their idolatries and commit outrages against the Faith.
These apostate Indians do themselves say Mass, and perform baptisms
and hear confessions; and they lead the others astray, persuading them to
live no longer in their pueblos, where they are instructed in Christian
doctrine and have political security, but to revert to the former mode of
life and to the savage freedom which prevails in this sierra, where the
curb of an enduring conversion has not yet been imposed upon the
Indians (Escalona 1744).

This evidence suggests that the synthesis of Indian and European cultures
was introduced already formed into many Rarámuri areas rather than being
created independently in each location following direct contact with the
Spanish. This conclusion is further supported by the uniformity of this contact
culture over the entire Rarámuri region today despite natural barriers to
communication and marked differences in the histories of different areas.
Even those Rarámuri who traditionally have rejected any affiliation with the
Catholic church and who the missionaries called "gentiles" share this culture,
including many of the same elements of Catholic religion that the baptized
Rarámuri maintain (Kennedy 1970a, 1978).

The similarities between "gentile" and "baptized" Rarámuri today may
also exist because many of the gentiles are the descendants of "apostates."
As the Jesuit José María Miqueo reported in 1745 from the mission of Yoquivo, located above the Batopilas canyon,

. . . these canyons are the common refuge of those who have fled other
missions; and according to what I have learned in the almost year and a
half since I came, the majority of the gentiles—of the many who live in
this rugged land—are not gentiles originally, but children or descendants
of bad Christians who, fleeing the pueblos or work in the mines, have
multiplied themselves, leaving their children with an abhorrence for the
pueblos and the Spaniards, a heritage of little appreciation for the
sacraments, and even a revulsion for the ministers of God.

Miqueo went on to complain that both gentiles and baptized Rarámuri had
their own sacraments that imitated those of the Catholic church and which
they considered to be as effective as those administered by the priests.

Because Basíhuare remained some distance from Spanish settlements
and missions throughout the colonial period, its residents probably were the
recipients rather than creators of the culture that emerged out of the contact

between the Rarámuri and Spanish. Presumably this culture was introduced to them by Rarámuri who lived closer to Spanish centers or who were fleeing into Basíhuare from these centers long before the Basíhuare mission was founded in the nineteenth century . If so, the Basíhuare Rarámuri would have been able to adapt this culture to local conditions free of direct intervention by non-Indians until the twentieth century.

Lartigue (1983: 96–98) has cautioned against exaggerating the isolation of the Rarámuri from the outside world and the autonomy of action they supposedly have enjoyed because of it. Despite the physical isolation of Basíhuare, the people who live there have been constrained in both the formation of their local society and culture and their interactions with outsiders by the economic and political conditions in the region and by a historical consciousness created out of an awareness of events that have transpired far beyond their ranchos. Nonetheless, for most of their history, the Basíhuare Rarámuri have been more isolated from outside influences than many other Rarámuri communities, and their contemporary society and culture reflect the relative autonomy afforded them by this isolation.

The establishment of a mission in Basíhuare in the nineteenth century and the arrival of Mestizo settlers in the twentieth diminished the extent of this autonomy but did not eliminate it entirely. By the time the mission was founded, the Catholic church had modified significantly its approach to missionization, especially the role that "reduction" would play. Although reduction remained a mission ideal, it had been abandoned as impractical in most of the mountainous areas and seems never to have been applied to Basíhuare (Spicer 1962: 38–39, 331–32). Basíhuare's *visita* status also suggests that the Rarámuri there would not have received strict instruction in Catholic doctrine. A *visita* would not have had a resident missionary, and the visiting priest probably would have remained only a few days at a time. Local Rarámuri probably were trained as catechists to lead prayers in the priests' absence and to teach the others Catholic doctrine, with considerable reinterpretation undoubtedly the result. The impact of Catholicism might also have been weakened because this mission appears to have been founded just after the Mexican Independence, when government subsidies of the mission system were disrupted and the missionary ranks depleted by the newly formed Mexican government's policy of deporting Spaniards (Arlegui 1851: 458). With the entire mission system struggling because of lack of personnel and resources, a minor mission like Basíhuare surely would have been neglected.

The Franciscan mission in Basíhuare appears to have existed no more than thirty years. It was reestablished by Jesuits in the early twentieth century, but again as a *visita* with no resident misssionary. Thus, the Rarámuri of Basíhuare have never had extensive contact with Catholic priests at any point in their history. They have maintained almost total control over their religious affairs and have incorporated Christian beliefs much more superficially than the Rarámuri of many other communities.

Similarly, because the Basíhuare Rarámuri have always greatly outnumbered local Mestizos, they have been able to retain possession over much of the best farming land, and despite some feelings of antagonism, relations between the two groups have been peaceful. Although Mestizos have controlled the local *ejido* organization for much of its existence, they compete among themselves for offices in this organization, which they can win only by cultivating the support of the Indians. The Rarámuri thus are in a position to manipulate the local economic and political situation to their advantage. In 1987, in fact, they elected Rarámuri men to lead the *ejido*.

Given the small number of Mestizos in the area, the Rarámuri of Basíhuare have experienced less pressure to adopt Mestizo culture than have the Rarámuri of many other communities. Since around 1970, however, several changes have taken place. Spanish has replaced Rarámuri as the principal language of interaction between Rarámuri and Mestizos, and, while most Rarámuri women continue to wear distinctively Rarámuri clothing, most men have exchanged their loincloths and headbands for pants and cowboy hats. They also have begun purchasing larger quantities of luxury items from Mestizo culture, like radios and tape players, and have increased their use of chemical fertilizers and tequila.

These recent modifications in local culture have resulted primarily from more extensive involvement of Rarámuri men in the regional wage economy and greater participation of Rarámuri children in the Mexican educational system. Throughout the 1970s, most local Rarámuri men worked as laborers on construction crews upgrading the main road through this section of the Sierra. In the 1970s and 1980s, a number of younger men also left the area to work for a few weeks or months at a time on large agricultural projects in central Chihuahua and the adjacent states of Sinaloa and Sonora. In both settings, these men came in close contact with Mestizos who ridiculed the Rarámuri's traditional clothing and poor Spanish, causing many to adopt Mestizo dress and to speak Spanish more frequently, even among themselves. These work experiences also exposed the Rarámuri to a wide variety of manufactured goods and provided them cash with which to purchase them.

The Mexican government has operated elementary schools in and around Basíhuare since the 1920s (Basauri 1929: 15–16), but attendance was poor until the 1950s, when the local representatives of the government began pressuring Rarámuri parents to send their children to school. In the 1970s, the government built a new school complete with dormitories and dining room in Basíhuare, and the Jesuits established a similar boarding school in Rejogochi. By 1980, the Jesuits had converted the Rejogochi school into a day school because they felt that, by keeping children away from home much of the year, they were undermining the transmission of Rarámuri culture.

Most of the teachers in these elementary schools have been non-Indians or acculturated Rarámuri from outside the Rarámuri area, and they have relied on textbooks provided by the Mexican government in their classes. The impact of these schools on Rarámuri culture has been blunted by the erratic attendance of many students and the difficulties of cross-cultural education. On the other hand, most students have gained a basic competency in Spanish and have begun wearing Mestizo clothing as a result of their experiences there.

These changes possibly mark the beginning of a period of extensive acculturation that will culminate in the radical transformation of contemporary Rarámuri life and the greater integration of the Rarámuri into the national economy and culture of Mexico. Yet by the end of the 1980s, most of the changes that had taken place were superficial. Overall, culture change in Basíhuare in the 1970s and 1980s has conformed to the same pattern as that for the Rarámuri as a whole throughout their postcontact history: new elements have been incorporated while the core of the Rarámuri's distinctive culture has remained intact.

RARÁMURI SERMONS AND
THE REPRODUCTION OF KNOWLEDGE

THE REPRODUCTION OF KNOWLEDGE

The reproduction of knowledge is one aspect of the more general processes of cultural reproduction. In American anthropology, cultural reproduction or, as it is often called, cultural transmission, emerged as a major focus of investigation in the first half of the twentieth century within the context of culture-and-personality studies. This approach was directed primarily toward elucidating the processes by which individuals become competent members of their cultures. Its advocates emphasized socialization and enculturation as the principal mechanisms by which the transmission of culture was accomplished and focused on the more psychological dimensions of this process, paying particular attention to the inculcation of values and cognitive schemes (Ortner 1984: 154; Harris 1968; Honigmann 1967). In recent years, some of the contemporary heirs of this intellectual tradition have argued that the study of cultural transmission must be undertaken within a broader perspective that takes into account "the driving forces and incorporative patterns of the larger society" (Comitas and Dolgin 1978: 166). However, the learning of culture by individuals, in both informal settings and formal educational contexts, remains a central focus of inquiry (cf. Hansen 1979; Hefner 1983).

The transmission of culture to the individual is a crucial dimension of cultural reproduction, but of equal importance is the reproduction of culture within the society as a whole. In the following pages, I examine the reproduction within Rarámuri society of the fundamental ideas about the universe in terms of which people act and interpret their experience. My primary concern is how this theoretical knowledge is made available for learning through various social practices and how this process in turn affects the distribution of the knowledge among the members of the society. In this sense, the reproduction of knowledge is directly tied to the reproduction of social life in general.

The most sophisticated perspectives on the reproduction of social life available today are found in the work of Pierre Bourdieu (1977, 1984) and Anthony Giddens (1976, 1979, 1984) (cf. Karp and Maynard 1983 and Sahlins 1981). Both Bourdieu and Giddens regard social life as a concrete historical process produced through the activities of sentient human beings. The focus of their inquiry is the relationship between human action and the systemic and structural properties of social formations. Of particular concern to both is how asymmetrical social relations of domination and subordination are created and perpetuated through the actions of the members of society.

Giddens (1979: 189) envisions human action to be motivated by the pursuit of interests, which he identifies as the possible modes through which people can fulfill their "wants." These wants emerge out of the fundamental conditions of human existence as well as the more specific circumstances of membership in particular societies and social classes. Structure both enables and constrains action and is linked to it through generative structural principles called "rules," which order action, and "resources," the power relations among the members of a society in terms of which action can take place. For Giddens (1979: 63ff.), structure is virtual, existing not as a totality in space and time but only partially and momentarily in its instantiations, that is, in practices. Thus, by virtue of structure, action is possible, and through action, structure is perpetuated (Giddens 1984: 374).

Bourdieu's ideas about the relationship between structure and human agency revolve around his notion of "habitus." He defines the habitus as a system of enduring dispositions or propensities that incline individuals to act in certain ways in given circumstances (1979). While the habitus is situated ontologically in individuals, it is socially constituted, the product of social conditions that in turn are produced by the material conditions of existence. Bourdieu avoids a complete material determinism of social action by envisioning material conditions to determine the social only "in the last instance" and then only negatively, by constraining the range of possibilities rather than specifying particular ones. Nonetheless, because of the direct connections between them, the social conditions of existence and thus the habitus are consistent with the material conditions with which they are associated (cf. Bourdieu 1984: 483–84).

Bourdieu focuses on the generative aspect of the habitus as the immediate source of individual interests and schemes of perception, conception, and action. Like Giddens, he regards human action as motivated by the need or desire to pursue interests. This action is accomplished by following strategies formulated in reference to both these interests and interpretations of the social and material contexts of action. The structures of the social and material worlds are internalized by the habitus, which in turn organizes the interests, strategies, and actions that produce practices. As a result, these practices embody and reproduce these structures.

Both Bourdieu (1977; 1984: 474) and Giddens (1979: 39ff.; 1984: 5–6) consider most social practices to be the product of habitual action based on what they call "practical" knowledge, in essence, the skills or expertise required to produce particular practices. They differ, however, in the importance they attribute to actors' explicit understandings of their world in the production of social action. For Bourdieu, explicit knowledge orients practices but does not produce them, typically serving as the basis for ex post facto rationalizations of action that disguise social reality, especially relations of inequality, in order to perpetuate it. In contrast, Giddens emphasizes that what people think explicitly about their world has a definite effect on their behavior and consequently on the products of their behavior. He (1984: 3–7) proposes a "stratification model of personality" that distinguishes three levels of consciousness: the unconscious, which is not directly accessible to actors; the practical consciousness, which while not unconscious cannot be expressed verbally by actors; and the discursive consciousness, which consists of what actors are able to talk about. In his view, all three levels of consciousness are implicated in the production of all social action.

Giddens also regards the reflexive monitoring of action by actors as a critical element in the production and reproduction of social life. He recognizes such monitoring as intrinsic to everyday action and the source of the understandings that the members of society have about their own activities and those of others as well as about the physical and social contexts of action. These understandings provide the basis not only for rationalizations of behavior but for future action as well. By reflecting on their actions, people also reproduce the tacit and discursive knowledge that makes their action possible in the first place.

Yet, events cannot be understood exclusively in terms of the knowledge and intentions of the actors who produce them. While actors know a great deal about their society and the circumstances of action within it, they are never totally aware of all the conditions that impinge upon their actions nor are all the consequences of these actions intended by them. As Giddens argues, "The escape of human history from human intentions, and the return of the consequences of that escape as causal influences on human action, is a chronic feature of social life" (1979: 7).

Bourdieu's and Giddens's models of the production and reproduction of social life provide a general framework within which the reproduction of theoretical knowledge can be investigated, but it is precisely in this area that their models most need development. Because the principal object of their inquiries is the process by which social relations are constituted, perpetuated, and transformed, both Bourdieu and Giddens emphasize the role that knowledge plays in the production of practices and only secondarily the role of practices in the reproduction of knowledge. In addition, they concentrate almost entirely on knowledge that is closely linked to practices, which, given the routine nature of most social behavior, is largely tacit, practical knowledge rather than explicit, discursive knowledge. As a result, they tend to ignore the reproduction of theoretical knowledge that is not directly implicated in the production of practices.[1]

My goal here is to shift the focus of inquiry from the reproduction of practices to the reproduction of knowledge in order to incorporate the complexities of cultural reproduction into a model of the reproduction of social life. Doing so risks committing the idealist fallacy of regarding culture as a mental phenomenon that exists apart from and logically if not temporally prior to practices. I avoid this pitfall by taking the reproduction of knowledge to be a concrete social process and by placing equal emphasis on both knowledge and practice. I begin this undertaking by classifying different kinds of knowledge on the basis of the characteristics that are most relevant to their reproduction and by examining the different kinds of practices required to reproduce them. I then consider the various social contexts within which the Rarámuri convey theoretical knowledge, focusing on the public speeches they deliver during gatherings at the pueblo center.

Kinds of Knowledge and Reproductive Practices

The perennial philosophical concern with the nature of knowledge has engendered a prodigious array of overlapping and sometimes contradictory characterizations of knowledge. Distinctions among different kinds of knowledge have been based on several criteria: the content of the knowledge in question (technological versus cosmological versus linguistic, etc.), its logical form (propositional versus nonpropositional), its relation to practice (practical versus theoretical), its social or psychological locus (public versus private, conscious versus unconscious), and so on. In terms of the manner in which it must be reproduced, however, the most important characteristic of a body of knowledge is whether it can be expressed verbally. I refer here to knowledge that can be rendered in explicit, verbal form as "discursive knowledge" in contrast to "nondiscursive knowledge," which cannot be formulated in propositions or other verbal expressions.

Nondiscursive knowledge includes both knowledge how to perform specific activities and the more experiential and evaluative dimensions of knowledge, which are related to the emotions as well as such things as the aesthetic sense (Bourdieu 1984). Such knowledge is by definition tacit since it cannot be expressed verbally. Discursive knowledge, on the other hand, can be either tacit or explicit. Tacit discursive knowledge often remains unspoken because it is so abstract, so grounded in experience, or so obvious that the need to formulate and express it verbally seldom arises (Sperber 1975: x). As Giddens (1984: 6) points out, the tacit typically is made explicit only when people confront puzzling events or need to justify an action that deviates from social conventions or expectations.

All explicit discursive knowledge is based upon tacit assumptions and connected to them by relations of logical contingency and presupposition. Such discursive knowledge also rests upon some nondiscursive knowledge, not because of logical connections between the two but because nondiscursive knowledge provides the experiential ground and thus the conditions for the existence of discursive knowledge. Ultimately all forms of discursive and nondiscursive knowledge are grounded in the unconscious, which, while incorporating both potentially discursive and intrinsically nondiscursive knowledge, remains inaccessible to conscious thought except perhaps through dreaming or the probings of psychotherapy.[2]

Discursive and nondiscursive forms of knowledge require different kinds of practices to be reproduced. Like the knowledge they reproduce, social practices are either discursive or nondiscursive in nature, that is, either verbal or nonverbal.[3] Certain kinds of discursive knowledge can be reproduced almost entirely through nonverbal practices. For example, a great deal of information about gender relations can be learned simply by watching men and women interact. In fact, while such relations can be described verbally, characterizing them explicitly often serves as the first step toward undermining their reproduction, particularly where they involve domination and subordination. On the other hand, in order to interpret such interactions, actors require some discursive knowledge not intrinsic to the acts themselves. In addition, many other kinds of discursive knowledge do not lend themselves to such portrayal through nonverbal acts and must be transmitted verbally to be reproduced.

In a similar way, the reproduction of nondiscursive knowledge must take place ultimately through nondiscursive practices. Verbal statements, like explanations of how to perform a particular action, can set the stage for the transmission of nondiscursive knowledge, but these statements only supplement and contextualize the nondiscursive practices by which the reproduction is accomplished. Moreover, the reproduction of most forms of nondiscursive knowledge remains incomplete until the person receiving the knowledge applies it in practice.

Whether discursive knowledge is explicit, tacit, or unconscious also has implications for its reproduction among the members of a society. The reproduction of tacit and unconscious forms of knowledge would appear to be more complicated than that of explicit discursive knowledge because they seldom appear in public discourse (Berger and Luckmann 1966; Douglas 1975), but such is not the case. Tacit knowledge and unconscious knowledge tend to be more fundamental than explicit discursive knowledge and to be logically presupposed by many different ideas. The explicit expression of any of these ideas necessarily entails the indirect transmission of the tacit and unconscious knowledge upon which the ideas are contingent. Similarly, in the course of producing practices, actors reproduce more or less automatically the nondiscursive knowledge that enables them to act. Such a relationship between knowledge and practice, in which the knowledge and practice directly reproduce one another, is the simplest form of reproduction. In contrast, much explicit discursive knowledge can be reproduced only through the verbal expression of the ideas in question because they are neither presupposed by other ideas nor so embedded in practices as to be directly conveyed through their production.

The processes by which knowledge, practices, and social life in general are reproduced are all interrelated and mutually dependent. Knowledge is reproduced among the members of a society only if some information is made available through public practices. At the same time, knowledge motivates the performance of these practices and provides the frameworks within which they are interpreted. On a broader scale, the existence and persistence of all kinds of knowledge depend upon the reproduction of the social forms through which practices are accomplished and of the more general social and cultural environments in terms of which the knowledge is rendered reasonable and thus worthy of acceptance (Hefner 1985; Eickelman 1979). These social forms and general contexts are themselves reproduced through the practices of social actors operating in terms of their knowledge of the world.

The Reproduction of Rarámuri Theoretical Knowledge

Rarámuri theoretical knowledge, like theoretical knowledge in all societies, has explicit as well as tacit and unconscious dimensions. While it is composed of ideas that can be expressed verbally, it is grounded ultimately in the conscious and unconscious assumptions that the Rarámuri make about the world. It also is linked to a variety of practices, the performance of which depends upon essentially nondiscursive knowledge.

As a body of discursive knowledge, Rarámuri theoretical knowledge requires some explicit formulation and transmission to be reproduced, but the Rarámuri maintain no formal educational institutions to instruct their children in such knowledge. Teaching of all kinds of knowledge is extremely informal, usually accomplished within the context of individual households through examples or brief statements rather than detailed explanations. Every sort of knowledge the Rarámuri possess is conveyed here: the basic values of the society, dress, postures, elementary skills like cooking and using an axe, advanced skills like weaving and playing musical instruments, as well as cosmological ideas and other theoretical knowledge. There seems to be no fixed time for the transmission of any particular kind of knowledge, which simply occurs in the course of daily life as the various subjects arise. Discussions of more theoretical topics, however, often take place in the evenings and early mornings as the members of the household relax before going to sleep or beginning the activities of the day.

A child's principal teachers are his or her parents and elder siblings, who assume many of the day-to-day responsibilities of child rearing. Grandparents also play a prominent role in raising their grandchildren. They often live in the same houses, or if not, the children may be sent to their grandparents' homes for a few days, weeks, or even months. The Rarámuri think of the grandparent-grandchild relationship as particularly close, characterized by warmth, affection, and considerable joking, especially about sex. Such older people also are regarded as rich sources of knowledge and serve as the arbiters of interpretations of events both present and past. They are called *anayáware* (ancient ones or ancestors) because they have lived in the past and thus are closer than the others to the events of the past and the knowledge that God gave the first Rarámuri at the beginning of the present world. Many people told me that they learned about the Rarámuri's deities, the organization of the universe, and similar cosmological matters primarily from their grandparents.

Households vary in the range and depth of the knowledge conveyed to their members. For example, I discovered that one five-year-old neighbor knew a great deal about medicinal plants—more in fact than some adults because his father was fascinated by the subject. Individuals with specialized knowledge like herbalism or more esoteric curing techniques tend to transmit this knowledge within the household or at least to their close relatives. Skills like oratory, which are not explicitly taught, also seem to follow family lines, presumably the result of boys emulating their fathers.

The informal exchange of theoretical knowledge among the members of different households takes place primarily during visits to one another's homes and drinking parties. People in Rejogochi are inveterate visitors, dropping in on one another with great frequency, usually in the morning soon after sunrise or in late afternoon. A visitor may come to a home simply to chat or to conduct some business, ask advice, or eat. Early morning visits often focus on dreams of the night before, a topic that almost invariably includes some cosmological information. If a household includes a particularly knowledgeable person, some visitors may arrive to seek his or her assistance in the interpretation of dreams or the diagnosis of illness. Occasionally the

Figure 11. A Rejogochi family. September 1977. Relaxing between their chinked log home and maize field, the woman feeds her baby while the son repairs his sandal. The family's dog laps up ground parched maize mixed with water from a plastic bowl, a cooking pot to one side. The man's hat rests on the base of an olla used for fermenting maize beer. The woman later repaired the hole in the olla's side, from which a rag protrudes, because such large ollas are difficult to replace.

principals in the conversation will move away from the house, but more often the other family members hear the exchange and even contribute to it. In my experience, however, conversations during most visits tend to be quite mundane, usually about community events and especially drinking parties.

Typical visits involve only the members of two households, but drinking parties draw together people from many different households. During these get-togethers, the Rarámuri often make offerings to their deities or the dead and perform curing rituals and other ceremonies. Considerable theoretical knowledge is conveyed through such activities, as I will discuss in chapters 5 and 6. In addition, near the beginning of the drinking, community leaders occasionally deliver speeches that outline proper drinking behavior and the general cosmological situation of the Rarámuri. This kind of knowledge may also appear in discussions during the drinking. People seldom talk about much of anything when they first arrive at a party, but conversation picks up after a few rounds of drinking. At this stage, the men (for I never sat with the women) may pursue more theoretical topics, with a number of different individuals participating and most of the others listening. Examples of topics I heard discussed at drinking parties include: where the sun and moon go after they set, why the moon does not appear every night, whether God drinks the beer that is offered to him, how restaurants in Mexico's cities produce ice, and why beer creates intestinal gases. Of course, these group conversations touch upon a wide range of additional subjects, including in particular recent events and community affairs.

As the drinking continues, the group tends to break down into smaller units and the conversation to shift to more personal topics. Frequently pairs of men move away from the others to talk privately. When I have been called aside, my partners often wanted me either to bring them things (sunglasses, radios, false teeth) or to do something for them (write a letter, for example). However, on some occasions these discussions focused on more philosophical matters, as they reportedly do among the Rarámuri men themselves, as for example when a man with moderate curing abilities consults with a more accomplished curer who performs a curing ritual during the party. These private tête-à-têtes obviously do not enter into the general conversation.

THE PUBLIC PRESENTATION OF THEORETICAL KNOWLEDGE

The Rarámuri present theoretical knowledge explicitly and consistently to large numbers of people from many different settlements only in the pueblo

Figure 12. A maize beer drinking party. Rejogochi, July 1981. The man in the foreground extends a gourd dipper of maize beer to the host of the party (not in view) after tossing some of the beer to the cardinal directions as an offering to Our Father. The man in the white hat to the right played his violin during the offering. Ollas of beer sit under the lean-to next to the house, the men and women entering from opposite sides to drink.

center, during speeches by the pueblo officials. As a result, these speeches are especially important in the reproduction of theoretical knowledge within the society, but much of Rarámuri theoretical knowledge, including the concept of soul, does not appear in them. The kinds of information these speeches convey as well as their overall efficacy as vehicles for the reproduction of theoretical knowledge is determined primarily by the role these speeches play in Rarámuri political process and the oratorical conventions that guide their production.

For the Rarámuri, the primary purpose of such speeches is not to communicate new information but to reiterate time-proven advice for the proper conduct of life. This purpose is reflected in their two terms for "speeches": *nawésare* and *nátiri*. These terms share the root *na-*, which means "to think," but *nawésare* and *nátiri* name not random thoughts or spontaneous opinions but well-worked-out thoughts and carefully considered opinions. The moral force the Rarámuri ascribe to these speeches is indicated by their tendency to choose the Spanish word *sermones* (sermons) as a more appropriate translation for these terms than the more common Spanish words for speeches, *pláticas* or *discursos*.

Speech-giving is part of the larger pattern of advice-giving that pervades Rarámuri social life. Adults regularly give advice to their children and to one another in both informal conversations and formal speeches. On certain ritual occasions they also deliver advice-filled sermons to the dead, imploring them to leave the living in peace, and to their crops and domestic animals, encouraging them to be productive and not to become disheartened by the late arrival of rain or the prospect of slaughter. Such advice is required, they feel, if people are to behave properly. They envision thought to precede and determine all behavior and regard the moral quality of people's actions as a direct expression of the quality of their thought, which in turn reflects the quality of the advice they have received.

People who act properly—who are kind to others, fulfill their responsibilities, are quick to share their food and labor, and refrain from being aggressive—are characterized not only as "good people" (*we ga?rá pagótame hu*)[4] but as "good thinkers" (*we ga?rá nátame hu*). Children become good thinkers by incorporating the advice offered by their elders, usually parents, grandparents, and older siblings. For adults, good advice is required to reinforce the ability to think well or to transform the bad thought of a person who fails to act in accordance with the standards of proper behavior. Many trials conclude with a short speech in which the presiding official scolds the offender and outlines the principles of proper behavior that should guide his or her behavior in the future. Such advice is considered fundamental to the individual's reform.

The Rarámuri of Rejogochi say that all good thought derives ultimately from their principal deities, whom they call "Our Father" and "Our Mother" and associate with the Sun and Moon.[5] Sometimes these deities convey their thinking to the Rarámuri in dreams, but most of this advice has been handed down from generation to generation, deriving from the original counsel they gave the Rarámuri's earliest ancestors. Bad thought comes exclusively from the Devil, who encourages people to fight, kill, bewitch, steal, and commit adultery. While most people consider the thought of Our Father and Our Mother to be superior to that of the Devil, they say that each individual decides which kind of thinking to follow in life, indicating through actions the choice that has been made: proper behavior indicates the selection of the thought of Our Father and Our Mother, improper conduct that of the Devil.

Rarámuri orators often portray their sermons as the words of Our Father and Our Mother. This rhetorical device for establishing authority and veracity is reinforced by the speakers' position within the society, usually as leaders or former leaders of the pueblo political organization who were selected for office because they are good people. Oratorical ability also provides concrete evidence of the speakers' moral, intellectual, and emotional strength. The most accomplished orators deliver their speeches at an incredibly fast pace, about 60 percent faster than normal conversation.[6] Their ability to speak so forcefully is taken as direct evidence of their ability to think well.

Speeches can be given any time people gather: to drink and work, to perform a ceremony, to conduct a trial, to bet on a footrace, and so on. The content of each speech is tailored to the events at hand but invariably includes advice on how people should conduct their lives. The most elaborate speeches tend to be those delivered by the pueblo political officials at the church in Basíhuare. The audiences for these speeches are composed of scores and at times hundreds of people from widely dispersed settlements who congregate in Basíhuare on Sundays and Catholic holy days.

These speeches typically follow the recitation of prayers in the church led by Rarámuri religious officials or the celebration of Mass, if a Catholic priest is present.[7] At the conclusion of these activities, the congregation files out of the church and reassembles in front, replicating their arrangement inside: women and children on the right, men to the left, all facing the church. The pueblo officials form a line across the portal and south side of the front wall of the church, facing the crowd and holding the canes that symbolize their authority. The leading pueblo official, the "governor" (siríame), usually delivers the speech, although in his absence or at his request, one of the other two leading officials—designated by the Spanish titles of teniénte (lieutenant governor) and alakánte from alcalde (mayor)—may do so.

When all are in place and hushed, the speaker begins. He stands erect and immobile except for the movement of his lips and an occasional emphatic gesture with his hand. His words flow in an intense monotonic stream, increasing in pitch steadily but nearly imperceptibly as he progresses. The crowd is attentive but impassive during the speech; only if the speaker falters will the listeners offer encouragement by shouting "Have strength!" (iwérasa.).

Examples of Rarámuri Sermons

The following speech was delivered in front of the Basíhuare church on January 1, 1978, by the governor of the Basíhuare pueblo. This was his last sermon as governor, after a tenure of six years. On this day he oversaw the

Figure 13. A sermon in Basíhuare. August 1981. The Basíhuare governor, grasping his cane of office, delivers a Sunday sermon. The lieutenant governor stands to his right, four other male officials to his left, while a tenánche leans against the church wall next to the steps. The men in the congregation, their hats removed, always assemble in front of the speaker, the women and small children to the side.

appointment of his successor by the men of the pueblo, an event to which he calls attention in the concluding section of the speech.

Yes, you good people who gathered here earlier to ask forgiveness of Our Father and Our Mother. May each of you arrive with strength back at the homes from which you came this morning. Come again to ask forgiveness here.

Follow the path of Our Father and the path of Our Mother. Do not be sad or disheartened. What good is being sad? Do Our Father and Mother get discouraged as they go caring for us here on earth? Everyone seek a long life. Vigorously pursue another day, another night, another year. Our Father and Our Mother never miss a day or year. They always are here on earth.

Like it has been from the beginning, this house [church] is standing here in which to ask forgiveness. Follow the path of Our Father and also the path of Our Mother. May you encounter old age a long way away. Grasp the staff of Our Father and also the staff of Our Mother, the flower of Our Father and the flower of Our Mother. In this way each of you who is standing here will have strength. Do not be unduly discouraged. Do Our Father and Mother become discouraged as they unfailingly provide light so that we can go around contentedly?

Do not fight. Always greet one another peacefully. That is good. Do not become angry as you sit together whenever someone makes beer to get some work done. Always ask permission to drink. Do not drink in secret. Sometimes bad things happen during drinking, causing people to cry. Fighting while drinking always makes a lot of work for your leaders. This is what I have to say to you people standing here.

Yes, you women who have gathered earlier, come here again to ask forgiveness of Our Father and Our Mother. Each of you walk vigorously along Our Father's path and Our Mother's path. Return again on Sunday. You women are not coming here in large numbers on Sunday. When you are drinking with other women, encourage them to come here on Sunday. Do not drink on Sundays. It will be good if everyone gathers here. In this fashion I speak to you people. In this way I give you my thought.

Others will now care for you and give you advice. From now on I will be resting. Listen well, you people: from now on I will be resting. I will simply sit when I drink with you. Realize, you people, that two new officials have been appointed. Listen you people who are standing here so that you will know who will help and care for you. In this fashion I speak to you people. Is this talk not good?

The crowd replies in unison, "It is good." The governor responds with, "Good bye. Thank you," and the crowd says "Thank you" in return. Then the governor tells them they may leave.

This speech develops three major themes. The first is the relation between the Rarámuri and their principal deities, designated as Our Father and Our Mother. These deities are portrayed as caring for the Rarámuri and offering them an approach to life—represented as a path, a staff, and a flower—for them to follow. That they also provide for their material needs is suggested by reference to the light emanating from the Sun and Moon, the most tangible gift of the most concrete manifestations of these deities. In return the Rarámuri are expected to come regularly from their homes to the church to "ask forgiveness" of their heavenly parents.

The words *wikála tána* mean "to ask forgiveness," *wikála* meaning "forgiveness" or "pardon" and *tána* "ask." The Rarámuri's conception of how this act is accomplished and the implications it has for their lives differs radically from that of more orthodox Christians. People "ask forgiveness" simply by entering the church or participating in ceremonies. They need not actually formulate their request verbally, in prayers, for example, or even in their thoughts. Moreover, salvation in the afterlife seldom is given as the reason for asking forgiveness. Rather people ask forgiveness to ensure God's continued beneficence by assuaging his anger at their misdeeds or their failure to fulfill their ritual responsibilities to him. In fact, many Rarámuri told me that *wikála tána* does not mean "to ask forgiveness" but "to ask God for good crops, rainfall, long lives, and protection from sickness," or "to give thanks to God" for such things. Asking forgiveness is the only obligation of the Rarámuri toward their deities specified in the sermon, but that it is fundamental to their relationship with Our Father and Our Mother is indicated by its reiteration throughout the speech, in both the men's and women's sections.[8]

The second theme of the speech is relations within Rarámuri society. Two overlapping sets of relations are mentioned: those among members of the community in general and those between the Rarámuri and their officials. In the speech, these two sets of relations are both portrayed in the specific context of drinking get-togethers. These gatherings are the most frequent interhousehold social event and the context within which most overt expressions of violence occur. Such an aggression-prone setting provides an appropriate backdrop against which to advocate the virtues of calm, restraint, and nonaggression in social relations. Drinking parties also are a principal context within which the pueblo officials fulfill their responsibility to care for the members of the community by intervening in their conflicts. The governor aptly captures the significance of his stepping down from office by indicating that in the future he will simply sit while drinking rather than involving himself in resolving interpersonal disputes.

The relation between the Rarámuri and their officials is more explicitly developed in the penultimate section of the speech, where the governor tells his audience that his successor has been appointed. Here the officials are portrayed as guiding, helping, and providing for the members of the community. There is an implicit but by no means unintended analogy here: that the relation between the members of society and their officials is comparable to that between the Rarámuri as a whole and their deities.

The final theme of the speech is the approach the Rarámuri should adopt toward life. The orientation of the sermon is entirely this-worldly; completely absent are references to the afterlife and the possibility of reward or punishment there as motivation for good behavior in this life. Emphasis is placed

on action, vitality, and fortitude. People are encouraged to pursue life vigorously, to be enthusiastic, to avoid becoming sad or discouraged. The Rarámuri's deities are held up as models for people to emulate, for they exemplify
these qualities daily in their unfailing journeys across the sky.

These same three themes are developed differently in a second speech,
delivered by the man who was appointed governor the day the first speech
was given. The date was February 11, 1979, and the occasion the Sunday
upon which the men of the pueblo selected the four leaders of the "Pharisees"
(*pariséo*), one of two special groups which organize the elaborate Holy Week
ceremonies. The Pharisees are portrayed as the Devil's allies and are opposed
symbolically to the "Soldiers" (*sontárasi*), who represent God's allies and are
directed by the four permanent pueblo officials known as "Captains" (*kapitáne*). Between the day of their appointment and Easter Sunday, however,
the Pharisees join the Captains to serve as the messengers and police of the
pueblo political organization. Because the Pharisees smear white pigment
over their faces and bodies, the governor refers to them in his speech as "the
white ones."

This sermon was delivered at the Basíhuare church following prayers
led by a local Mestizo woman. The officials and audience arranged themselves
in front of the church exactly as described above and the governor began:

> Listen you good people who have come here to ask forgiveness of Our
> Father. I say to you: May you have strength for the journey back to the
> places from which you came this morning. Return contentedly to your
> homes along the paths of Our Father and Our Mother. Do the Ones Who
> Walk Above caring for us ever falter in their journey? Therefore, you
> should be strong and contented.
>
> Return here again next Sunday, I say to you. Never fail to come here
> to ask forgiveness of Our Father and Our Mother. By doing so, you will
> always walk with strength. Do not be sad. Do not follow the One Who
> Lives Below for if you do you will end up crying. Be strong and
> contented wherever you go. Are the Ones Who Provide Us Light lazy as
> they walk above? I say to you: They watch over me and over all of you.
> Therefore, take heart and go with strength. Do not be sad. Return
> contentedly here again on Sunday.
>
> Whenever you assemble to drink the beer that someone has
> prepared, do so in this way. Be happy and content. Do not fight. Sit and
> talk with one another in a beautiful fashion. Why should you want to hit
> your brothers? If there is money on the ground, you will not see it if you
> are swinging your fists and throwing stones.
>
> Young men, always think well. You often fight when you drink, but

you also should be contented whenever you are drinking. Do not fight among yourselves. What will fighting do for you? What will you gain by fighting?

All of you should give fiestas and dance. Do not be lazy when fiestas and dances are being performed. Send to God that which God has put here, a calf, a kid. Everyone should pool their food, each contributing a little, and place it on the dance space to send to God. This is how it is. If you do these things, you will be given more days to live. Give fiestas with force and you also will have force.

Think when you act, you young men, and all you good people who are standing here. Do not fight. Be calm and contented when you are together, I say to you. Do not fight among yourselves. Drink contentedly.

Always ask permission of the *Presidente* before you sponsor a drinking party so that he will help you should anyone fight or do bad things while they are drinking. If people fight and you have not asked permission to drink, then he will charge you a fine. Always advise him before drinking. Some of you people who live far from here have been drinking without asking permission. Ask permission when you drink, I say to you. This is what the *Presidente* has said to me.

If you fight when you drink, you will give your leaders a lot of work to do and you will tire out the white ones who have now been appointed. They will pursue for me people who commit misdeeds, helping the Captains perform their job. This is the way it will be now. If you fight, they will follow you wherever you go in order to capture you and bring you back. Be contented. Do not fight among yourselves.

Treat the Pharisees well, I say to you. Do not fight or quarrel with them. Do not tell them they are worthless. This is the way it was established here in the beginning. This is the way it is. Be strong and happy. When the Pharisees go around telling the people to assemble for a talk, give them beer so that they may be full. This is my thinking. May you return to your homes with force.

And now you good women, I say to you. May you have strength as you return to the homes from which you came to ask forgiveness of Our Father and Our Mother. May you return contented. Do not be sad or give up. Do the Ones Who Walk Above watching over all of us ever give up? Return contentedly here on Sunday to ask forgiveness of Our Father. You should come here every Sunday. Do not stay away from the church. If you do not always ask forgiveness, in the end you will be sent to the One Who Lives Below.

This thinking has been sent to help all the people. Very few of you have been congregating here. You should come here to the church all the time to ask forgiveness of Our Father and Our Mother.

This is all that I have to say to you. Do you consider to be good

what I have said, which is the word of Our Father and the word of Our
Mother?

The crowd then responds in unison, "It is good. Thank you," to which the
governor replies, "Thank you. You may leave now."

In this sermon, the relation between the Rarámuri and their deities is
presented in much more detail than in the first speech. Here the Rarámuri's
heavenly parents are portrayed almost exclusively as "The Ones Who Walk
Above," that is, as the Sun and Moon, and their attitudes toward the Rarámuri
are represented metonymically by the activities of these celestial bodies. More
importantly, a third deity appears: "The One Who Lives Below," a euphe-
mism for the Devil.[9] The governor warns his listeners of the sad consequences
that will befall them should they choose the Devil's path over that of their
Father and Mother. While sharing the this-world emphasis of the first speech,
this sermon also holds up the threat of being sent to the Devil in the afterlife
as punishment for failing to ask forgiveness regularly.

The relation of reciprocity that the Rarámuri believe exists between
themselves and their heavenly parents is more explicitly spelled out here than
in the first sermon. In addition to the obligation to ask forgiveness, the Rarámuri are encouraged to balance the benevolence of their deities by sponsoring
fiestas, dancing, and making food offerings, performing these activities with
the same constancy and force that their deities exemplify in caring and providing for the Rarámuri. The reward for maintaining a balance in these relations is strength for living and the continued goodwill of Our Father and
Our Mother.

With the exception of encouraging people to cooperate in providing food
offerings, the governor's commentary on the nature of proper relations within
the society focuses, like that of his predecessor, on drinking party behavior.
He singles out young men as the group most prone to fighting during drinking, and he uses the violence associated with drinking to outline the functions
that the newly appointed Pharisees will perform. He also fulfills his role as
the mediator between the Rarámuri community and the national government
by instructing people to ask the local representative of the government (the
section president) for his permission before staging drinking parties.

The governor's depiction of the proper attitude people should take toward
life is the same as that in the first speech. He encourages people to be vigorous
and contented, using the actions of their heavenly parents as examples of
how they should approach their own lives. But unlike in the first speech,
the behavior of these deities is portrayed here not just as a model to emulate

but as a justification for adopting a positive attitude toward life. Because Our Father and Our Mother unfailingly protect and provide for the Rarámuri, people have every reason not to become sad, discouraged, or disheartened.

The Cosmology of Rarámuri Sermons

These two speeches provide a feeling for the content and tone of Rarámuri sermons, but they should not be considered representative of the entire genre. Between 1977 and 1984, I recorded thirty-four speeches given by seven different men, all from Basíhuare. Each speech is unique, reflecting idiosyncracies of oratorical style and differences in the community's activities at the different times when the speeches were given. Yet, since many of these activities are organized into a recurring annual cycle, speeches from the same times of different years tend to be very similar. Moreover, speeches throughout the year focus on the same three themes as the two speeches presented above: the relations between the Rarámuri and their deities; the relations within Rarámuri society; and the proper approach to life. To be sure, these themes are developed in different ways by different speakers, but they are evident even in Rarámuri speeches from other places and other times (Lumholtz 1902, I: 348–49; Bennett 1931).

These public speeches convey a specific view of the universe which differs significantly from the cosmology I recorded in formal interviews and informal conversations. To simplify the discussion, I will refer to the former as the cosmology of the speeches and to the latter as the cosmology of everyday life. The two cosmologies differ primarily in their treatment of space and time and the relationships among beings in the universe.

The speeches divide the universe into three levels: the domain of the Rarámuri's heavenly parents is above, that of the Devil below, with the Rarámuri in the middle. In their everyday cosmology, the Rarámuri often organize the universe into a hierarchy of seven levels, although the relations among the levels remain the same as in the sermons. We live on the fourth or middle level, with the three levels above associated with God and God's wife, the three below with the Devil. They call the levels above the earth *riwigáchi* (sky or heaven), which they preface with *siné* (first), *osá* (second), and *bisá* (third) to distinguish each successively higher plane from the others. God and his wife reside in the highest heaven, called *bisá riwigáchi*. The Rarámuri tend not to name the levels below the earth separately, referring to them collectively as *riré* (below) or *riré pachá* (below underneath). There is nothing above the highest plane or below the lowest.

The Rarámuri conceive of each level as identical in most respects to all the others. Except for geological features like mountains and deep canyons, each plane is completely flat. The underside of each level is the sky of the level below, conceived of as a dome, the base of which approaches but does not join the outer edges of that plane. Beginning at the lowest level, columns rise from the edge of each level to support the sky and by extension the next higher plane. Earthquakes occur when the Devil shakes the columns that support the earth.

The only horizontal references in the speeches distinguish between the site of the church and the places where the Rarámuri live. In the very pueblo-centric view of the speeches, the pueblo center—specifically the church and its yard where the dance space mentioned in the second speech also is located—is the preeminent moral space in the Rarámuri's world and the most appropriate site for the conduct of their religious affairs. All other areas, including those inhabited and cultivated by the Rarámuri, are called *kawichí* (wilds).

Outside these speeches, *kawichí* has several meanings and multiple connotations. It can refer with increasing degrees of specificity to "earth," "land," "mountains," and "one's land or homeplace." In a relational sense it means "outside" with respect to areas where the Rarámuri concentrate their activities. It means "forest" and "uncleared land" in contrast to "cultivated land" (*wasachí*) and "living area" (*bitérachi*). Because clearing and cultivating land are considered to be the occupations God ordained for Rarámuri men, the areas in which such activities do not occur are seen as lying somewhat outside the moral order. Lands characterized as *kawichí* are described as being "to one side" (*chakéna*) to distinguish them from cultivated fields. *Chakéna* also denotes behavior or thinking that deviates from God's teachings, which are characterized as "straight" (*wachíame*). Together with bodies of water, especially deep holes in streams, *kawichí* is associated with the Devil while cultivated land is associated with God. *Kawichí* thus has connotations of non-human, wild, and potentially evil as opposed to the values of human, domesticated, and potentially good attributed to areas of more intensive human activity.

The speeches' focus on the church and surrounding settlements also excludes other regions of the world that figure in the Rarámuri's everyday cosmology, including other Rarámuri settlements, Mexican cities and towns, and foreign countries. Similarly, the speeches do not provide an image of the world as a whole. The Rarámuri conceive of the earth as an island surrounded by a dike, which is guarded by little people known as the *suwé piréame* (those who live at the edge). Small in stature but exceedingly tough, these people fight off the animals that emerge from the water to breach the dike and flood the earth. No mention of these people or their responsibilities appears in the speeches.

The temporal frame of the speeches, while appearing at first glance to have considerable breadth, is rather restricted. The speeches link the Rarámuri's contemporary society and culture to events that occurred at the beginning of the world, but they contain no allusions to recent history nor to the numerous ancient events that the Rarámuri recount in their stories and myths as having had a formative influence on the current state of their world (Lumholtz 1902, I: 295–310, 330–55; López Batista 1980; Mares Trías 1975). The speeches also portray time as strictly linear. Both the world and Rarámuri customs are conceived to have had a beginning, and the possibility of an end to the world sometimes is suggested. Cyclical time is entirely absent from the speeches even though it is basic to the everyday cosmology, appearing both in the annual agricultural and ceremonial cycles and in the view that the present world is the fourth in a never-ending cycle of creation, destruction, and replacement.

The Rarámuri also postulate the existence of many more kinds of beings than are mentioned in their speeches. In the speeches, only three general categories of beings appear: humans, represented exclusively by the Rarámuri; the Rarámuri's heavenly parents; and the Devil. Various segments of Rarámuri society are designated explicitly—men, women, young men, and officials—but except for the behavior desired between officials and the general populace, the relations among these segments is not mentioned. Rather the speeches prescribe how individuals should treat one another and how the Rarámuri as a whole should act toward their deities. Only in speeches given during the Easter season is the relationship between God and the Devil mentioned. Then, the Rarámuri say, God and the Devil drink together and the Devil tries to harm God while he is vulnerable. In his speeches, the leader of the Easter ceremonies describes God's condition and encourages the Rarámuri to perform the Easter rituals assiduously to protect God and his wife until God has recovered.

Among the many classes of beings that are not mentioned in the speeches are a number of malevolent beings who constantly threaten the Rarámuri with death or disease. All are considered to be the Devil's allies and to live in the underworld or in marginal areas of the earth, underneath streams and lakes and in the wilds (Merrill 1981: 118–22). These include the water people (*ba?wichí piréame*), water monsters (*walúluwi*), rainbows (*konomí*), whirlwinds

HEAVEN
Our Father and Our Mother
Our Father's and Our Mother's offspring
(*sukrísto, sánti*)
Our Father's and Our Mother's helpers
(Rarámuri souls, soldiers)

	EARTH	
Water people	Humans	People of the edge
Water monsters	(Rarámuri, Chabóchi)	Plant people
Rainbows		(*bakánawi, híkuri,*
		uchurí, rikúhuri)
		Sorcerers' animal familiars
		(*oromá*, coyotes, etc.)

UNDERWORLD
The Devil and the Devil's wife
The Devil's helpers
(Chabóchi souls, soldiers, diseases, whirlwinds)

Figure 14. Beings in the Rarámuri universe

(*pibíware* or *pipibíri*), and a variety of beings known collectively as the Devil's "soldiers" (*sontárasi*). These soldiers appear principally as coyotes, foxes, and strangers, both Indian and non-Indian, and attempt to injure or kill the souls of Rarámuri while they are dreaming. Many of the dreams Rarámuri people told me included accounts of their encounters with these soldiers and the ingenious means they adopted to avoid being harmed by them (Merrill 1987).

In comparison to the Devil's allies, those of God and God's wife are rather colorless. They live in heaven and serve these deities as their peons, providing them with food, performing chores and errands, and fighting the Devil's allies. The souls of most Rarámuri enter the ranks of these peons at death. Exceptions are small children, whose souls are transformed into stars, and people who have committed acts such as sexual intercourse with non-Indians or murder, for which their souls are sent to spend eternity with the Devil or destroyed.

Also living in the third heaven are the offspring of the sexual union of God and his wife. The sons of this union are known collectively as *sukrísto* (from Spanish *Jesucristo*, "Jesus Christ") and the daughters as *sánti* (saints).[10] The sukrísto are associated with metal crucifixes, the *sánti* with saint medallions, and they protect the people who own these religious icons. In addition, God bestows a *sukrísto* on each person to whom he assigns curing responsibility. These doctors receive the ability to cure from God in their dreams and then purchase metal crucifixes to indicate their new status and to use as part of their curing paraphernalia.

Four other categories of beings are associated with special plants. These are *bakánawi* (probably a bulrush, *Scirpus* sp.); *híkuri* (various "peyote" cacti, including *Lophophora williamsii*); several spiny cacti known as *uchurí* (*Echinocereus*, *Coryphanta*, and *Mammillaria*); and *rikúhuri* (*Datura* spp.) (Bye 1979a). The Rarámuri do not clearly affiliate these plant beings with either God or the Devil. *Bakánawi* and *híkuri* protect people from harm and help them, particularly in competitive games, if the people feed them and observe a few taboos. If people fail, *bakánawi* and *híkuri* will capture their souls and hold them for ransom. *Uchurí* and *rikúhuri* never help the Rarámuri but they will attack people who step on or otherwise harm them by causing their heads to ache. They may also guide sleeping offenders to the tops of tall cliffs from which they will fall to their injury or death.

Three important categories of human beings also are omitted from the speeches. The first of these is sorcerers (*sukurúame*).[11] The Rarámuri of Rejogochi assume that both Indians and non-Indians and both men and women can become sorcerers, but they maintain that the majority of sorcerers as well as the most dangerous ones are Rarámuri men. These evil practitioners harm people in a number of ways. They (or rather their souls) travel during dreaming to capture the souls of their victims or they petition the Devil in their dreams to make their enemies sick. Sorcerers also dispatch the predatory animals they own—usually one of the evil birds called *oromá*, which are identified with shooting stars—to attack their victims. Once captured, the souls are held prisoner for a few days and then boiled and eaten by the sorcerers, often joined by their animal familiars and the Devil. When a soul is taken, the victim immediately becomes seriously ill and will die if a doctor cannot rescue the soul before it is destroyed. Children live only a day or so after their souls are stolen because they are not as "tough" (*biwárame*) as those of adults.

In addition to stealing souls, sorcerers intrude a variety of objects into their victims' bodies while they sleep. These objects enter through the mouth or penetrate the skin leaving no external trace. Once inside, they interfere with the normal operation of the body, inducing in the victim a lingering illness that leads to death if the souls find the condition of the body intolerable. For example, sorcerers tie wires around people's genitals and their waists to prevent or impede elimination. To cause vomiting and loss of appetite, they insert into their victims' stomachs small glass bottles, pocketknives, or the spherical, fiery hot chiles called *korí síbari* (in Spanish, *chile piquín* or *chiltepín; Capsicum annuum* var. *glabriusculum*). They also send small stones (*sukí*) or worms (*nowí*) into their enemies, both of which are alive and consume the victims' flesh from the inside. These objects can only be extracted by a doctor whose powers rival those of the attacking sorcerer.

Because they are evil, sorcerers sometimes bewitch people in distant settlements with whom they have had no personal contact. They also use their powers to influence the outcome of competitions like footraces by disabling the members of the opposing teams (Kennedy 1969; Irigoyen Rascón and Palma Batista 1985). Usually, however, their attacks are directed against people with whom they are angry, unless these are members of their immediate family, whom they typically do not harm. By insulting or scolding sorcerers, neglecting to offer them food or beer, or refusing to comply with their requests, a person risks causing offense that will be redressed through sorcery. In some cases the offended sorcerers will attack their enemies indirectly by harming their children or livestock.

Individuals become sorcerers by accepting black or dark-colored sheets of paper from the Devil during their dreams. Their souls keep these papers, which give them the knowledge to bewitch. The Devil also gives them *sukrísto* (the beings associated with crucifixes) and animal familiars to assist their evil work along with the harmful objects they put into their victims. People who possess dark papers are capable only of bewitching; they have no curing abilities. God gives to doctors comparable white or light-colored papers that convey knowledge in keeping with God's thinking, like the good advice parents give their children. Some people have both dark and light papers and care for people until they become angry, at which point they resort to sorcery. The recipients of light-colored papers have the capacity only to cure but nonetheless can harm people who anger them by requesting that God take their souls. Thus doctors as well as sorcerers are to be feared.

The second major category of human beings omitted from the speeches is the Rarámuri who maintain no affiliation with the Catholic church, known locally in Spanish as *gentiles*, "heathens" (Rarámuri *hentíle*), and *cimarrones*, "wild people" or "fugitives" (Rarámuri *simaróne*) (see Kennedy 1970a, 1978).

The Rarámuri of Basíhuare claim that if gentiles enter a church, the walls will collapse around them. They also say that when gentiles die, God will not give them a light with which to illuminate their way, as he does for baptized Rarámuri. Sometimes people refer jokingly to unruly people as *si-maróne* and threaten to baptize them by throwing them into a stream.

Given these ideas, the gentiles would seem to be a logical subject for the sermons in the pueblo center, but they are never mentioned in the Basíhuare speeches.[12] Their absence perhaps reflects the baptized Rarámuri's belief that the gentiles are not immoral or bad but, like all Rarámuri, the children of God who live as much in keeping with God's thinking as they do. In fact, some baptized Rarámuri say it is not God's intention that gentiles should be baptized. Baptism is a prerequisite for entry into heaven, and God wants the souls of the gentiles to remain on earth in the afterlife to fulfill a special commission with which he has entrusted them: to guard the columns that support the sky.

Finally, non-Indian people do not figure in the speeches. The Rarámuri call all non-Indians, both men and women, *chabóchi* (hereafter "Chabochi[s]"), which means "whiskered ones" (*chabó* "whisker[s]" plus the nominative suffix *-chi*). The selection of facial hair as the distinguishing feature of non-Indians is appropriate since most Rarámuri have few whiskers and very little body hair. In fact, they sometimes refer disparagingly to Chabochis as "hairy asses" (*kosichí bowéame*).

This term "Chabochi" emerged early in the colonial period (Ratkay 1683: 35) and today is used not only by the Rarámuri but by the local Mestizos to refer to all people who display non-Indian physical features or identify with and practice a non-Indian way of life. Thus, both physical and cultural factors enter into the classification of a person as Rarámuri or Chabochi. When presented with pictures of American and African blacks, several Rarámuri men were inclined to classify them as Rarámuri, mainly because they consider their own skin color to be *chókame* (black or dark). However, had they had more information about the cultures of these people, their responses probably would have been more equivocal. When asked the affiliation of acculturated Rarámuri or individuals of mixed Rarámuri-Chabochi descent who culturally are not Rarámuri, people will note their genetic heritage but point out that they live or think like Chabochis. Similarly, non-Indians who exemplify Rarámuri values in their behavior or who adopt aspects of Rarámuri culture sometimes are characterized as being "like Rarámuri" (*napurigá* Rarámuri).

Today the Rarámuri distinguish among several types of Chabochis, based both on their personal contact with them and on references they hear on the radio or from local non-Indians. The terms for these subcategories are derived from Spanish and include: *gríngo*, often pronounced *bríngo* or *brínki* (American); *ransési*, from the Spanish *francés(a)* (French); *alemáne* (German); *rúso* (Russian); *chíno* (Chinese); *haponése* (Japanese); and so on. Sometimes all foreigners who in any way resemble Americans are lumped together under the label *gríngo* as are light-skinned and fair-haired Mexicans from outside the area. At this level of discrimination, "Chabochi" often is used to refer specifically to local non-Indians rather than to non-Indian outsiders.

The concept "Chabochi" contrasts primarily with that of "Rarámuri." "Rarámuri" has several meanings of varying specificity.[13] In its most general sense, "Rarámuri" means "human being(s)" and includes both Indians and non-Indians. In a more restricted sense, the term encompasses all Native Americans while excluding non-Indians, or Chabochis.[14] The Rarámuri also use the term even more specifically to mean "the Rarámuri proper," distinguishing themselves as Rarámuri from other Native people, whom they label with specific tribal names like Tepehuan, Yaqui, and Mayo. In its most specific sense, "Rarámuri" denotes "Rarámuri men" as opposed to Rarámuri women, who are called *igómele*, the plural form of *mukí* (woman). *Igómele* also denotes females at a particular stage of their life cycle—maturity—and contrasts with other life stage distinctions the Rarámuri make: mature men, old men, old women, young men, young women, boys, girls, and babies. The terms for these stages are applied to all human beings, Rarámuri and non-Rarámuri alike.

As the dominant population in the region, non-Indians are extremely important in the Rarámuri's lives and cosmology. They are conceived to be the children of the Devil and the Rarámuri's counterparts on the opposite side of the universe. The Devil cares for them as God cares for the Rarámuri, and they think like the Devil, tending to behave in evil ways that are detrimental to the Rarámuri. At death, their souls join the Devil in the underworld, but the Rarámuri do not see this as an unpleasant fate. They live there just as the non-Indians did on earth, helping their "father" in his endeavors like the souls of the Rarámuri serve their heavenly parents.

In addition to excluding the majority of beings in the Rarámuri universe, the speeches also simplify the relations among the Rarámuri and their deities. In the speeches, the Rarámuri's heavenly parents are invariably benevolently inclined toward them, the Devil misleads them, and God and the Devil are enemies. In both the speeches and in other formulations, these deities are located at opposite ends of the universe, providing the poles around which are clustered the basic oppositions that demarcate Rarámuri moral space.

Outside the speeches, however, the relations among these beings are much more complex and ambiguous.

For example, if the Rarámuri fail to reciprocate God's attentions by offering food and performing ceremonies, he will withhold the rain, send pests to destroy their crops, or withdraw his protection, leaving them vulnerable to the Devil. Some people suggest that, when angry, God also cooperates with the Devil to their detriment. Similarly, while the Devil's inclination is to harm the Rarámuri, he will leave them in peace if they give him food. When they slaughter animals for ceremonies, the blood that drips to the ground is intended for the Devil. In the same contexts, they frequently erect small crosses on the dance patio next to the large crosses designated for God and place bits of food in containers on the ground beside them. They call these crosses *nawirí* (disease[s]), and near the end of the event they bury this food for the Devil and *nawirí*, hoping to neutralize the threats from them. One Rarámuri man also proposed to me that if the Devil is pleased with the Rarámuri he occasionally will help as well as refrain from harming them.

Two Cosmologies or One?

To clarify the role that the Rarámuri's public speeches play in the reproduction of theoretical knowledge within Rarámuri society depends first upon defining the relationship between the cosmology presented in the speeches and that of everyday life. Two alternative views of this relationship can be proposed: first, that the two cosmologies present alternative views of the universe, the cosmology of the speeches being the Rarámuri's adaptation of a European Christian world view derived from Catholic missionaries while the cosmology of everyday life is predominantly indigenous; or, second, that the two cosmologies are in fact one, with the cosmology of the speeches being a simplified version of the other. Evidence can be marshaled in support of each of these hypotheses but, as I will explain below, the second is more likely.

A European Christian origin of the cosmology of the speeches is suggested by both the content of the speeches and the circumstances out of which they emerged as an institution in Rarámuri society. Many of the cosmological ideas conveyed in the speeches correspond quite closely to European conceptions. These include a tripartite universe, a linear organization of time, the human predicament of being caught between divine and diabolical influences, the clearcut opposition between God and the Devil, and their unambiguous association with good and evil respectively. In addition, while oratory appears to have been an important feature of the Rarámuri political process before European contact and the structure and performance style of modern speeches bespeak indigenous roots, the practice of pueblo officials delivering sermons at the church unquestionably was established by Catholic missionaries (Velasco Rivero 1983: 123–31). Because these speeches were initially intended to reiterate the missionaries' teachings, their content would have been influenced by Christian cosmology. Also, because most of the early missionaries were competent in the Rarámuri language, they presumably were directly involved in translating Christian concepts into Rarámuri terms, which would then have been adapted by the Rarámuri pueblo officials in their speeches. In addition, they would have monitored these speeches to ensure that the information they conveyed conformed to Christian ideology.

The conclusion that the cosmology in these speeches has Christian origins and exists compartmentalized from more aboriginal ideas is consistent with the analysis of Rarámuri society and history offered by Jacob Fried (1977). Fried argues that contemporary Rarámuri society includes two distinct and somewhat contradictory modes of religious and political organization, the first being the aboriginal rancheria system, the second the introduced Jesuit-Spanish pueblo system. The rancheria system is characterized by a dispersed settlement pattern, diffuse social ties, informal leadership, and religious practices directed toward local and often individual concerns. The pueblo system in contrast has a centralized focus with a formal hierarchy of officials to direct its political and religious affairs and an orientation toward communal values and projects.

Fried proposes that the dichotomy between the two systems extends beyond social and political relations to the realm of cosmology. He characterizes the rancheria cosmology as based on a belief in a "quixotic and unorganized spirit world" populated by supernatural beings whose powers are ambivalent and often directed toward harming people. He portrays the pueblo cosmology, on the other hand, as derived directly from the Jesuits and as including only Christian deities, whose powers are unambiguously benign and good. He argues, however, that the "true religious feelings" of the Rarámuri are those associated with the rancheria cosmology while the Catholicism found in conjunction with the pueblo organization represents not so much religion as "an *ideological* tool used to validate the authority of pueblo officials" (1977: 267–68, original emphasis).

Contemporary social and political practices in the pueblo of Basíhuare confirm the connection that Fried proposes between pueblo religion and political process but they also suggest that his dichotomy between pueblo and rancheria formations is overdrawn, especially in the degree of compartmentalization he sees in the two systems. For example, the political officials of the Basíhuare pueblo function in both pueblo and rancheria contexts. In speeches they mention their role in resolving conflicts at drinking parties, which occur almost exclusively at individual rancherias rather than the pueblo center. They are also regularly consulted on local rancheria affairs. Similarly, pueblo and rancheria religious practices include both introduced and indigenous elements: the Spanish-derived matachine dancers perform at both pueblo and rancheria celebrations as do the indigenous "chanters" known as *wikaráame;* some rancheria ceremonies are scheduled according to the Catholic ritual calendar and coordinated with the ritual activities at the church, and so on.

There also are compelling reasons not to regard the cosmology presented in the pueblo speeches as predominantly Christian. Fried (1977: 267) reports that Rarámuri pueblo officials invoke Jesus and Mary to legitimize their authority, but the crucial feature of their appearance in pueblo ideology is not that they correspond to Christian deities but rather that they represent a male-female pair. In the Basíhuare sermons, Jesus is never mentioned, but the principal deities remain male and female: God and God's wife, who are portrayed in the clearly aboriginal form of the Sun and the Moon. In addition, central elements of Christian theology like the Trinity, redemption through Christ's crucifixion, and a strong other-world orientation are entirely missing.

My conclusion is that the cosmology of the speeches is a highly simplified, even schematized, version of the cosmology of everyday life, not an alternative or competing view of the world. The speeches focus on a few specific themes and portray the cosmos in its most uncomplicated form, excluding mention of all but the most important beings in the universe and ignoring the ambiguities in the relationships among these beings. Yet, no themes or beings appear in the sermons that are not also present in the cosmology of everyday life. The association of God and God's wife with the Sun and Moon, their preeminence in the Rarámuri pantheon, and their benevolence is basically the same in both as is the figure of the Devil and his malevolence. The hierarchical structure of the universe and the association of good with above and evil with below is essentially identical. The linear organization of time also appears in the cosmology of everyday life, although linear chains of events often are encompassed by temporal cycles of longer duration.

The cosmological ideas that are consistently conveyed in pueblo sermons include only those that are directly related to the role of the pueblo political officials in the local society. These officials are supposed to serve as moral exemplars for their fellows, guiding them along the paths most likely to result in the continued well-being of the community. The Rarámuri regard the speeches of these officials as the principal vehicles through which they provide this guidance. In them, the officials describe the order of the universe, claiming that it was established at the beginning of time by the Rarámuri's heavenly parents whose images they evoke as the ultimate symbols of this order. They portray this order as defining the attitudes toward life that people should adopt as well as the actions they should perform if they are to maintain positive relations with one another and their deities.

This information also indirectly justifies the collective activities of the pueblo, most of which are ceremonies intended to fulfill the Rarámuri's obligations to their deities. At the same time, the officials use the speeches, perhaps unconsciously, to establish the legitimacy of both the political offices they hold and of their personal claims to them. They portray the pueblo political organization as part of the inalterable order of the world. They also claim that the words they speak are of divine origin and, while they state that they simply convey these words, the obvious implication is that they are worthy to do so. By presenting good advice through skilled oratory, they demonstrate the qualities for which they were selected for office and from which their rather tenuous claim to authority largely derives.

Even this limited information appears in the speeches in condensed form. This further simplification of the cosmology of everyday life reflects the constraints of the conventions of effective oratory in terms of which the speeches are produced. These speeches are examples of political oratory, not because they attempt to sway public opinion on specific issues but because they are intended to persuade people to accept a particular perspective on the world and to act in conformance with a standard of behavior that at times might conflict with their perceived self-interests. As Crocker notes, persuasion is the "most embracing rhetorical motive" (1977: 37), and it is the rhetorical intent of these speeches that shapes much of their form and content.

In their use of a restricted range of grammatical forms and intonational and gestural patterns, their focus on a redundant set of themes, and their presentation in highly structured contexts, Rarámuri public speeches closely resemble political oratory in societies around the world (Bloch 1975; Sapir and Crocker 1977; Paine 1981).[15] But the common feature that most affects the detail in which they present cosmological information is their reliance on figures of speech to get their messages across. Since the time of Aristotle's investigations of rhetoric, scholars have recognized the persuasive power of such figures of speech (Burke 1969; Sapir and Crocker 1977; Paine 1981).

In the creation of their speeches, Rarámuri orators employ most prominently two kinds of figures of speech: metonomy and synecdoche.

Sapir (1977: 4) describes metonymy and synecdoche in the following terms:

> Metonymy replaces or juxtaposes contiguous terms that occupy a distinct
> and separate place within what is considered a single semantic or
> perceptual domain. Homer will often be used instead of the *Iliad* ("you
> will read in Homer . . ."), where agent replaces act; or the phrase "deep
> in his cups," where "cups" as container stands for the sherry or wine
> that is contained. Synecdoche, like metonymy, draws its terms from a
> single domain; however, one term term always includes or is included by
> the other as a kind for type, part for whole: France for a specific
> Frenchman, sail for ship.

The significant feature of these figures of speech for the transmission of knowledge is that they are reductive and representational (Burke 1969: 503) in that a complex of elements is reduced to and represented by one element from the same domain.

Rarámuri speeches consist almost entirely of a limited number of metonyms and synecdoches, each of which uses a concrete image to represent a much broader universe of concepts and relations. A passing mention of the white paint of the Pharisees evokes the complex cosmological and social associations of the Easter season. The movements of celestial bodies summarize the relation between the Rarámuri and their principal deities. The food and beer that people are told to give to their community officials stand for the complicated relations of mutual respect and dependence between them and are analogous to the offerings they give their deities. Drinking parties and the behavior associated with them, both proper and improper, represent social relations as a whole.

These speeches are effective because they express complex and abstract ideas in concrete forms that are easy to grasp. The images they employ operate simultaneously on the sensual, emotional, and cognitive levels. Because they evoke concepts rather than presenting them in explicit detail, they also engage the members of the audience in the active creation of their arguments, mobilizing the experiences, values, and beliefs that they share with the speaker (Paine 1981: 13–14).

By adhering to these conventions, Rarámuri orators produce speeches that are rhetorically powerful and aesthetically pleasing but rather ineffective for the reproduction of Rarámuri theoretical knowledge. While these speeches establish some of the central ideas in Rarámuri cosmology, they do not elaborate on these ideas nor do they provide the extensive background information required to interpret them.[16] Moreover, these ideas represent only that small portion of Rarámuri theoretical knowledge which is directly linked to motivating and legitimizing the activities of the pueblo. The Rarámuri's ideas about souls do not appear in these speeches because they are relevant primarily to individual experience and action rather than the affairs of the pueblo. Of course, Rarámuri orators do not intend their speeches to teach such knowledge or to educate their audiences in the intricacies of the world, but no other institution in Rarámuri society transmits theoretical knowledge in a way that would ensure its diffusion and standardization within the society. Most Rarámuri knowledge, including the concept of soul, is conveyed less formally in more restricted settings, creating a greater opportunity for the emergence of variation in the ideas of different members of the society.

THE CONCEPT
OF SOUL

The concept of soul is fundamental to the Rarámuri view of the world. All of their explanations for their actions and their physical, mental, and emotional states are grounded ultimately in their theories about the nature and activities of their souls. This concept also motivates many activities that are central to Rarámuri life, such as curing and death rituals. Yet despite its importance the Rarámuri of Rejogochi make no special efforts to insure the reproduction of the concept, in part because it is so pervasive in their thought and action. Also the principal agents of the reproduction of knowledge in the society— a child's parents and other adult relatives and the community's political leaders—are more concerned with teaching and reinforcing the standards of proper social behavior than with providing frameworks like the concept of soul for understanding experience.

Most of the ideas about souls that people receive from others are transmitted in relative privacy at home. Household instruction in matters like the concept of soul is casual, accompanying the normal conduct of daily life, and often takes place indirectly through recounting myths and dreams, diagnosing illnesses that afflict household or community members, or discussing the circumstances surrounding recent deaths. The amount of information so conveyed varies considerably from household to household. Some people informed me that their relatives had told them many things about souls as they were growing up, but others reported having received little or no information on the subject.

Given the social context of the reproduction of this knowledge, it is more surprising that Rarámuri from different households agree on many aspects of the concept than that they hold some differing opinions. This agreement is in part the result of the obvious fact that the nuclear families upon which all households are based are each created through the marriage of individuals from different households; homogenization of knowledge is intrinsic to the reproduction of society. Also, some information about souls, albeit fragmentary, is communicated informally between the members of different households. For example, when people visit one another in the mornings they often discuss their dreams of the night before. Since dreams are considered to be the activities of a person's souls, such dream accounts necessarily include much information about souls. The most detailed instruction on the topic seems to be provided by Rarámuri doctors to their apprentices, but this instruction is essentially private, and apprentices often are the children or other close relatives of the doctor and thus members of the same household.

In Rejogochi, public discussions that include information about souls are predominantly discussions of health matters. When someone gets sick, the causes of the ailment become a major topic of conversation within the community, with people formulating diagnoses of the illness and evaluating those suggested by others. Since the Rarámuri believe that a person's condition at any time depends on the condition and location of his or her souls, some reference to souls is usually a part of such diagnoses. Ideas about souls also are conveyed implicitly in public activities like curing rituals. The performance of such activities enhances the likelihood that many different people will be exposed to these ideas and consequently that they will share them.

Any adequate model of the reproduction of knowledge must incorporate a concept of human agents as thinking actors. No one is given a full-blown view of the world to memorize. Rather people formulate their knowledge by thinking through the information they receive from many sources in a process that reveals, in Sperber's words, their "qualitatively determined creative competence" (1975: xi). Obviously the content of the ideas to which people are exposed guides their thinking, as do the complex circumstances surrounding their transmission: what is conveyed by whom to whom in what fashion and contexts and the relation of all these factors to more general social processes. But whether the transmission is exhaustive or fragmentary, public or private, explicit or implicit, and the assimilation coerced or voluntary, this social dimension by itself is insufficient to account for the reproduction of knowledge. The logical relations among the ideas involved must also be taken into consideration because these relations both enable the creation of knowledge and simultaneously limit the amount of individual variation that will be associated with it.

In this chapter, I describe the principal ideas that form the Rarámuri concept of soul and indicate the points on which people tend to agree or disagree. I then examine the logical relations among these ideas and the different approaches that individuals adopt in creating and organizing their knowledge. These factors, together with those associated with the public presentation of information about souls in curing and death-related practices to be discussed in chapters 5 and 6, are responsible for the pattern of individual variation and consensus that characterizes the concept of soul.

SOULS IN THE RARÁMURI UNIVERSE

The Rarámuri of Rejogochi employ two terms, *ariwá* and *iwigá*, for "soul(s)."[1] Both terms also mean "breath," although *iwigá* is more often used this way than is *ariwá*. The Rarámuri use the same terms for souls and breath because they consider them to be one and the same. Breathing indicates the possession of souls, but the Rarámuri do not believe that all beings who have souls breathe nor that breathing is necessary to maintain life. For them, souls are inherently alive and each soul-possessing entity is alive as long as its souls are present. Those beings who breathe do so because a little of their soul substance continuously moves in and out of their bodies, much as people enter and leave their homes. Thus, in their view breathing is not a mechanism by which a life-sustaining element like oxygen is brought into the body and wastes are expelled. In fact, they do not postulate the existence of "air" in the sense of an invisible, impersonal, and formless substance that pervades the world around them. They conceive of wind (*iká*) not as air in motion but as a being, usually portrayed as having human form, who in substance is like breath and runs across the face of the earth. Similarly they identify small whirlwinds (*pibíware* or *pipibíri*) as the souls of the dead or the souls of the living who have left their bodies during sleep and larger ones as beings who emerge from holes in the ground, sent by the Devil to harm people.

The Number and Classification of Human Souls

The Rarámuri conceive of human beings as composed of a body and one or more souls. They call the body *sapá*, a term they also apply to the fleshy portions of the body specifically and to meat generally. The body is supported by the bones (*ochí*) and prevented from drying up by the blood (*la*), which some people believe comes from the liquids they drink. They also assume that the body contains many internal organs like those of the animals they butcher and that these organs have necessary functions.

The body itself is animate only because of the soul or souls that live within it. People in Rejogochi disagree about the number of souls each person has and the relationship among these souls. Some people maintain that each individual possesses only one soul, identical in appearance to the person in whose body it resides. This soul flows to all portions of the body through the arteries and veins and forms pockets, like pockets of "wind" (iká), at the joints and other places where the body can move. When the soul leaves the body—for example, during dreaming or drinking—only a portion departs and most of the soul remains behind to care for the body. Death occurs when the entire soul leaves the body.

Much more widespread is the notion that each person possesses many separate souls distributed throughout the inside of the body. Each of these souls enjoys some autonomy; different souls can be in different places at the same time and can experience different fates after they leave the body at death. In this view, the souls within a single body are of two kinds, large souls and small souls. The many small souls reside principally in the joints but can also be in other parts of the body. There are fewer large souls but people disagree on their exact number. The typical response is that males have three large souls each and females four, since three and four are symbolic markers for males and females respectively. However, many people propose that males and females have an equal number of large souls, which can be three, two, or even one apiece.

The Rarámuri associate the large souls preeminently with the chest region, which they regard as the seat of life, vigor, emotions, speech, and, with the head, of thought. Some maintain that all the large souls reside exclusively in the chest. Others propose that the largest of the large souls, together with one or more of the others, lives in the chest while another lives inside the head. A compromise position holds that the largest or all the large souls live in both the head and heart and migrate between them.

Three different but related schemes are used to classify an individual's souls. The first is a basic rank ordering that can be applied to any set of unequal members. Usually only the large souls are ranked individually, as "largest" (waʔrubéra), "next largest" or "middle" (nasípa), and "smallest" (petabéra), with the remaining souls known collectively as "small souls(s)" (ta ariwá). This classification does not necessarily imply anything about the relations among souls. However, because it is used to distinguish among political officials and the members of certain classes of ritual participants, it has connotations of relative importance and, to a lesser degree, of relative authority.

The second model is the same as that employed to classify siblings, appropriately applied to souls because all the souls that live within a person are thought by some to be siblings of the same sex as that person. Rarámuri kinship terminology classifies siblings according to their relative ages. Although all of a person's souls are of the same age, their size differences are taken to reflect variations in maturity. The largest souls of an adult look and act like adults, they say, while the smallest souls of the same person are like small children.

When the sibling relationship among the souls is emphasized, sibling terms are added to the terminology of the basic rank ordering scheme. Thus a man's three large souls would be classified as follows: *waʔrubéra bachirúame ariwá* (largest older brother soul); *nasípa bonirúame ariwá* (middle younger brother soul); and *petabéra bonirúame ariwá* (smaller younger brother soul).[2] The small souls usually are not distinguished individually but rather are known as a group as *ta kúchile ariwá* (small children soul[s]) or *ta ranára ariwá* (small offspring soul[s]). However, the smallest souls, such as those found inside the knuckles, sometimes are called *petára sipáli bonirúame ariwá*, which means "smallest exactly younger brother soul(s)" or, in freer translation, "the very smallest younger brother soul(s)."

The third classification is based on a model of the relations between parents and children. Here the souls of each person include members of both sexes and there are only two large souls, the larger of which is identified as the father and the other as the mother.[3] The remaining small souls are seen as the children of the two large souls but of unspecified sex. In this model the largest soul is *waʔrubéra ariwá* (largest soul), the other large soul is his wife (*upíra*), and the small souls are their children, *ta kúchile* (small children) or *ta ranára* (small offspring).[4]

The Rarámuri use the second and third models more frequently than the first because they tend to think of a person's souls as kinspeople. These models are based directly on the image of the ideal relationships among the members of a Rarámuri household, appropriately so since the body is thought of as the souls' house. Like the older residents of a household, the large souls care for the small souls and, because they can think better than the small souls, they advise them on proper behavior. And again like a child's elders, the large souls maintain some authority over the small souls. For example, when the large souls decide that the body should perform some complex action like walking or chopping down a tree that involves the cooperation of souls in many parts of the body, they tell the other souls to perform the necessary movements. Yet the small souls, like Rarámuri children, enjoy significant individual autonomy and are fully capable of performing reflex movements and minor acts, like tapping the finger, on their own.

Other Soul-Possessing Entities

The Rarámuri think that plants and animals as well as people have souls. The information I collected from the residents of Rejogochi about plant and animal souls differs somewhat from that reported from a neighboring area fifty years earlier by Bennett and Zingg:

> All breathing things have souls. The animals and men have the same kind
> of souls. The soul of the birds is almost the same except that the birds
> whistle rather than sing—a slightly different manifestation of the soul.
> The fish have another soul, which is like water, since water is to a fish
> what air is to an animal. Trees have no souls, though some plants are
> attributed with soul possession (1935: 323).

In Rejogochi, people say that all living things, including trees and other plants, have souls, but they do distinguish between beings that breathe and those that do not. This distinction and its relation to the nature of the souls of different kinds of beings is the subject of an interview I conducted in Rejogochi in 1981. I asked:

"What are the souls of fish like?"

"They are the same as ours. Our Father gave them their souls; fish belong to him. He created them when he made the world. Since the time he came down to earth, there have been fish."

"Why do fish die when they are taken out of the water?"

"They are unhappy. If they leave the water, they'll die. They live in the water and will die right away if they are not in the water because the heat from the sun kills them. They become hot inside and their souls leave. They have a different kind of soul, a small spherical soul inside. Have you seen it? I enjoy eating this soul. When we catch fish, we eat this soul right away."

"Can you see this soul?"

"Yes."

"What exactly do you eat?"

"The fish's soul. This soul keeps the fish from drowning, gives them great endurance and the ability to swim deep under the water. They never drown. They're like otters. Otters are very skilled at swimming in the river. Have you ever seen one?"

"Yes, but not here. I've seen them in the United States."

"I saw one some time ago down at the river. They're very quick. You see them here and then all of a sudden they are over there."

"So they swim under the water."

"Yes, searching for fish."

'Why can't we do the same?"

"Well, we can but only for a short time, like when we dive for fish."

"Why can't we stay under the water longer?"

"Because we start gulping in water and will die. But fish grow up in the water; they have a different kind of soul. They never drown. They don't breathe. Their souls are closed up inside of them. If they should breathe, they would drown. If their souls leave, like when there is no water, they die right away."

"But why do we breathe?"

"Because Our Father made us that way."

"Do pine trees breathe?"

"No, they don't. They are very hard but nonetheless they grow."

"What are the souls of birds like?"

"They are the same as ours. They also breathe."

"Why do birds sing instead of talk?"

"They sing but don't talk because that's the way Our Father made them. No birds can talk but they breathe like we do. Chickens, for example, breathe."

"Do maize plants breathe?"

"No, they grow up differently. They don't breathe."

"What about tadpoles?"

"They don't breathe. Their souls also are closed up inside of them."

"And frogs?"

"Frogs do breathe. They are the tadpoles' mothers."

The fish souls described in this conversation as both visible and edible are gas bladders (also known as the air or swim bladders), which allow fish to control the depth at which they swim (Richard Vari 1986: personal communication). While everyone I asked agreed that this organ is called the fish's soul (*rochí ariwára*), some people said they did not know whether the organ itself was the soul or the soul was inside it.

The Rarámuri's responses to questions about the souls of maize show similar ambiguity. Some people refer to the germ of the maize kernel as its soul (*sunú ariwára*). A local insect pest (most likely the angoumois grain moth, *Sitotroga cerealella* [Olivier]; Ronald Hodges 1986: personal communication) sometimes deposits its eggs inside maize kernels and the larvae consume the germs before changing into moths. Because the Rarámuri see the moths only after the germs are destroyed, many have concluded that the souls of the maize kernels transform into the moths, which also are called "maize kernel soul(s)." Others, however, are unsure if the soul of the maize is in fact the germ or if it is distinct from it and invisible.

Although the Rarámuri do not clearly equate the souls of all plants and animals with breath, they use the same terms (*ariwá* and *iwigá*) for them as for human souls. Most people assume that plants and animals derive their animacy from souls and that their souls are comparable to humans' in sizes and interrelationships. People also think that, like human souls, plant and animal souls look like the entities in which they live. The souls of a few soul-possessing beings, however, do not resemble their external forms. Principal of these are the four classes of special plants mentioned in chapter 3: *uchurí, rikúhuri, bakánawi*, and *híkuri*. In all respects, the outer forms of these entities are plants but their souls look and act like human beings, described as having the appearance of either Rarámuri or Chabochis (non-Indians). A similar disparity is found in the case of *sukrísto* and *sánti*. The souls of these beings are people—the sons and daughters of God and his wife—but their bodies, so to speak, are the figures on metal crucifixes and saints' images, objects that appear inanimate.

There also is some ambiguity regarding whether God, the Devil, and their respective wives have souls or are intrinsically alive. The Rarámuri say that these deities are human beings, albeit special ones, and therefore assume that they have souls, but they conceive of the potential death of these deities as resulting not from soul loss but rather from their physical destruction after which they will no longer exist (although some people suggest they would come back to life). In this respect, the deities resemble inanimate things, which cease to exist in a particular form only when they are destroyed physically.

Inanimate Entities

When I asked people in Rejogochi, "Do rocks have souls?" the usual reply was, "No, rocks don't have souls. They *never* die." For the Rarámuri, death is possible only if life first occurs, and everything that is alive can die. Inanimate objects are inanimate primarily because they have no souls or, in the case of the bodies of soul-possessing beings, no longer have souls within them. However, the Rarámuri frequently present food and maize beer to God and during death fiestas give food, beer, clothing, sports equipment, raw materials, and tools to the dead. They do not view these offerings as merely symbolic but believe that the intended recipients do in fact take and use them.

To account for the unchanged appearance of these items after they have been offered, the Rarámuri attribute to them what I will call "parallel aspects." These parallel aspects vary in the extent to which they are visible. The parallel aspect of a knife or a pot, for example, is entirely invisible, but those of foods are tangible, identified with their aroma and the steam that rises from them during cooking. During fiestas people do not inhale the steam and aromas of the foods until they are offered to God because those are God's parts of the food.

There is no single term in Rarámuri for the parallel aspects of different objects. Depending on the object, they are called "aroma," "steam," "smoke," "that which God takes," "that which the dead take," and so on. A few Rarámuri suggested to me that all parallel aspects should be called "souls," a usage similar to that adopted by Lumholtz (1902, I: 301, 347) in writing that God consumes the "nourishing substance" or "soul" of the food that the Rarámuri offer him. The parallel aspects of inanimate objects do bear some resemblances to souls: they are invisible or only marginally visible and can be detached from the things with which they are associated. But the differences between the two are important enough that most Rarámuri prefer not to call them souls. Unlike souls, parallel aspects are as inanimate as the objects themselves, and these objects derive nothing from the presence of their parallel aspects nor are they affected by their absence. In fact, it seems that inanimate objects maintain inexhaustible parallel aspects as long as the objects themselves are not destroyed. For example, the living can offer the same hoe or other tool to the dead on several occasions.

The Responsibilities of the Souls

> One day God and his older brother, the Devil, were sitting together
> talking and decided to see who could create human beings. God took
> pure clay while the Devil mixed his clay with white ashes and they began

forming some figurines. When the dolls were ready, they fired them so they would be hard. God's figures were darker than the Devil's. They were Rarámuri people while the Devil's were Chabochis.

Then they decided to see which one could bring his figures to life. God blew his breath into his dolls and they immediately came to life but the Devil, blow as he would, had no success. He turned to God and asked, "How did you do that?" so God taught the Devil how to give souls to his creations.

Once the Rarámuri and Chabochis were alive, God and the Devil organized a footrace between them. Both sides placed their bets, which included money as well as goods, and piled them up at the starting line, which also marked the finish. The length of the race was set—a short distance of about ten kilometers—and the two teams of runners set out. While the race was close, the Chabochi runners arrived at the betting spot first, so they took the winnings and left. God was quite angry with the Rarámuri because they had lost. From then on, he said, they would be poor while the Chabochis would be rich and, while the Chabochis could pay their workers with money, the Rarámuri would have only maize beer to give to the people who helped them.

All subsequent generations of Rarámuri and Chabochi people are descended from these first human beings, the product of their sexual union. From the Rarámuri perspective, the formation of an individual, of a self, begins in the mother's womb when a nascent body is united with a set of souls.[5] The parents provide the basic elements of the new body. In sexual intercourse, a man introduces semen (*chi?wá*, a term which means both "semen" and "milk") into the menstrual blood (*la* "blood") which has accumulated inside his mate's body between her menses. This semen causes the blood to coagulate, thereby preventing it from flowing from her body. God (or in the case of Chabochis, the Devil) then places some soul substance inside this mass of blood and semen, which he shapes into human form with his own hands.

The Rarámuri see the body and the souls like a house and its inhabitants. The body gives the souls shelter and some protection against evil beings while the souls live inside the body and care for it just as people care for their homes. The degree to which any particular soul fulfills this responsibility varies according to its size relative to other souls in the body: the larger the soul, the greater its contribution. If the body is injured, the comfort and safety of the souls is jeopardized and if the souls are negligent or desert the body, the person will sicken and die just as a house falls into disrepair if its residents abandon it.

The souls keep the body warm inside, move the various parts of the body, give the body force, and do all the thinking. The connection of souls to strength and vitality is expressed linguistically in that the terms for these physical attributes derive from the same root, *iwi-*, as those for souls, breath, and life in general. Thus, *iwigá* means "soul(s)" and "breath," *iwíma* means "to breathe," *iwítima* means "to bestow life or breath," and *iwérama* means "to have force, vitality, or endurance."[6] The Rarámuri believe that a person's vitality and forcefulness directly reflect the strength of his souls, but when they characterize the souls as strong, they often mean in a mental and emotional as well as physical sense.

Gifted orators are said to "speak forcefully" (*we iwéame raʔícha*). Their vigorous style of presentation reflects the strength of their souls because the content of the speech, as well as the breath that conveys it, comes from the large souls that live inside the chest. By presenting an effective speech, a man also demonstrates that he is emotionally strong, unintimidated by having to speak in front of his fellows. In addition, the words that he conveys are considered to be a direct expression, an externalization, of his thought and are called "thought" or "advice" (*nátiri*). His ability to speak forcefully is contingent upon and therefore indicates his ability to think forcefully.

The inextricable interconnections the Rarámuri see among an individual's physical, mental, and emotional states are further exemplified in the meanings they attribute to the term *iwérasa*, the imperative form of the verb *iwérama*. *Iwérasa* means "Have force, strength, and stamina!" but also "Be determined!", "Be enthusiastic!", and "Be contented!" During the Rarámuri's marathon footraces, people jog beside the runners they have chosen to support, shouting, "*Iwérasa!*" or "*Wériga!*"—"Be strong! Be determined!" Calls of "*Iwérasa!*" also ring out during rituals to encourage the main participants to complete their performances, which often requires strenuous exertion for entire nights in the cold or rain.

In these and all other contexts, *iwérasa* is employed interchangeably with the phrase *tarakó siwésa*, composed of the strong negative *tarakó* and the command form of the verb *siwéma*. It means "Don't give up!", "Don't back down!", "Don't lose your enthusiasm!", "Don't be disheartened!" and, in a more general sense, "Don't be sad!" *Siwéma* is one of three verbs the Rarámuri employ to convey the meaning of "to be sad," all three of which are antonyms of *iwérama* and, like it, denote particular physical and mental as well as emotional states. *Siwéma* means primarily "to lack enthusiasm or stalwartness." The Rarámuri use it less frequently in its positive sense than in its negative command form *tarakó siwésa*, meaning generally "don't be sad in this fashion." The second term, *niʔwíma*, connotes a state of longing or homesickness, the feeling experienced by people separated from their families or homes. The third verb is *oʔmónama*, which has less specific connotations than either *siwéma* or *niʔwíma* and encompasses both. Of the three verbs, *oʔmónama* conveys most closely the connotations that "to be sad" has in English, but some states marked by *oʔmónama*—for example, a hangover—are not characterized as "sad" in English.

The Rarámuri are very sensitive to any expression of sadness. They interpret sighing, for example, as a sign that a person's souls are sad and are leaving the body, because sighing involves the rapid flow of breath (i. e., souls) from the body. When a person sighs, people immediately ask, "*Chu shíka oʔmóna muhé?*" "Why are you sad?" and attempt to cheer the person up. The Rarámuri tell each other not to be sad because being sad can have serious, even fatal, consequences. A person is sad because his or her souls are sad. If the souls are sad, they can be harmed or destroyed by malevolent beings because in their sadness they lack the energy and will to resist attacks. Or, being unhappy in their present location, the souls can choose to abandon the body, sometimes to join their parents, God and his wife, in heaven where they will live contentedly. The Rarámuri consider the likelihood quite high that unremitting sadness, like that caused by the death of a loved one, will lead to death. Therefore, they constantly try to avoid becoming sad or to change their sadness to contentment by emphasizing the lighter side of things, enjoying themselves whenever possible, and confronting disheartening events with humor and gaiety.

The extent to which a person's souls are able to remain content in the face of saddening events and unpleasant circumstances depends upon the degree to which they are tough. The term the Rarámuri employ to describe souls as "tough" is *biwárame*, which also denotes the hardness of a rock or piece of ground and the toughness of a cut of meat. The souls become tougher as they mature. The Rarámuri say that children are so susceptible to illness because their souls are not tough, and they invariably characterize old people as tough, much as English speakers refer to an old man as "a tough old geezer." The fact that they have arrived at an advanced age is irrefutable testimony to the toughness of their souls.

In its usage, the term *biwárame* is closely associated with but nonetheless distinguishable from *iwéame*, which means "strong" or "with strength." If a person's souls are tough, they also are strong, but the toughness and strength of the souls are not necessarily reflected directly in the body. A young man can have a strong, tough body which he strengthens through exercise and exposure to the elements without his souls being equally strong and tough. Conversely, an older person can have strong, tough souls but a weak body.

In addition to endowing the body with warmth, force, and movement, the souls are responsible for performing a person's thinking. The Rarámuri say that people think in their heads and in their hearts because that is where their large souls are located, but they also attribute a crucial role in thinking to the brain (*mochogóare*). If people have no brains, they say, they cannot think, and if someone appears entirely incapable of learning or comprehending something, people ask, "Why can't you think? Do you have water inside your head instead of brains?"

The English verb "to think" finds its closest Rarámuri equivalent in the verb *natáma*. The Rarámuri use *natáma* in two senses, first to denote thinking in general, understood as the performance of mental operations, and second to designate thinking that allows and constrains an individual to act in conformity with conventions of proper behavior. In both cases, people's behavior testifies to the quality of their thought because, from the Rarámuri perspective, human action is a direct externalization of thought.

The Rarámuri consider reflex actions and simple body movements to require little or no thinking. The small souls in the body control basic behaviors and also care for the body when the larger souls are absent, but a person will sicken and die if his large souls are gone too long. None of the souls of babies and small children are larger than the smallest souls of an adult. They are almost incapable of coordinating their movements; they jabber instead of talk and are wholly dependent upon their elders for protection and sustenance. As children mature, they "think a little" (*pe náta*), but people emphasize that they think only about their parents, playing, and eating. The limited range of their thought is regarded as comparable to that of animals: cattle are said to think only about grazing, coyotes only about stealing, otters only about eating fish, and so on.

A child's body and souls mature together. As the souls grow, their strength and thinking abilities improve, but the discrepancies among the different souls within the body increase. The size and capacities of the small souls increase only slightly during a person's lifetime while the size, strength, and thinking ability of the large souls increase dramatically. At maturity, the large souls are adults but the small souls, despite their age, still look, think, and act like small children.

In Rejogochi they say that people usually can think (or think well) by the time they reach puberty. Of course, the development of their thinking ability does not cease at puberty but continues for the rest of their lives as they grow in knowledge and experience, at least until they become senile. Older people are said to think better than younger people in part because they have thought about many more things. They have had more experience in the world and can deal more effectively with unexpected events. They are not easily intimidated and are more capable of controlling their emotions, all of which indicate their souls are tough. As a result, they will not be given to melancholy or at the least will be able to recover quickly from sadness, avoiding its dangers. They will not scare easily, which makes them less likely to suffer soul loss. They also will be able to withstand and repel the attacks of malevolent beings to the extent that the toughness of their souls surpasses that of their assailants. However, all mature individuals do not have equally tough souls. The souls of people who have received special knowledge from God or the Devil are tougher than those of all others. From this knowledge, these specially endowed individuals derive the ability to act to their best advantage in a variety of threatening situations, defeating their enemies and protecting themselves and, in the case of doctors, other people from harm.

The Rarámuri of Rejogochi usually base their evaluation of the thinking ability of adults on two characteristics: the attitude they assume toward work and the way in which they relate to other beings in the universe. People are said to "think well" or to be "good thinkers" (*we ga?rá nátame hu*) if they initiate work projects on their own and demonstrate an ability and willingness to work without supervision or coercion. Working and thinking well imply one another as do laziness and bad thinking.

Calling someone lazy is one of the more serious insults a Rarámuri can make. The negative connotations of laziness derive in part from the idea that if people are unwilling to work, they will steal from others in order to survive. This connection between laziness and stealing is a constant theme in many accounts of events of the distant past, most of which describe Rarámuri people who transformed themselves into wild animals to avoid having to work for a living, as in the following example:

> A long time ago, when the world was new, there was a man who was
> very lazy. One day the people scolded him for not planting his maize so
> he took a planting stick and walked down to his field, but he did not feel
> like working. He decided instead to go sit by the creek and rest for
> awhile. There he began to think, "I'm tired of having to work so hard for
> my food. I think I will be a raven and then I can steal all the food I
> need." So he bathed in the creek and changed into a raven, his planting
> stick becoming his long beak. Then he flew away to the mountains where

ravens live today, returning to his former home only when he needed to steal food from the people.

Thinking ability is also indicated by the way a person acts toward other people. People are characterized as good thinkers if they are faithful to their spouses, quick to share their food and labor, responsible in fulfilling their duties to family and community, and not given to anger or violence. Their actions toward their deities also are important. For example, all Rarámuri people are supposed to sponsor as many fiestas for God as possible because it is during such fiestas that they return to God the food that he has provided for them and of which he is said to be the ultimate owner. If people who own many domesticated animals seldom sacrifice them for God, the Rarámuri say they do not think well. God will probably become angry at them for hoarding and will kill the animals himself or will make the owners or members of their families sick.

The Rarámuri consider the best thinkers in the community to be those individuals, regardless of age, who can cure other people. To be a doctor a person must possess esoteric knowledge and be able to dream well. God gives doctors permission to cure and provides them with the special knowledge from which they derive their curing abilities.[7] By applying their knowledge and dreaming abilities to benefit others, doctors demonstrate that they are good thinkers. However, anyone who can cure people can also choose to hurt them. Such people get their abilities to harm others from God, the Devil, or both, but if they ally themselves exclusively with the Devil, they are unable to cure.

These sorcerers injure their victims by capturing and destroying their souls or by putting foreign objects into their bodies. To do these things, they must be able to dream well, which requires highly developed mental abilities. Therefore, the Rarámuri hesitate to say that such people cannot think well so they describe their thinking in other terms: "they think in an ugly fashion" (*we cháte nátame hu*); "they do not think very straight" (*ke tási me ga?rá wachíniga nátame hu*); or "they are thinking apart" (*we waná nátame hu*), "apart" meaning apart from God's thinking and in conformance with the Devil's. Yet, when "thinking" is used in the sense of that which generates proper actions, such people unquestionably fail to think well since their sorcery is the epitome of improper behavior.

Whether people think well or not—that is, whether they think like God or the Devil—depends on the advice (*nátiri*, literally "thought") they received while growing up. This does not mean that adults cannot change their thinking

or that the Rarámuri do not attempt to transform the thinking of a person
who violates social conventions from bad to good. To the contrary, the giving
and receiving of advice among adults are prominent features of various kinds
of social interactions, from private, informal conversations to the public
speeches discussed in the last chapter.

Despite the pervasiveness of good advice in the Rarámuri milieu, people's
actions do not invariably reflect it. Whenever people consistently ignore good
advice and fail to behave properly, the Rarámuri not only say that they do
not think very well but that they are also crazy.[8] Anyone whose behavior is
bizarre or whose actions do not conform to the standards of proper behavior
qualifies as insane, but people who act improperly are more likely to be
characterized as insane than those who act strangely. A Rarámuri man and
woman who lived near Rejogochi were at least marginally insane by Western
standards. The man expressed himself only with difficulty and had little
control over his emotions, laughing or crying inappropriately. The woman
lived alone year-round in a rockshelter, wandered in the forest at night, and
reportedly ate meat raw "like a coyote." The Rarámuri viewed their behavior
as abnormal but disagreed as to whether they should be classified as insane.
Some people insisted that they were insane because they acted strangely but
others thought they were not insane because they worked for their food and
did not harm other people.

The Rarámuri are not ambivalent when judging those who violate the
norms of proper social conduct. Such people are unquestionably crazy because
their souls are crazy, a condition usually attributed to their failure to receive
and incorporate proper advice during their maturation, although sometimes
people are said to be crazy because they got drunk before they were able to
think well. Children can drink maize beer in quantities sufficient to become
inebriated, however, only if they first receive the permission of their parents
or other older relatives. If these relatives allow the children to drink before
they can think well, they display their own inability to think well. As a result,
they probably cannot give their children the advice they need to prevent their
souls from growing up insane.

Individuals are considered to be permanently insane only if they consistently behave improperly. If someone who normally displays good thinking
ability starts a fight or has an adulterous liaison, he or she is considered
insane only during the time of the misdeed. "Temporary insanity" usually
occurs in connection with drinking and reflects short-term aberrations in
thinking ability often induced by some outside influence such as the Devil.

Being insane and being incapable of thinking well are two ways the Rarámuri explain improper behavior and describe a person who exhibits such behavior. Both characterizations are employed interchangeably with a third: being shameless. To say that someone has no shame, the Rarámuri use the phrase *ke tási riwéri*, which consists of the negative *ke tási* plus the present tense form of the verb *riwérama*. *Riwérama* has no one-word equivalent in English; its meaning can be conveyed only through a composite gloss such as "to have pride, shame, self-esteem, honor, and a well-developed sense of appropriate behavior." The Rarámuri use this term in its negative sense to characterize anyone who behaves improperly, regardless if he or she has committed a major crime like murder or theft or only a minor breach of etiquette such as entering someone's home without first being invited. When employed positively rather than negatively, *riwérama* can mean either "to be ashamed or embarrassed" or "to know how to act in a proper fashion." These two senses are not as distinct as they might at first appear, since being ashamed and acting properly are two sides of the same coin.

Characterizing someone as shameless is a grave criticism because it means that the person is not easily shamed and thus not easily controlled by the other community members. Shaming is the major means for maintaining social control in Rarámuri society. In the not too distant past, the pueblo officials publicly flogged certain kinds of offenders, usually thieves. Today a person who physically harms other people or their property can be fined or, in the case of more serious crimes such as murder and grand larceny, turned over to authorities of the Mexican judicial system to be jailed. Regardless of their severity, however, all offenses are punished at least in part by shaming and for most offenses shaming is the only punishment.

Shaming usually takes the form of scolding. Sometimes people are scolded behind their backs as it were, through gossip which is communicated in private but always seems to eventually get back to the subjects. People also scold others directly in public gatherings, particularly during drinking get-togethers, if the person has slighted them or otherwise acts improperly. These scoldings are made before a limited audience, usually a group of neighbors, but if someone complains to the pueblo political officials about another person's conduct, the offender can be shamed before the members of many different settlements.

When such a complaint is filed, the pueblo officials dispatch a messenger to tell the accused to appear in the pueblo center on the following or a subsequent Sunday. On that day, the person is called before the officials, who are seated in a row on a long bench, holding their canes of office in their hands. The accused sits or kneels on the ground in front of the officials with his or her accuser to one side. The merits of the case are heard with the protagonists presenting their sides, their statements often being supplemented by interjections from the members of the crowd. If the accusation is judged valid, the governor or another political official questions the offender about the motivation for the improper behavior and admonishes him or her to modify his or her behavior in the future, usually outlining general standards of proper behavior in the process. When the lecture is over, the person moves away showing no expression but, according to what several Rarámuri told me, feeling ashamed and thoroughly castigated.[9] As Bennett and Zingg write of such official scoldings, "The social disgrace stings almost as sharply as the whip" (1935: 332).

Most Rarámuri parents raise their children to be very sensitive to shaming. Parents seldom strike their children for misbehaving, reprimanding them only by scolding and shaming them. When people are shamed, they usually withdraw, resuming their normal interactions when their embarrassment has receded to a tolerable level. Although their neighbors may gossip about the transgression for months or even years thereafter, they usually treat the person exactly as they did before the shaming took place. However, sometimes certain individuals will commit several offenses and appear totally unaffected by any advice or scolding they receive. If the offenses are serious—for example, if they fight every time they drink and particularly if one of their fights leads to someone's death—the community members then shun them.

Shunning among adults usually means refusing to invite the offender to drinking parties. This sanction derives its strength from the extreme importance of drinking get-togethers to the Rarámuri. In the context of such gatherings, people hear news and gossip about the community and the outside world, settle disputes, and coordinate their plans with those of others. Drinking parties are their main form of recreation and are a break from the normal course of daily household-centered affairs. Social life beyond the household revolves around drinking parties, and participation in them usually takes precedence over the performance of all other activities.

Consistent exclusion of a person from drinking get-togethers is a serious sanction because it involves the disintegration of the ground of a person's social being. When faced by such community rejection, most Rarámuri attempt to modify their behavior. If, however, shunning has no impact on the individual's actions, then the Rarámuri consider his or her souls to be irremediably insane.

INDIVIDUAL VARIATION IN THE CONCEPT OF SOUL

I encountered almost complete consensus among the Rarámuri of Rejogochi on the basic ideas about souls and animacy just discussed. In fact, disagreement was restricted almost entirely to ideas about the number and organization of an individual's souls, but whether a person is believed to have one large soul that is divisible or many separate souls makes little difference since the basic position is the same: that living human beings are soul-possessing entities, their souls are distributed throughout their bodies, and one portion of their total souls can be alienated from another. I also found that the people who conceived the body to have a single soul sometimes adopted the multiple soul model, for example, to portray the relations among souls as comparable to those among members of a household. Similarly, some people used the single soul idea when discussing situations in which all of a person's soul substance was proposed to be either completely outside or completely inside the body, but adopted the multiple soul idea when the soul substance was thought to be divided between the inside and outside. In other words, these people maintained both the single and multiple soul ideas, employing one or the other depending upon which was simpler or otherwise more appropriate in a given context.

By far most of the individual variation associated with the concept of soul occurs when the concept is used to explain specific existential states, in particular deviations from a person's "normal" condition of being alive, awake, sober, content, and healthy. I will focus on five of these states here: sleeping, dreaming, intoxication, illness, and death. Rarámuri explanations of these existential states rest upon the general assumption that a person's condition at any given time directly reflects the condition of the souls, the location of the souls with respect to the body, or both. However, only the condition of a person as revealed by his or her internal monitoring or external symptoms usually is known, not the condition or location of the souls. Determining whether the perceived change in the person's state reflects a change in the condition of the souls or a shift in their location with respect to the body and deciding what factors are responsible for this change become matters of speculation and potentially a point on which individual variation will occur.

In some cases, certain alternatives can be eliminated. For example, shifts in mood are attributed to changes in the emotional states of the souls since they are not radical enough to involve the departure of a person's souls. Similarly, if a person is deathly ill, one can assume that more than a minor change in the location and condition of the souls has occurred. Frequently, however, the information at hand is insufficient to determine with certainty what has generated the condition.

Sleeping and Dreaming

All the Rarámuri I consulted agreed that sleep and most events that happen during sleep are produced by the activities of the souls, but individuals disagree somewhat on the details of these matters. To indicate the nature of these variations as well as to provide the reader with a better sense of the relationship between what the Rarámuri told me and my presentations of their ideas about souls, I consider in detail the theories of sleeping and dreaming offered by the two men with whom I worked most closely.

The theory of the older man, Mariano Sikóchi, is the simpler of the two and has many more adherents in Rejogochi than that of Cornelio Rowhárare. Mariano offered a synthesis of his view during an interview taped at my home in Rejogochi on November 26, 1978.

I broached the subject by asking, "Why do we sleep?"

Mariano immediately responded, "Why not? That's the way things are. Why not? We get very sleepy."

Because I was interested in the role that souls play in sleep rather than its ultimate or immediate cause, I got to the point:

"So we are able to sleep when all the souls are inside the body?"

"Sure we can," he replied. "Everything sleeps. The souls themselves sleep. They go to sleep first, then we fall asleep. This is how God set things up—to sleep at night—from ancient times. From the time that he first placed souls in people, this is how it has been. 'Sleep,' God said. The souls themselves sleep, then the body, the house [of the souls], sleeps."

"So when the souls sleep, we sleep, too?"

"We sleep, everything sleeps. No, the body is just a house. The souls sleep inside the chest. They go to sleep first. Then later they wake up. This is how things were established."

"But can the souls also leave the body?"

"Yes, when they wake up. They open their eyes and sit up. Now they are thinking well again. The head is thinking well. Then when the time comes, they sleep again. They are just resting. They don't talk, but they are thinking. Then, if we dream something evil, they begin thinking. If something attacks me, that's what they do. If some Rarámuri arrives to attack me, they begin to think, they wake up. Dreaming begins right away."

"Do the souls go outside the body?"

"They go outside."

"While we dream?"

"They go outside."

"But if they are inside, we don't dream?"

"No, even then we dream. When the souls are thinking well, when they are awake. They wake up inside and they think. They think very well when they are awake, but if they don't wake up then they don't think. Like goats don't think. They [the goats] just wander off into the woods."

To explore his ideas about the process of falling asleep, I asked, "Why do we yawn?"

"Well," he said, "because the souls are sleepy. When we are tired, we yawn. Like after we work a lot, we're exhausted and we yawn."

"Are the souls tired, too?"

"Yes, they become sleepy. We don't want to become overly tired, because the souls won't be contented. If we're not ill, we don't get sleepy and can work very hard. Doing things like drinking maize beer makes us sleepy. The souls are not contented and we can fall ill. They are sad. Eating bitter foods makes us nauseous and the souls are unhappy inside. We want to sleep."

"If all the souls are not inside, then we become sleepy?"

"We become very sleepy if most of the souls are gone and we become sick. We are very weak and sad. We can't work very well. Like when people around here are ill, they can't work. They are not contented and can't work. They walk very slowly, like Patricio when we were drinking or Basilio" [two old men in the community].

From this and similar interviews, I arrived at the following synopsis of Mariano's theory of sleeping and dreaming. In his view, the external state of a person directly reflects the state of his souls inside his body. The person feels drowsy when his souls feel drowsy and falls asleep when his souls fall asleep inside his body. Dreaming begins when the largest soul wakes up but the other souls continue sleeping. This soul can then leave the body and its activities outside are experienced as dreams. When it returns, it can either resume sleeping or remain awake, but the person awakens only when all his souls wake up. The largest soul does not leave the body or even wake up independently of the other souls every night; therefore, a person does not dream every night.

The theory of Cornelio Rowhárare also emerged during formal interviews in my home, but because he was a competent speaker of Spanish, much of our conversation took place in that language rather than Rarámuri. I took notes during the interviews instead of recording them on tape so here I can only paraphrase what he said. The following are a sample of his ideas.

August 28, 1978: When we sleep, only the largest souls leave the body. The medium-size souls stay in the chest and the small souls in the rest of the body. Because these souls remain in the chest, we breathe heavily while we sleep. I drink a lot while I sleep. The souls make maize beer themselves and join other souls to drink in the night. I get drunk on a lot of nights.

September 7, 1978: At night the only soul to leave the body is the largest. When it wants to leave, we get drowsy and when it departs we fall asleep. When it returns we wake up. Only this soul goes out at night. The two medium-size souls stay inside the body caring for it.

October 4, 1978: We yawn when we are sleepy because our souls want to leave, and we sleep because our souls go outside our bodies. Only one soul leaves, the largest one that lives in the middle of the chest. The other two large souls that live inside the chest and head stay behind with the small souls. No, I think the large soul in the head also leaves because our eyes close when we sleep. Only the large soul in the chest remains inside with the small souls. The two souls that leave go around together in one body. If the Devil grabs them while they are outside, the Devil keeps the largest one and the other returns to the body.

October 28, 1978: While we are sleeping all of the large soul is outside. The breath that remains inside the body is the souls that stay behind. We can't move around while we are sleeping because the small souls that remain inside the body are too weak. Only when the large souls return can we get up.

November 1, 1978: Sleepwalking is called *uchuwásari*. I never walk in my sleep but my younger brother has. People walk in their sleep because they have offended the *uchurí* or *rikúhuri* [the plant people discussed above] by hitting or cutting them. They come to these people's homes in the night while they are sleeping and carry them off to high cliffs from which they push them off. They take the body with the small souls inside. The large souls are outside the body then so the sleepwalker isn't aware of what is happening and doesn't remember anything afterward.

November 28, 1978: When we sleep our souls go outside the body and wander around. I don't know if they sleep outside the body but they don't sleep while they are inside us. When the souls return, we wake up right away. I usually wake up several times during the night but when I have drunk maize beer I sleep all night long because my souls go farther away. You and Cecilia sleep all night long without waking up because your souls have a long way to go to get back to the United States and Mexico City. You dream a lot of the United States because you don't want to live here anymore and want to return to your home in the United States.

March 2, 1979: When the souls decide to leave, we become sleepy. When they leave we go to sleep. The small souls never leave the body except at death. We dream when our souls talk with other souls. If our souls don't encounter other souls in their wanderings, then we don't dream.

Cornelio's theory is more complex than that of Mariano because he introduced several permutations of it during the months we worked together and because it is based on a different assumption than the first, an assumption that requires more elaborate ideas. This assumption is that the souls never sleep inside the body and probably do not sleep when they are outside the body. Therefore, the state of the body during sleep cannot be explained simply as a reflection of the activities of the souls inside the body. According to Cornelio, sleep takes place only when one or more of the large souls leave the body. On different occasions, he suggested that the largest soul alone, the largest soul and the large soul that lives in the head, and all three large souls depart when sleep occurs. People feel sleepy when their souls decide to depart, but the souls themselves do not feel sleepy; they feel only that they want to leave. Their desire is indicated by yawning, that is, a more active movement of breath, or soul, into and out of the body than occurs in normal respiration.

In Cornelio's theory, the fact that falling asleep usually occurs gradually is accounted for in several ways. When two or all three large souls are said to be involved, a person experiences the transition from drowsiness to sleep because the souls leave the body in succession rather than together, with the person getting sleepier as each soul leaves, finally sleeping when the last soul departs. As an alternative explanation, which is even more reflective of the way a person falls asleep, each departing soul gradually flows from the body. In the explanation that has only the largest soul leaving, the person remains awake but drowsy while this soul is close by but becomes increasingly sleepy and eventually falls asleep as it moves farther from the body. When one or more of these souls are outside the body, the sleeper is immobile because the souls that remain inside are not strong enough to move the body. He wakes up as soon as the souls return.

The activities of the soul(s) outside the body are experienced as dreams but, since sleep occurs only if a soul or souls leave the body, the problem arises as to why a person does not dream the entire time he is asleep and on some nights does not dream at all. According to Cornelio, an individual dreams only if his soul or souls encounter other souls during their wanderings outside the body, failing to dream if no such encounters take place. However, other

factors also can preclude dreaming. Once I accompanied a man from Rejogochi to some ancient cave burials and inadvertently touched one of the
bones there. When I related this event to Cornelio, he told me that I would
be unable to dream for a few days because the dead people buried in the
caves would lock my souls up, preventing them from traveling around and
having experiences.

The individual variations in the explanations of sleep occur because people have no information about whether sleep is caused by a change in the
condition of a person's souls or a change in their location. Mariano attributed
sleep to a change in the condition of a person's souls inside the body while
Cornelio explained it as caused by a change in the souls' location. I asked
Cornelio why he did not choose the simpler explanation and he gave the
following reason. The souls' major responsibility, he said, is to diligently
care for the bodies they inhabit. If a person's souls were to fall asleep inside
the body, they would be unable to maintain their vigilance. He considered
the relationship between people and their souls to be analogous in some respects to that between God and the Rarámuri: the souls care for the Rarámuri
from the inside just as God cares for them from the outside. In fact, he
viewed the connection between God and the souls in caring for people to be
even closer than this analogy suggests because God gave the souls this responsibility. Cornelio felt that if sleep were caused by the souls going to
sleep, the constancy of God's care for the Rarámuri would be called into
question. Since the idea that God continuously watches over them is a basic
premise of Rarámuri world view, he rejected the simpler explanation.

Despite their differences, both accounts of sleep explain dreams as the
activities of one or more of a person's souls while the person is asleep. These
men could have proposed that dreams are simply the imaginings of their
souls, but because the Rarámuri rely on dreams to provide them access to
information and beings, like God, that they feel are crucial to their survival,
they are committed to the reality of dreams (Merrill 1987). If dreams are
considered to be as real as is waking life and if people are animate and sentient
only because they have souls, then the conclusion that dreams are the activities
of the souls is unavoidable. People act in dreams but their bodies are dormant;
the actors must be their souls.

Inebriation

All the Rarámuri I consulted generally agreed on how a person becomes
intoxicated (Merrill 1978). When a person drinks maize beer, they say, the

beer settles in the stomach. The souls dislike the smell of the beer so one or more of them leave, and the person becomes intoxicated. Neither the souls that remain inside the body nor those that depart drink any of the beer and none is intoxicated during the time the individual is drunk. During and after drinking, the beer gradually passes out of the body as waste. As the beer is eliminated from the body, the soul or souls return and the person becomes sober.

The Rarámuri also show general agreement on the implications of soul departure during drinking for their physical and mental states and general behavior, but again people do disagree on some details. They explain the deviations from a state of sobriety that occur during drinking primarily by reference to two variables: the amount or number of souls that leave the body and the proximity of these departed souls to the body. The explanations of inebriation proposed by different people vary because they emphasized one of these variables over the other or maintained different ideas about how these variables interact to produce intoxication.

Everyone concurs that the smaller souls remain inside the body during drinking, caring for the body just as children stay at home when their adult relatives go to drink. Explanations of inebriation thus focus on the activities of the large souls. These explanations are of three kinds, each with its own permutations, according to whether one, two, or all three of the large souls are thought to leave the body during drinking.

Explanations that involve the departure of all three large souls during drinking propose that these souls abandon the body in succession rather than simultaneously. The first to leave is the largest of the three, which lives in the heart, followed by the large soul in the head and then by the third large soul, which also lives in the heart. As each soul departs, the drinker becomes increasingly intoxicated, with the degree of intoxication being directly proportional to the number of large souls that leave. When the person stops drinking, the souls return in reverse order of their departure and the drinker becomes more nearly sober as each soul reenters the body.

When only two large souls are envisioned to leave the body, again they depart and return in succession, the largest soul in the heart leaving first and returning second, the large soul in the head the opposite. The other large soul in the heart remains inside the body to supervise its care. The large soul in the head is assumed to leave because a major effect of alcohol consumption is giddiness in the head. During drinking the Rarámuri frequently will inquire of one another in a humorous vein, "In what part of your body are you drunk?" (*Churigáchi rikúti?*), to which the expected reply is, "In my head" (*mo?ochí*).

The explanation of inebriation that appears to be the most popular attributes intoxication to the departure not of two or three large souls but of the largest soul alone, which is associated with the heart. All the other souls stay inside the body and are responsible for its care. The increasing intoxication that comes from continued consumption of alcohol is explained in one of two ways: either this largest soul flows from the body gradually or it leaves all at once and then moves farther and farther from the body as the drinking continues. Some of the people who propose that more than one soul temporarily leaves the body during drinking also incorporate one or the other of these two notions into their theories of intoxication in order to better account for the continuity of the inebriation process.

The Rarámuri say they tend to behave improperly when they are drinking because the smaller souls that remain inside their bodies cannot think very well. They also suggest that while God gave them beer to drink, the Devil encourages and sometimes forces them to drink a lot. They assume that the Devil invariably arrives when people are drinking to get them to behave improperly. The Devil knows that his chances for success are greater when the large souls are outside the body because the smaller souls are less able to resist him. If he is successful, the drinkers will be more likely to fight among themselves, commit adultery, and perform other improper acts, all of which please the Devil.

People who think well when sober usually do not indulge in undesirable behavior even when very drunk because, before leaving, their large souls tell the small ones how to act and care for the body in much the same way as an elder advises a child on proper conduct. People whose large souls do not think well behave improperly when drunk because these souls have no advice—or only bad advice—to give when they leave.

While not all people behave the same way when drunk, general similarities characterize their drinking behavior. People in Rejogochi frequently say that drunk people act like children and point to several correspondences between the behavior of drunk adults and of children. Neither small children nor drunk adults are adept at motor activities such as walking and talking. Further, small children have limited memory, and adults usually cannot remember all the details of their activities while they were drunk. In addition, drunken people laugh, cry, shout, chase each other around, and generally behave in ways that the Rarámuri consider to resemble the behavior of their children. The Rarámuri believe these similarities exist because when people are drunk the souls that remain inside their bodies approximate in size and thinking ability the largest souls of small children.

People do not speculate much about what souls do while they are outside the bodies of drinkers. One man suggested that his souls travel to heaven during this period to visit with their parents, God and his wife, but upon reflection he said that while he found such a possibility pleasing, it was unlikely because of the immense distance the souls would have to travel in such a short time. He then proposed that his souls remain near his body when he drinks to care for it from the outside, a view shared by the majority of people I consulted. The soul or souls that leave the body during drinking continue to contribute to its care by communicating with the souls that remain inside. When people leave one drinking party to go to another or to return to their homes, the souls outside their bodies trail along to protect them.

To account for intoxication the Rarámuri can choose between alternatives similar to those that explain sleep: they can attribute intoxication either to the intoxication of the souls inside the body or to the departure of some of the souls from the body. However, everyone I consulted rejected the intoxication of the souls themselves as the cause of inebriation, for one of two reasons. The first derives from the analogy they propose between the relationship of the body to its souls and a house to its residents. If a house is pervaded by an unpleasant smell, its residents will leave until the odor clears. The souls do likewise when strong-smelling maize beer or other alcoholic drinks fill their home, except for those souls who must remain behind to care for the body. The second reason is associated with the idea that God is pleased by beauty and displeased by ugliness. As God's creations, souls partake in his likes and dislikes. Consequently they leave the body during drinking because the unpleasant smell of maize beer is considered ugly. They do, however, maintain their vigilance over the body by remaining nearby.

Illness

From the Rarámuri perspective, people remain healthy as long as their souls are content while inside the body and return unharmed from their excursions outside the body. Anything that alters this situation jeopardizes the person's health. Innumerable factors undermine a person's well-being, either by altering the condition of the body or by threatening the souls. People are in greatest danger when one or more of their souls are injured or captured by a malevolent being. If the affected souls cannot be healed or rescued, the people will die. Ailments that primarily affect the body tend to be less serious than those involving the souls directly but even seemingly insignificant illnesses can have portentous implications if they cannot be quickly cured. If a sickness renders the body—the house of the souls—an unpleasant home, the souls may decide to leave. While the souls seldom abandon a body sick with a temporary and minor ailment, they are increasingly inclined to leave if the condition persists.

People generally agree on the factors that cause different kinds of illnesses but are less certain about which of these factors is responsible for causing a particular instance of sickness. This disagreement is possible because, except for the most and least serious ailments, the symptoms of most illnesses can be attributed to a change in either the condition or the location of the afflicted person's souls. In addition, because many factors can affect the condition or location of a person's souls, any one of a variety of explanations potentially may account for any particular set of symptoms. Determining the actual cause of the ailment involves a process of elimination in which treatment is initiated based on the likeliest diagnosis and, if the illness remains, pursuing alternative diagnoses and treatments until the patient is cured or dies. In the next chapter, I will examine in detail one case from Rejogochi that illustrates the diversity of possible diagnoses and treatments for a prolonged sickness.

Death

All the Rarámuri people I asked attributed death to the total absence of souls from a person's body. Given their belief that souls are intrinsically animate and the fact that death is a state of inanimacy, this conclusion is unavoidable. Of course, they could say that death occurs when all the souls inside the body die but this alternative is unlikely because they believe that some aspect of a person continues to exist after death.

This consensus on death itself contrasts with the diversity of Rarámuri ideas about the fate of souls in the afterlife. Most people agree that every individual has many souls, each of which may have a fate distinct from that of all the others, and that the souls of different people may experience different fates in the afterlife. People disagree on the application and development of these ideas, and sometimes one person may apply contradictory notions about souls to explain different aspects of the afterlife.

When the souls abandon the body at death, they undertake a journey. In one view the souls of the deceased travel to all the places visited in life, following the footprints left behind on previous trips and bidding farewell to friends and relatives. For some people a major purpose of this journey is to allow the dead to retrieve their footprints, which they must present to God when they arrive in heaven, together with their hair cut during their lives.[10]

Souls can travel at great speeds when unencumbered by their bodies, so they complete the journey in three days if the deceased is male, four if female. Then members of the deceased's household prepare offerings of food and other goods for the souls of the deceased to carry on their journey up to heaven.

In an alternative view of this journey, the souls of the deceased travel to the edge of the world where the arch of the sky approaches the earth's plane and then complete a circuit of its circumference. This journey does not repeat the travels of the deceased during life because it is much too long for a living person to accomplish. At each of four points along the edge stands a cross that the souls of the dead circle counterclockwise, crossing themselves and turning counterclockwise at each side. The Rarámuri do this during their ceremonies and call it "greeting God." When the dead greet God, it signifies their separation from the earth and their integration into God's celestial realm. In this view, the dead goes to his or her household after three (or four) days to collect the offerings there before ascending to heaven. Most people agree that the souls of dead Rarámuri then reside in heaven for eternity unless they have committed capital offenses. If so they are sent to the Devil to be destroyed. The souls of Chabochi people automatically go to the underworld when they die, but they are not punished because the Devil is their father.

In this view, the universe is composed of three levels—earth, heaven, and the underworld—but another view of the afterlife, considered plausible by a few people, is proposed for a universe of seven levels. In this conception, when a Rarámuri dies on earth, the souls travel up to the third heaven to greet God, who then dispatches them to live in the first heaven, the level immediately above the earth. There they inhabit a second body, identical in all respects to the previous body. The new person begins life at the age at which the earthdweller died, essentially picking up where the original body left off. When the souls abandon this second body, they again return to heaven, and God sends them to live in the second heaven in a new body that continues the life of its immediate predecessor. At the end of this third life, the souls again abandon their body, but this time all but the smallest of these souls themselves die, becoming like ashes although they are not burned. The smallest soul becomes a moth (called *nakarówili anayáwari*, "ancestor moth" or *nakarówili ariwá* "soul moth") and returns to the earth where, through its own carelessness, it eventually falls into one of the fires of the living. When this moth is destroyed, all that remains of the person are the ashes that were his souls and the decomposed remains of his successive bodies. The eventual destruction of the souls is not seen as a punishment for misdeeds but as the natural conclusion of existence. In this view, Chabochi people also live and die three times on successive levels of the universe, but their movement is downward rather than upward.

Several variations on this scheme all have to do with the ultimate fate of the souls. In one variation, after the third death the smallest soul becomes a moth but the remaining souls, rather than dying, ascend to the third heaven to live for eternity with God. Another variation excepts little children. According to some people, all the souls of children ascend directly to heaven after death. Others say that children, like adults, pass through a series of lives and deaths, but after the third death God makes their smallest souls into stars in the third heaven.

In keeping with some of the distinctions made between the fates of children and adults, most Rarámuri maintain that everyone's small souls go to heaven because small souls are like children, whom God exempts from punishment and protects from harm. However, people tended to offer this view only when I inquired specifically about the fate of the small souls in the afterlife. When I asked about the fate of a person's souls in general, people seldom distinguished among the souls because of size except when proposing that one or more small souls transform after death into, for example, a coyote or moth.

The moths that figure in this account as people's ultimate forms are interpreted by others as the souls of people who have committed incest. Because these moths are irresistibly attracted to flames, they in effect punish themselves. People who do not think these moths are the souls of the incestuous do agree, however, that people who commit incest are punished by God, who sends their souls to be destroyed by the Devil in a fire.

The Rarámuri propose a variety of punishments in the afterlife for offenses committed during life, the details of which will be presented in chapter 6. They range in severity from gentle scolding to complete destruction of the souls. Some individual variation is associated with descriptions of these punishments and the crimes for which they are applied but all agree that whatever its form, punishment is swift but brief. There is no eternal damnation and suffering in the Rarámuri scheme of things.

THE PRODUCTION OF VARIATION AND CONSENSUS

In this description of the Rarámuri concept of soul, I have included only a sampling of the diversity of ideas about souls that different Rarámuri people maintain, but these examples illustrate the variation and consensus that exist. The Rarámuri share many ideas about souls, but not because they consciously attempt to establish homogeneity within their society on the concept of soul. Rather, this agreement reflects the operation of factors that place constraints on the possibility for variation during the course of the reproduction of this knowledge. These constraints tend to be implicit and unconscious, deriving both from the transmission of ideas about souls in public contexts and from the logical relations among the ideas that comprise this concept. Here I will consider the logical relations within the concept of soul and the constraints on variation associated with them, examining in chapters 5 and 6 the kinds of information about souls that are conveyed through public practices.

The ideas that constitute the Rarámuri concept of soul are propositional in form and linked to one another primarily by relations of contingency or presupposition. They can be organized into a hierarchy according to the degree to which any given idea presupposes or is presupposed by other ideas. Higher-level ideas are those that are contingent upon few or no other ideas within the concept of soul while lower-level ideas presuppose several higher-level ideas.[11]

To say that two ideas are linked by a relation of presupposition means simply that one is contingent upon the other. The lower-level idea that people derive their animacy from their souls, for example, presupposes the higher-level idea that souls are animate. Such a relation is, from lower to higher levels, one of logical requirement: if souls give a person animacy then they necessarily must themselves be animate. However, the relation in the opposite direction, from higher-level to lower-level ideas, is considerably weaker, and can be characterized as one of "suggestion" (Quine and Ullian 1978). People may attribute animacy to souls without concluding that they derive their own animacy from them, although such a conclusion is "suggested" by the assumptions that souls are animate and people have souls.

A few propositions in the concept of soul are related to one another in deductive arguments, in which one idea logically follows from the others. For example, as discussed above, the idea that people's dreams are the activities of their souls is a conclusion that can be drawn from the Rarámuri's ideas about the reality of dreams, the role of souls in providing people with animacy and sentience, and the souls' ability to operate independent of the body. For the most part, however, the higher-level ideas in the concept of soul do not logically entail lower-level ones and the lower-level ideas cannot be deduced from higher-level ones. In other words, this concept is not a deductive system of knowledge in which the majority of ideas included within it can be derived from a few general assumptions.

Thus far I have mentioned three kinds of relations that exist among the ideas within the Rarámuri concept of soul: contingency, suggestion, and logical implication. All of these relations can be subsumed under a more general category I call "relations of support." The propositions involved in these relations are mutually reinforcing, each idea lending credence to the others so that the acceptance of one of them increases the likelihood that the others also will be accepted. However, the support that one idea gives another is greater when it logically requires or is required by the other idea, as in the case of relations of logical presupposition and implication, than when the ideas simply suggest one another.

Different ideas within the concept of soul often presuppose different higher-level ideas, which means that the concept is compartmentalized along the lines laid down by vertical relations of contingency. Ideas that fall at about the same level of the hierarchy neither presuppose nor are presupposed by one another, but they can be involved in relations of support that cut across the compartments created by relations of contingency. An example of such horizontal mutual reinforcement is seen in the relationship between the Rarámuri's explanations of inebriation and of serious illness. Both intoxication and serious illness are characterized by radical changes in a person's condition. Therefore, attributing intoxication to the departure of one or more of a drinker's souls reinforces the idea that grave illnesses also are caused by soul departure, and this explanation of illness simultaneously supports the explanation of inebriation.

The many interconnections among these propositions contribute to the overall coherence and stability of the concept of soul but do not preclude its flexibility. By flexibility, I mean the ability of one part of the conceptual scheme to undergo modification without requiring comparable changes in other portions. The compartmentalization of the concept of soul contributes to its flexibility because ideas in different compartments, or domains, deal with somewhat different matters and can be modified independently of one another. Thus, the Rarámuri could reject the proposition that people's thinking is performed by their souls without jeopardizing their view that individuals derive their vitality from their souls. Similarly, they could decide that intoxication is not produced by the departure of one or more souls from the body without having to modify the idea that dreams are the activities of souls outside the body during sleep.

Such flexibility does not exist in those sets of ideas about souls that are linked to one another in deductive arguments because the rejection of one or more premises of a valid deductive argument usually entails rejecting or at least revising the conclusion and vice versa. This flexibility also is not found among the higher-level ideas in the concept. The rejection of a higher-level idea requires rejecting all the lower-level ideas contingent on it. Because higher-level ideas often are presupposed by several different lower-level ideas that can fall within different domains of the concept, the rejection of higher-level ideas can result in considerable modification. For instance, if one rejects the idea that some of an individual's souls can temporarily leave the body without fatal consequences, this eliminates the possibility of explaining dreaming, intoxication, and serious illnesses by soul departure. Such lower-level explanations, however, can be altered or rejected without undermining the higher-level ideas they presuppose. A person can decide that serious illness is not caused by soul loss but still believe that souls can leave the body temporarily without causing death.

Given the logical relations among the ideas that make up the concept of soul, the number of alternative ideas is greater at the lower levels of the hierarchy and the consequences for the concept as a whole of choosing one lower-level idea rather than another also are more limited. There is, in other words, more opportunity for people to vary on lower-level ideas than higher-level ones. The pattern of consensus on higher-level ideas about souls and variation on lower-level ideas reflects these possibilities, but the Rarámuri do hold some lower-level ideas in common. Such consensus on lower-level ideas exists in some cases because these ideas are logical conclusions of higher-level ideas, but in others people have selected the same idea even though viable alternatives exist.

By "select" I do not necessarily mean conscious choice. People may not be aware that there are alternatives to many of the ideas they hold, or, if they do consciously choose among ideas, they rarely can choose from options already formulated by others; more often they think of their own alternatives. Nonetheless, by adhering to a particular idea, people reject, consciously or unconsciously, its alternatives, although a person may employ alternative ideas in different contexts.

If the construction of knowledge involves, even metaphorically, making choices among alternative ideas, the next question must be: what motivates making those choices? Various concerns may motivate a person to select one idea over its alternatives. Some of these concerns stem from the position the person maintains in the society or from other features of his or her life history. People who perform the same social roles or who have similar backgrounds probably will be motivated by some of the same concerns and therefore will make some of the same choices. Many studies of intracultural variation amply demonstrate that correlations can be established between such factors and patterns of sharing and variation in what different people think (see, for example, Burton and Kirk 1979, the essays on intracultural diversity in *American Ethnologist*, vol. 2, no. 1, 1975, and the various studies cited by Boster 1986). On the other hand, sharing a social position can engender disagreement as well as agreement as, for instance, when Rarámuri doctors offer different diagnoses of an individual's ailment in order to undermine the competence of their competitors in the eyes of the community.

The concerns that influence an individual's choices also may be more personal, giving rise to what Burton and Kirk (1979: 842) have termed "random" variation and Pollnac (1975: 89) "idiosyncratic" variation, that is, variation that cannot be correlated with other sociocultural variables (cf. Berger and Luckman 1966: 106). In some instances, random variation derives from the ways different people organize and evaluate ideas, as illustrated by the alternative explanations of sleep presented above. Mariano Sikóchi preferred the explanation that the souls sleeping inside the body causes sleep because of its simplicity. He did not regard the higher-level idea that God constantly cares for the Rarámuri as immediately relevant to his own theory of sleep. Cornelio Rowhárare, in contrast, explained sleep by the departure of the large souls from the body because he considered the vigilance of the souls to be a direct commentary on God's vigilance over the Rarámuri. Cornelio, but not Mariano, established direct connections between lower- and higher-level ideas from separate domains of Rarámuri world view, giving more general significance to the lower-level ideas and enhancing the overall coherence of his conceptual scheme.

In some cases, different people establish similar connections between the same higher- and lower-level ideas, producing consensus rather than variation. Such consensus is seen in the view that intoxication is caused by the departure of one or more of a person's souls. Since people in Rejogochi believe that the souls themselves get drunk while outside the body, attributing intoxication to the intoxication of the souls seems to be a viable alternative explanation. However, they share fundamental ideas about the relationship between the body and souls and between the souls and God that appear to preclude their adopting this interpretation. These ideas imply that the souls and God reject the beer, reflecting, I suggest, the association of intoxication with improper behavior. Since such moral ambiguity is not an issue with sleep, people seem to be less concerned with connecting their explanations of sleep to more general cosmological ideas.

Individual variation also can result when people bring different higher-level ideas to bear on a single topic. A good example of such variation is seen in the Rarámuri's ideas about the fate of a person's small souls after death. In one view, the large and small souls are regarded as collectively responsible for a person's behavior so they experience the same fate in the afterlife. In a second view, God invariably takes a person's small souls to heaven even if the large souls are destroyed as punishment for wrongdoing in life. This treatment of the small souls reflects the Rarámuri's idea that there is no original sin and that the small souls, like children, are not responsible for the misdeeds of their elders. In a third view, which I did not mention above, the souls from the upper half of the body rise to heaven while those of the lower half, all of which are small, descend to the underworld to live. Here the body and souls are seen as a microcosm of the universe, which is polarized between divine and diabolical powers.

I recorded these ideas not only from different people but in some cases from the same people on different occasions. When I pointed out the contradictions among them to some of these people, they said things like, "I don't know how that can be, but that's what people say." They did not attempt to resolve the contradictions, I think, for three reasons. First, these ideas have no consequences for behavior. Second, the Rarámuri are not as concerned that such lower-level ideas be mutually consistent as they are that higher-level ideas be consistent among themselves and that lower-level ideas be consistent with the higher-level ideas to which they are related. Third, the contradictions cannot be resolved except by rejecting two of the three alternatives. These alternative lower-level ideas support different higher-level ideas, all of which are important in Rarámuri world view. Because these higher-level ideas are established by convention rather than by empirical observation, they cannot be confirmed by appeal to external reality. They must instead be supported by sources within the system of ideas of which they are a part, in this case by lower-level ideas.

These lower-level ideas also provide distinct perspectives on the place of death within the cosmos. Eliminating any one of them would represent to the Rarámuri a reduction in meaning. Seen logically, the claim that inconsistency enhances meaning is a non sequitur. Obviously, pervasive inconsistency in a set of ideas would be chaotic, but insisting on absolute consistency (even if it could be achieved) would only impoverish meaning. Rarámuri thought is not pervaded by contradictions nor are the Rarámuri unable to recognize contradictions when they occur. But they seem to prefer to ignore some inconsistencies in minor details if resolving the inconsistencies diminishes the richness of their world view.

CURING
PRACTICES

In March of 1978, a man in his late twenties named Calistro Sawárare began experiencing a dull pain in his right hip, which hindered his walking. At the time, he was living in Rejogochi with his wife and three small children in a log house he had built next to his wife's land, across the creek from his wife's parents' home and about a two-hour walk from his own parents' home. Over the next two weeks the pain increased, so Calistro asked his wife's parents and siblings for their help in diagnosing and curing the ailment. After some discussion they concluded that Calistro's malady more than likely had been induced by *bakánawi*.

Bakánawi, it will be remembered, are a class of beings, human in form but small in stature, who are associated with the underground tubers of a plant, probably a bulrush (Bye 1979a: 35–36), that grows in the deep canyons that dissect the southwestern portions of Rarámuri country. Rarámuri who live near these canyons supply these tubers to Rarámuri in other areas, but few people in Rejogochi acquire them because they are afraid. *Bakánawi* will protect and assist the people who own them but only if these people "feed" them by making offerings of incense and unsalted chicken meat and broth. Calistro's father, rumor had it, owned several of these tubers but seldom offered them food. Calistro's in-laws suspected that the *bakánawi* had become angry with Calistro's father and decided to return to their home in the canyons. But before departing, the diagnosis went, they tied an invisible cord around Calistro's leg and kidnapped his largest soul, which they were now holding captive in the canyons.

On April 10, a Rarámuri doctor who specialized in recovering souls captured by *bakánawi* arrived in a nearby settlement from his rancho thirty kilometers away to perform a *bakánawi* ceremony. Calistro's in-laws attended the ceremony and asked the specialist to stop by Rejogochi on his way home to see Calistro. Although he was exhausted from performing the long ceremony through snow and drizzle, the doctor went to Calistro's house the next morning and examined him. After questioning Calistro about his illness and consulting his *bakánawi*, he agreed that *bakánawi* had captured Calistro's soul. He then performed a short version of the *bakánawi* ceremony in which he succeeded in convincing the *bakánawi* to return Calistro's soul in exchange for food and other items.

Calistro began recovering almost as soon as the *bakánawi* specialist finished, but over the summer he relapsed. By mid-August he could not walk without pain, had no appetite, and had lost a lot of weight. His in-laws tried to convince him to enter the Jesuit-run clinic in Creel, about fifty kilometers away, but Calistro was afraid he would die there. He finally agreed to go if the clinic staff could cure an old Rarámuri man from Rejogochi whom they were treating. The old man died in the clinic a few days later.

On August 13, a Sunday, I walked with Calistro and several other young men the ten kilometers from Rejogochi to the church in Basíhuare. Calistro dragged along, constantly falling behind, so we stopped every fifteen minutes or so to let him catch up. His companions joked with him about his slow pace, and began calling him by the nickname "Rawhide," in reference to the old-style rawhide-soled sandals that his father had used long after everyone else had begun to wear tire rubber soles. Along the way Calistro told me he believed he was sick because a yellowish mucus-like substance called *awagásine* had accumulated inside his body. *Awagásine* comes from bitter things that people consume, like maize beer and the water in which greens are cooked, and causes loss of appetite and heaviness in the legs. Along the trail, he pointed out a plant that is used as an emetic to eliminate *awagásine* from the body (called *nawá*, *Wedelia* sp.) but said he had not yet used it. Throughout his illness, Calistro seemed passive and somewhat resigned, not refusing advice or cures but not actively securing treatment himself.

By mid-September, Calistro was seriously ill, able to walk only by supporting himself with a stick and spending most of his day lying on his bed or sitting on a blanket outside his house. Thus debilitated, he decided to move in with his wife's parents so they could help her care for him. About this time, the director of the local Jesuit-sponsored school, who believed Calistro had bone tuberculosis, began Calistro on a series of injections. After a couple of weeks, Calistro refused the injections, saying they were too painful and were not helping him.

In the ensuing weeks, Calistro continued to lose weight and to talk, cry, and breathe heavily in his sleep. His in-laws were worried about his condition and puzzled by the failure of the *bakánawi* specialist's cure. They asked Calistro about his past, trying to find something he might have done that would have led to his present state. They learned that when he was a small child, a peyote ceremony had been held at his parents' home. Just after the ceremony ended, Calistro started playing on the patio where the performance had been staged and consequently, his in-laws reasoned, had come in contact with peyote.

The Rarámuri identifiy peyote, which they call *híkuri*, with several kinds of cacti, principally *Lophophora williamsii* (Bye 1979a). Their ideas about peyote are very similar to those about *bakánawi*. They conceive of peyote as a special class of beings who have human forms and who are capable of either helping or harming people. To acquire the assistance of peyote or to cure an ailment caused by peyote, people must sponsor a series of rituals—three for males, four for females—which involve making food offerings, dancing, and consuming a mixture of ground peyote and maize beer under the direction of a peyote specialist. These rituals are performed within a partitioned-off area open only to those individuals who are to partake of the peyote and actively participate in the ceremony. Everyone else must remain outside or risk having their souls captured by the peyote people (Lumholtz 1902, I: 356–79; Bennett and Zingg 1935: 291–95; Velasco Rivero 1983: 104–16; Deimel 1985). By entering the peyote patio, Calistro had somehow violated this restriction and had angered the peyote who now, years later, had grabbed his largest soul. His in-laws concluded that he talked and wept in his sleep because he was communicating with the peyote people and that his breathing was labored because the souls that remained inside his body were leaving.

The obvious course of action to take was to request a peyote specialist to perform a peyote ceremony in which he would offer food and other articles to the peyote in return for Calistro's soul. However, because the maize had not yet been harvested, a peyote ceremony could not be held. The Rarámuri believe that performing either a peyote or *bakánawi* ceremony during the maize growing season will anger God who will send hail and worms to destroy the maturing crop. To seek advice on what they should do, Calistro's father-in-law journeyed thirty kilometers to the home of the *bakánawi* specialist who had previously treated Calistro. The doctor said that he had no connection with peyote and could not help Calistro himself, but he offered to speak with a peyote specialist he knew who lived another ten kilometers away. He would request that the specialist contact the peyote people in his dreams, asking them to have respect for Calistro and telling them that Calistro would pay them later, as soon as the harvest was completed.

Calistro's health continued to decline, but he was convinced that peyote had nothing to do with his illness. He felt instead that he had been bewitched by some members of the Rejogochi community. Shortly before his illness began, he had been drinking maize beer with several other men at a drinking party in Rejogochi. When all the beer had been consumed, he noticed two men—both suspected sorcerers—walking together to their homes. Calistro believed that on this night the men had conspired to bewitch him. He also attributed the recent death of one of his children to the same suspected sorcerers, but he apparently never acted upon his suspicions.

In early October, Calistro's in-laws invited the *bakánawi* specialist to perform another *bakánawi* ceremony for Calistro and scheduled the fiesta for October 18. By mid-morning of that day, most of the residents of Rejogochi and other nearby communities had assembled at Calistro's in-laws' house to work. The men helped Calistro's brother-in-law cut, tie, and store bundles of cornstalks that would feed his cattle in the winter; the women joined Calistro's wife and female relatives in preparing the food.

Around 2:00 P.M., a man began performing the *tutubúri* ritual in front of a single wooden cross erected on a cleared space a few meters from the house. The *tutubúri* precedes the offering of food to God during fiestas such as these. At about 4:00 P.M., shouts from lookouts announced the arrival of the doctor, who was accompanied by his wife, his two sons, and a nephew. After eating some ground parched maize mixed with water and drinking a little maize beer, the doctor asked that Calistro be brought to him. Calistro was unable to walk or stand so four men carried him out of the house on his blanket and placed him on the ground before the doctor. An expression of shock and dismay passed across the doctor's face. Calistro weighed only about thirty-five kilos, about half his normal weight, and with his shriveled skin and sunken cheeks looked like an old man. I had known Calistro quite well but had not seen him in weeks. I barely recognized him.

After chatting a few minutes with his patient, the doctor called Calistro's in-laws and parents to join him, together with other members of the community who were familiar with *bakánawi*. When the group had assembled, the doctor explained that almost all of Calistro's souls had left his body and that there was little he could do to help him. He said that he did not want to perform the *bakánawi* ceremony because if Calistro should die, the Mexican government officials would put him in jail. However, Calistro's father-in-law, an accomplished orator, convinced the doctor to proceed.

The doctor first performed a standard curing rite for Calistro to strengthen Calistro's body and the souls that remained inside him. He removed his crucifix from around his neck and, pressing it to Calistro's chest, began speaking words of encouragement in a style reminiscent of public sermons but very low, almost in a whisper. Then dipping his crucifix in a metal cup containing a decoction of agave hearts and water (called *me* or *misagóri*), he outlined the form of a cross on the top of Calistro's head and on his chest and shoulders. He placed the necklace bearing the crucifix around Calistro's neck and then gave him several sips of the agave drink from a metal spoon. At the same time, he grasped a piece of the agave heart and with it outlined the form of a cross on the top of Calistro's head and shoulders and then on his elbows and hands, concluding at the chest. From a gourd dipper he administered three sips of maize beer to his patient and then dipped the spoon in the beer to make crosses on Calistro's chest, the top of his head, and his elbows, touching the spoon to his own chest before replacing it in the cup. He then lifted the crucifix from Calistro's neck and placed the base of the cross in Calistro's mouth. Aligning his own mouth near the top of the cross, he blew a series of short breaths along its surface and into Calistro's mouth. Then he pressed the crucifix to Calistro's head, shoulders, elbows, wrists, and palms, speaking words of encouragement to him. Taking Calistro's right hand in his, he passed it across his own chest and then with his left hand pressed his crucifix against the middle of Calistro's back. He concluded by speaking again to Calistro in the same quiet but energetic tone as before. Calistro then thanked the doctor and four men carried him back to the house in his blanket. The doctor and his elder son then performed this curing ritual for each of the other people present.

While this curing was taking place, Calistro's father-in-law and a few other men enlarged the patio where the *tutubúri* was being performed to about eight meters in diameter. Three crosses were placed in a row running north to south so that when facing them the doctor would look southwest toward the *bakánawi*'s home. A sapling was placed upright behind the crosses to hold cuts of goat meat, and an earthen jar of maize beer was placed on either side. A plank in front of the crosses would, during the course of the ceremony, hold the other food and goods that were to be given to the *bakánawi* in return for Calistro's souls.

About nightfall, the doctor moved to the patio and sat on a wooden plank opposite the crosses. He placed a half gourd on the ground before him and then pulled from his jacket pocket a plastic bag containing four light-gray tubers that are the manifestations of *bakánawi* visible to ordinary people. He gently opened the bag and placed it on his lap next to a crucifix that he had removed from around his neck. He then began talking to the *bakánawi*, telling them to travel to the *bakánawi* homeland in the canyons to find out if Calistro's soul was being held captive there.

While he was talking, the other people present began assembling at the patio. Calistro's relatives sat in a semicircle around the doctor, the women to his right, the men to his left. Calistro was placed to the doctor's immediate left and reclined against the bench wrapped in his blanket. The remaining people arranged themselves behind this group, sitting on the ground or standing next to two fires kindled to ward off the autumnal chill.

Calistro's father-in-law arrived with a metal bar to loosen up the dirt in front of the doctor, who excavated a shallow depression there and placed the half gourd over it. He then began to sing, accompanying himself by rasping two special sticks on top of the gourd. His songs were directed to the *bakánawi* he had sent to the canyons. During the next five hours, the doctor continued his singing and also performed a series of acts designed to cure and protect Calistro and his family. Offerings of maize tortillas, ground parched maize, goat meat, boiled chickens, blankets, money, and maize beer were brought up from the house and put around the crosses to be given to the *bakánawi* upon their return.

Around 2:00 A.M., the doctor interrupted his singing to exclaim, "Here they come! One is riding a pinto horse," but only he could see the *bakánawi* people as they approached the patio. He began to talk with them and then told the others what the *bakánawi* had said. They had been told by the *bakánawi* in the canyons that they no longer held any of Calistro's souls, having returned all the souls they had previously taken during the ceremony performed in April. However, they said, they had learned that God was causing Calistro's illness because he was angry that Calistro had never sacrificed any of his cattle to give him meat. Therefore, the doctor explained, God had taken Calistro's own flesh, causing him to lose so much weight.

The *bakánawi* specialist told Calistro to sponsor a fiesta for God right away, slaughtering one of his cattle, and to give one fiesta each year for two more years, killing a head of cattle each time. After the first fiesta, the doctor said, Calistro would begin to recover and would be completely cured after all three fiestas had been performed. Calistro agreed to follow the doctor's advice, but he privately expressed doubts that he had displeased God because he owned only a few cattle.

On November 2, Calistro's wife and in-laws organized a fiesta in which they sacrificed one of Calistro's cows and sent the meat to God. Calistro did not participate, lying completely incapacitated inside his in-laws' house. Following the fiesta, Calistro's condition worsened rather than improved. His in-laws were at a loss as to the cause of his illness but, after considering his symptoms once again, they concluded that he was suffering from *bikarí* (from *biká*, "to rot or putrify"). A disease contracted through sexual intercourse with a Chabochi, *bikarí* characteristically causes a swelling of the abdomen; Calistro's stomach was distended and inflamed, with the skin over it cracked and peeling.

Calistro denied having had sexual intercourse with any Chabochi women or Rarámuri women contaminated by contact with Chabochis, but his in-laws did not believe him. They offered to buy medicine for him in a pharmacy located in the Mestizo town of Creel, but he refused. On November 6, Calistro's father-in-law consulted with a Rejogochi doctor of some repute who agreed with the family's diagnosis. The following morning, the doctor descended into a nearby canyon and collected a plant reputed to cure *bikarí*, administering a drink made from the medicine to Calistro the same afternoon. Two days later Calistro died, and on November 10 the men of his wife's family and a few other men of the community buried his body in the Rejogochi cemetery.

Calistro's decline and death were both sad and disconcerting to the people of Rejogochi. Despite all the material and intellectual resources they had marshalled to cure him, a very active young man had been reduced in less than a year to a helpless invalid, a cadaver before he died. The distress that his parents-in-law felt was deepened by their loss over the next five years of another of Calistro's children, two other grandchildren, and three of their own adult children. Although other families in Rejogochi endure their share of sickness and death, none in recent years had been affected as drastically as Calistro's in-laws.

With the passing of time, interest in Calistro's sickness and death faded as the community turned its attention to more pressing concerns, but because of its complexity, his case continued to come up occasionally in general discussions. By 1981 most people in Rejogochi had concluded that the venereal disease called *bikarí* was the most plausible cause of his death and that the other diagnoses and treatments had been misguided. Calistro's brother-in-law told me that the only result of the fiesta that they had sponsored for God had been the waste of one of Calistro's cattle.

RARÁMURI CURING PRACTICES

Etiology

The history of Calistro's decline and death reveals much about how the Rarámuri conceive of illness and the practices they adopt to diagnose and cure
it.[1] They use the verb *kanírema* to mean that they are healthy, content, and
in good spirits, the verb *nayúma* to say that they are sick. The semantic scope
of *nayúma* corresponds closely to that of its English gloss "to be sick" except
when "sick" refers to mental illness or moral depravity. They do not consider
aches and pains caused by such things as overexertion, bruises, and cuts to
be illnesses and, unless these problems are extremely serious or persistent,
they do not employ *nayúma* when speaking of them. Instead they use the
verb *okórema*, "to hurt" or "to experience pain," which designates any state
characterized by pain regardless of cause.

The Rarámuri have specific names for the various ailments they recognize, but for the most part they do not organize these illnesses into general
categories. García Manzanedo (1963: 65) has suggested that these ailments
can be divided into those with natural causes and those with supernatural
causes, but this is not a distinction made by the Rarámuri, who do not dif-
ferentiate between the natural and supernatural. A better distinction is drawn
between the ailments they think are intentionally caused by other beings and
those that are not. This division is more in keeping with their view of illness
and of the universe in general and more reflective of the differences in their
practices to prevent and cure illness. It also corresponds fairly closely to their
distinction between illnesses that result from threats to the souls and those
that affect the body primarily. Ailments intentionally caused by other beings
usually involve direct threats to a person's souls and have serious, often fatal,
consequences. Ailments not caused by others tend to have the most impact
on the body rather than the souls and while they are unpleasant they seldom
result in death.

Ailments Not Intentionally Caused by Other Beings.   These varied ailments
include some self-induced problems. For example, by eating or drinking
bitter things, people promote the formation inside their bodies of *awagásine*,
the yellowish bitter substance that causes appetite loss and weakness, which
Calistro once thought caused his illness. Another danger is staying in the
sun too long or eating too much green corn, which can bring on diarrhea

(*witabúa*), a common affliction. Sleeping on moist ground can cause one's insides to become humid, and a specific kind of mushroom (*amaséware*) will grow in the stomach, interfering with digestion. These mushrooms also can grow when a person eats on an empty stomach. The Rarámuri say people should eat whenever they start to feel hungry or risk encouraging the growth of these mushrooms or of worms (*sikówiri*) that grow inside the stomach and make growling noises when people are hungry.

All these maladies arise because people create the fostering circumstances. People also can become ill because they come in contact with entities who should be avoided. For instance, the mixing of body fluids that occurs during fighting or sexual intercourse with Chabochis can result in illness, including venereal diseases (*bikarí*), although the Rarámuri say that Chabochis are not adversely affected by such contacts. In addition, contact with the souls of the dead or with food or drink they have touched will at the least upset a person's stomach. Chabochis and the dead need not intend for the person to become ill; improper contact itself can cause illness.

Sometimes ailments arise from the malfunctioning of the body, a circumstance over which an individual has little or no control. For example, babies often are sick with vomiting and diarrhea, which the Rarámuri attribute to their fontanelles falling. A bone running between the fontanelle and the roof of the mouth is believed to drink the babies' blood, causing them to dry up inside. If the dehydration process cannot be reversed by raising the fontanelle, the children's souls will leave and they will die.

A similar threat comes from the white threads (*rumugá*) that the Rarámuri say grow from the crowns of all people's heads. One of the first obligations of a newborn's parents is to have a doctor burn away his or her *rumugá*, which is accomplished with smoldering corn cobs in a series of three rituals for male children, four for females. During these rituals the doctors name the children and thereafter are responsible for protecting them from harm during dreams and for curing their illnesses. If the *rumugá* are not burned away, they will inhibit the children's growth and will attract hail and lightning, endangering not only the children but their families, their neighbors, and the community's crops as well. Despite being destroyed when children are small, the *rumugá* continue to grow throughout their lifetimes. When the *rumugá* become several feet long, they can wrap around the body and cause illness. To prevent this, doctors periodically perform a ritual, usually in conjunction with a fiesta, in which they burn or cut the *rumugá* of all the participants.

Figure 15. Destroying the rumugá. *Rejogochi, June 1981. As part of a cooperatively sponsored fiesta to cure maize and livestock and send offerings to the dead, women kneel with their babies along the edge of a dance patio to be cured. Two doctors cut and burn the* rumugá *from the crowns of their heads while an assistant (obscured from view) gives them agave water. To the left, a chanter performs the* tutubúri *while matachines dance behind. The men, cured first, watch from the hillside.*

Ailments Intentionally Caused by Other Beings.   From the Rarámuri perspective, whether people are healthy or sick usually reflects the quality of their relations with other beings in the universe, all of whom potentially can affect them. Consequently, much of their thinking about health, particularly about serious illness, is organized around an opposition that structures much of their view of the world, the opposition between cooperation and competition. They see beings in the universe as divided between those who tend to help preserve health and those who tend to undermine it, but whether these beings protect or harm the Rarámuri depends upon how the Rarámuri act toward them. Health for the Rarámuri is thus a matter of cosmological proportions pervaded by moral implications.

The beings the Rarámuri cite most frequently as threatening their health are the following: (1) the four classes of beings associated with the plants *uchurí, rikúhuri, bakánawi,* and *híkuri;* (2) God; (3) the Devil and his subordinates; and (4) sorcerers. *Uchurí* and *rikúhuri* never help the Rarámuri nor do they try to hurt them unless provoked. If people harm these plants by cutting, trampling on, or throwing a stick or stone at them, the plants will become enraged and take revenge. They can, for example, cause people to have persistent and painful headaches or to become very drunk from only a little drinking, often resulting in dangerously irrational behavior like wandering off into the mountains alone. Or the plants will lead people while they sleep to clifftops from which they will fall to their injury or death. If children offend, the plants can make them grow up violent and mean. *Bakánawi* and *híkuri*, in contrast, help and protect people as long as the individuals who own them reciprocate by feeding them. If people become negligent in their duties, *bakánawi* and *híkuri* will harm them by tying up portions of their bodies and kidnapping their souls or those of their relatives or neighbors.

God is usually benevolent to the Rarámuri because they are his children, but as with *bakánawi* and *híkuri*, their relationship with God is based ultimately on balanced reciprocity. The people repay God for his care and encourage his continued benevolence by offering him food in fiestas and acting in conformance with his teachings. If people fail to maintain the balance or to act properly, God will withdraw his care, thus giving the Devil free rein to harm them. If he is extremely displeased, he will ask the Devil to send illnesses, a request with which the Devil readily complies. God also can work harm more directly. For example, if people whom God has blessed with prolific herds refuse to return a portion of these animals to him by sacrificing them during fiestas, God will take the souls of these animals himself and may further punish the misers by reclaiming their souls or those of one or more of their children. The *bakánawi* specialist, it will be remembered, thought such an offense had caused Calistro's illness. If parents neglect or are unduly harsh with their children, God will call the souls of the children back to heaven where he and his wife can care for them, thereby causing the parents anguish and sorrow. Also, the Rarámuri suspect that a slow and painful death is God's punishment for crimes such as thievery or sorcery.

The Devil is the relentless adversary of the Rarámuri, constantly trying to undermine their well-being by devious means. The Devil and his cohorts, including his soldiers and certain wild animals like coyotes, wander about at night searching for the souls of dreamers to pummel, capture, or kill, or the Devil may send his subordinates alone while he remains at his home on the bottom level of the universe. He also controls several diseases (*nawirí*), including head colds, measles, and scarlet fever, which he can dispatch at any time. The Rarámuri conceive of the *nawirí* as being like fog (*bimorí*) or wind (iká), but sometimes they appear in dreams as beautiful women to men or handsome men to women and coax the dreamers to accept their offers of food and maize beer or to have sexual intercourse with them. If the nawirí succeed, the dreamers will be sick upon awakening.[2]

Other beings, considered to be associates of the Devil because they follow his directives, also are a threat to Rarámuri souls. Most notable of these are the "water people" (ba?wichí piréame) who capture the souls of people startled at or near water and carry them to their homes below the water to be their spouses or peons. The Devil also has allies among the Rarámuri themselves. These individuals consider the Devil's way of thinking to be better than God's and thus have become sorcerers. The Devil encourages sorcerers and gives them the knowledge and means to pursue their work.

The Rarámuri are very afraid of sorcerers because they believe them to be responsible for most serious illnesses and especially most fatal illnesses. The possibility of sorcery is a constant feature of Rarámuri social life because any adult can be a sorcerer. However, individuals who profess an ability to cure are considered more likely to be sorcerers than those who do not, with men and older people more likely candidates than women and younger people. In addition, suspicions of sorcery usually are directed toward people unrelated to the victim. During the years I lived in Rejogochi, I heard of only one case in which a man was suspected of having killed his wife through sorcery, and I encountered no cases of a victim accusing close relatives of bewitching him.[3] Often people suspect a resident of a distant settlement and view all strangers as potential sorcerers. People in Rejogochi particularly fear the members of several adjacent pueblos: Narárachi, Tehuerichi, Norogachi, Choguita, and Pamachi. According to the Rarámuri, Chabochis also practice sorcery but not as competently as do the Rarámuri.

Whenever I requested detailed descriptions of how sorcerers actually accomplish their goals, I invariably was told, "I don't know. I don't work that way." People do not admit to being sorcerers, but if they are suspected they may cultivate the image without actually acknowledging its validity in order to intimidate others. They can do so with impunity because few people will make public accusations of sorcery for fear of retaliation, and finding evidence is difficult since sorcery is performed secretly, principally in dreams.

Nonetheless, people do sometimes accuse others of sorcery and one person occasionally will threaten to bewitch another. Such threats usually are made in the heat of arguments that occur during drinking parties and propose a confrontation between the antagonists' souls that the Rarámuri think, and say, is like the fighting between people that occurs at these parties. In a typical exchange, the challenger sardonically inquires, "How tough are you?" (meaning, "How tough are your souls?") to which his opponent responds, "I'm not afraid of you," or "We'll see who is more of a man." This confrontational language reflects sorcery's image as an alternative expression of interpersonal conflict and a way, albeit improper, to resolve such conflict. Sorcery also provides the Rarámuri with a way to avenge wrongs done to them by Chabochis, with whom physical violence is inadvisable given the Chabochis' control of the judicial system. Almost invariably when a Chabochi falls ill, the Rarámuri (and sometimes the Chabochi) will attribute his or her illness to bewitching by a Rarámuri whom the Chabochi has offended.

Sometimes sorcerers bewitch complete strangers who live some distance from them but usually they act only in anger. Most of the things that make sorcerers angry involve some breach of etiquette or thwarting the sorcerers' wishes. When people insult or anger a sorcerer, the Rarámuri say he becomes "very angry" (*we yo*) or "ugly sad" (*cháte oʔmóna*). Instead of thinking "straight" in conformance with God's thinking, he begins contemplating how he will bewitch his victims, thinking "apart" (*chakéna*) in line with the Devil's teachings.[4] The relationship that develops between offended sorcerers and their intended victims is phrased in terms of opposition and competition: they "oppose" (*saérama*) one another with the more powerful of the two overcoming the weaker. A person says that a sorcerer attacks him because "he hates me" (*tamí kichísa*). This hatred is diametrically opposed to the feeling that the Rarámuri say motivates doctors and God to help people: *tamí nitimá* "they feel sorry or feel compassion for me."

To harm his enemies, the sorcerer sometimes puts foreign objects into their bodies, inducing painful and often lingering illnesses. Wrapping a wire around the stomach of a pregnant woman, for example, keeps her from giving birth, thus killing both mother and child. The sorcerer also can place a second child inside a pregnant woman so that she will give birth to twins, an undesired occurrence, or turn the baby the woman is carrying sideways in her womb to prevent its birth. If the sorcerer is angry because someone has refused to sell him some livestock, he may send lightning to strike the corrals and kill the animals.[5]

Sorcerers may attack people with whom they are not angry because they are on opposing sides in competitions. People suspect that sorcerers attempt to affect the outcome of any competition in which they are involved, especially footraces between two or more pueblos, when large amounts of money and goods are bet. Although the sorcerers seldom compete in the races, they try to disable the opposing runners, usually by concealing a dangerous object along the path. For example, they reportedly take human leg bones from ancient cave burials and grind the bones into powder, which they mix with the dirt of the trail. They tell their own runners to avoid this spot, but when their opponents step there, the bones grab their legs, usually at the knee, temporarily crippling them and making them weak and sleepy. When the race is over, the bones release the vanquished runners, sometimes permanently injured.

By far the most radical sorcery technique is the capture and destruction of souls. Sorcerers or their animal familiars steal their enemies' souls as they sleep. The victims of these attacks wake up extremely ill, experiencing excruciating pain in the chest or ribs and usually bleeding from the nose and mouth. Unless doctors can find and release the souls before their captors cook and eat them, the people will die.

The Process of Diagnosis

When a person falls ill, the first step toward a cure is diagnosing the ailment and deciding on the appropriate treatment. Diagnoses are based not only on an evaluation of the patients' symptoms but also on a consideration of the things that they have done and the events that have transpired in their lives that might have caused the illness. For example, if people feel weak and experience swelling, particularly in their legs, and have been startled recently at or near water, they usually suspect that the water people captured their largest souls when they were frightened. They attribute their sluggishness to the absence of these souls and the swelling to water filling up inside their bodies because their souls are held captive below water.

Usually the severity of an illness indicates whether a person's souls are directly threatened. There is no question, for example, that a person's largest soul has been captured by a sorcerer or some other evil being when the victim suddenly becomes very ill with severe pain in the chest. Similarly, people know that common ailments like colds and diarrhea do not jeopardize their souls. Diagnosis is most difficult when the illness is neither trifling nor grave. Such mid-range ailments resist diagnosis because the same symptoms can have different causes. For example, a loss of appetite can be attributed to the accumulation of *awagásine* in the body or to the presence of an object inserted by a sorcerer. Even when the symptoms are sufficiently severe or persistent to indicate that the patient's soul is being held outside the body, the identity of the captor is not always apparent. Possible culprits include the water people, God, *bakánawi*, and peyote, among others, and until the culprit can be identified the proper cure cannot be performed. Quite frequently, as Calistro's case illustrates, people propose several diagnoses and try different treatments until they cure the illness or the person dies.

When suffering from mild ailments such as colds, for which the diagnosis is obvious, people usually take home remedies or commercial medicines like aspirin. If, however, their illnesses are severe, their personal treatments ineffective, or the diagnoses not apparent, they or members of their families will request the assistance of Rarámuri doctors.

When called in for consultation, doctors first discuss the symptoms and the possible causes with their patients. During these discussions, the doctors often run their hands over the patients' bodies and stare fixedly at them to feel and see any illnesses or irregularities that might be inside. They then think about what they have learned to determine the cause of the malady and the possible treatment. As Bennett and Zingg write,

> the doctor spends much time during, before, and after a cure in
> "thinking." In doing this, he is analyzing the patient's illness and aiding
> in his recovery. The power of the shaman to analyze and cure in his
> dreams is an extension of the same idea. His helpers too are supposed to
> "think" (1935: 261).

The diagnosis of illness is one of the few areas of Rarámuri life where meaning is literally negotiated. Besides differences of opinion on the proper interpretation of symptoms and assignment of causes, the patient, the doctor, the family, and neighbors all manipulate the possibilities in the process of determining who ultimately is to blame for the illness. Arriving at the correct diagnosis and treatment is everyone's first concern, but seldom are the symptoms so definitive that one cannot choose between different diagnoses to assign or avoid responsibility for the ailment. A review of the diagnoses offered in Calistro's case illustrates the process.

Calistro never accepted direct personal responsibility for his sickness. His conclusion early on that he suffered from the accumulation of bitter substances (*awagásine*) inside his body involved no assignment of blame since this condition results from eating foods that are so basic to the Rarámuri diet that they cannot be avoided. Similarly, the diagnosis of bone tuberculosis attributed responsibility to no one, but it was entertained seriously only by the non-Indian director of the local school.

The diagnosis to which Calistro and his family adhered the longest and consequently that which stimulated the most activity involved *bakánawi*.

Bakánawi had bound Calistro's leg and taken his largest soul not because of some shortcoming on his part but because his father had failed in his obligation to these beings. When the *bakánawi* ceremonies did not cure Calistro, his relatives proposed that peyote may have been responsible because peyote and *bakánawi* cause similar illnesses. Here Calistro's failure as a child to observe a prohibition against contact with peyote was assumed to have instigated the attack, but his father's (or parents') negligence was blamed rather than Calistro himself.

Calistro never gave much credence to the diagnosis implicating peyote, perhaps because this diagnosis implied that he participated, albeit unwittingly, in causing his illness. Instead, he suspected the outright malevolence of two of his neighbors, who he believed had bewitched him. Calistro's symptoms were consistent with a diagnosis of sorcery because, like *bakánawi* and peyote, sorcerers are thought to tie up people's extremities as well as steal their souls. Such attacks often are felt to occur when the victim has offended the sorcerer, but sometimes evil sorcerers will harm someone simply because they are malevolent. Calistro characterized his assumed assailants in this light, reinforcing this image by claiming that they directed their evil toward his defenseless child as well as toward him. To recover from sorcery, the victims must convince Rarámuri doctors to confront the sorcerers and force them to undo their evil. I never heard that Calistro engaged a doctor for this purpose, but such arrangements usually remain secret.

Calistro's adherence to diagnoses in which he was not held directly responsible for his illness contrast with those proposed by his in-laws and doctors. In the early stages of the illness, these people concurred on diagnoses in which Calistro was not personally responsible for his misfortune. As the disease worsened, however, they increasingly placed the blame on him. By the end, they assumed that he was suffering from a venereal disease deriving ultimately if not directly from Chabochis.

The point of transition in the progression of the diagnosis came at the second appearance of the *bakánawi* specialist. By performing the first *bakánawi* ceremony for Calistro, the doctor acknowledged *bakánawi*'s role in the ailment. He agreed to perform the second ceremony unaware of the extent of Calistro's decline in the intervening six months. When he saw the severity of Calistro's condition, he immediately shifted the responsibility from *bakánawi*, over whom he proclaimed some control, to God and ultimately to Calistro for his failure to fulfill his obligations to God. Since lingering illness is usually interpreted as God's punishment, such a conclusion was accepted as reasonable by everyone but Calistro.

Calistro's family, neighbors, and doctors were not trying to hurt Calistro by blaming him for his ailment. They were desperate to find a cure and assumed that such a terrible illness must have been punishment for something he had done. Severe illnesses tend to be diagnosed as caused by beings who are angry with the patient. Such diagnoses always imply that the sick person is at least partly responsible, so suggesting that Calistro had done something to bring on his illness was not unusual. What was unusual was Calistro's refusal to accept responsibility. Most patients willingly admit their short-comings because they can be cured only if the cause of their illness can be determined. Calistro did not do so, I think, because he had not committed adultery and truly believed he had not done the other things the diagnoses implied, like offending peyote or God. Yet he did not resist the treatments arranged for him by his wife's parents even when these treatments were motivated by diagnoses with which he did not agree. He accepted these treatments because the other measures taken to alleviate his illness had failed. As his health declined, he also became increasingly resigned to the possibility of his death and willing to place his fate in the hands of others.

The Prevention and Alleviation of Illness

The Rarámuri engage in a variety of activities to prevent or alleviate illnesses. They characterize most of these activities with one or another of the synonymous verbs *óoma* and *oméa*. The simplest translation of these terms is "to cure," but they have broad connotations. In fact, people who translated them into Spanish for me said they meant "to care" (*cuidar*), not "to cure" (*curar*). This translation reflects in part the Rarámuri's view of curing as both preventative and alleviative. It also is consonant with their view of the ideal relationship between doctors and their charges. Doctors are the caretakers of the community, "caring for" or "watching over" (*tibúma*) their neighbors in the night to protect them from evil beings and helping them regain health when they are ill. They assume this and their other responsibilities because they "care" or "feel compassion" (*nitimá*) for them. The rituals doctors perform for their patients are expressions of their care for them.

Preventing Illness. Some of the measures the Rarámuri take to prevent sickness do not require the special services of a doctor. For example, during fiestas people often erect one or more small wooden crosses near the large crosses designated for God. These crosses mark the places where the Rarámuri bury bits of food as offerings to the Devil and the personified illnesses known as *nawirí*. They make these offerings so that these beings will not afflict them but will pass on to other people who have not given them food.

To foil sorcerers who try to come in the night to steal their souls, people sometimes arrange a clever trap on their door sills. They place a small clay bowl of ground parched maize near the edge of the sill closest to the inside of the house. Behind the bowl, toward the outside of the house, they put up a small wooden cross to mislead the sorcerers into thinking that a fiesta is in progress at which they can find food. However, to reach the food, sorcerers must cross the outside half of the sill. Here the inhabitants of the house scatter several extremely hot chiles (*korí síbari*) and a few spiny prickly pear pads, which burn and stick the sorcerers, causing them to flee. The Rarámuri of Rejogochi also place prickly pear pads and other spiny plants on top of the baskets that cover ollas of maize beer. The stickers are intended to prevent the Devil and the dead from contaminating the beer by drinking it during the night, for if they should succeed, the people who later drink it will become sick.

When children have been frightened or when a death occurs in their homes, their parents mark a cross with ashes on the children's foreheads. During the principal fiesta for the dead, participants put such ashen crosses on their foreheads to prevent the dead and other dangerous beings from taking their souls (see chapter 6). Sometimes parents also prepare necklaces of red coralbeans (*Erythrina flabelliformis;* in Rarámuri *aposí*) to protect their children from the water people and hang small wooden crosses or saint medallions around their necks to ensure their general safety. Adults wear these medallions and metal crucifixes for the same purpose and keep portraits of saints and the Virgin Mary in or around their homes to ward off evil beings. Some people also acquire *bakánawi* and peyote for protection.

Other more elaborate activities designed to prevent sickness can be performed only by doctors. To eliminate possible contamination of the maize beer for a fiesta or drinking party, a host sometimes asks one or two doctors to pass a flaming pine torch around the ollas containing the beer and to sprinkle drops of water cooked with agave hearts into the beer before the drinking begins. This agave decoction is said to protect and strengthen the souls and is featured in many ceremonial contexts where it is sprinkled over the crosses and offerings and sipped by the people in attendance. Frequently the cup of agave water is simply handed around, each person sipping a little before passing it on to the next person. Certain individuals recognized as people of knowledge will, after sipping the water, take the spoon or a piece of the agave from the cup and outline crosses on the top of their head and the center of their chest. However, people who lack the requisite knowledge cannot cross themselves with the agave water but must have the rite administered to them by a doctor.

The administration of agave water along with several other stereotyped acts constitute what can be considered the basic curing rite of Rarámuri medical practice. The goals of this ritual, which I will examine in some detail below, are to fortify people's souls so they can defend themselves against harm and to make them content so they will not abandon the body. The basic curing rite is a central component of all alleviative curing rituals but usually it is performed for all the people in attandance, not just those who are sick. In addition, about once a year, community members participate in a ritual in which doctors burn and cut away the *rumugá*. On this and other occasions, people prepare a smudge of cedar or juniper boughs, inhaling and bathing their bodies in the aromatic smoke. The agreeable odor is said to please their souls. The Rarámuri also stage similar preventative curing rituals

Figure 16. Curing goats. Rejogochi, June 1984. A doctor protects a corral of goats from harm by blowing his breath, or soul, over them along the length of a wooden cross. As part of the curing, the doctor also sprinkles medicines over the animals and advises them in a speech on how they should live.

*Figure 17. Curing maize.
Rejogochi, June 1984. With a
pine needle brush, a doctor
sprinkles medicines carried by his
assistants over a maize plant to
promote its growth and to protect
it from pests. He selects one
plant in each field for this
special treatment, planting a
wooden cross next to it. He cuts
the plant's* rumugá *with a knife
and completes other ritual acts to
keep the Devil and hail away.*

to protect their maize and domesticated animals (typically only their goats,
sheep, and cattle) and to encourage their productivity.

Alleviating Illness.   If the measures the Rarámuri take to prevent illness
fail and they become ill, they resort to alleviative curing. After reaching a
diagnosis, either themselves or in consultation with their families, neighbors,
and perhaps doctors in the area, they must decide how to go about treating
the illness. Their two alternatives are to attempt a cure themselves or to seek
a doctor's help. If they believe that their souls are in jeopardy, they will
contact a doctor immediately, but if the illness seems minor they usually
initiate treatment themselves, calling in a doctor later if their efforts fail.

The Rarámuri treat most minor ailments with one or more of a variety
of plant, animal, and mineral substances, all of which God gave them in the
distant past to use as medicines (Bennett and Zingg 1935; Pennington 1963;
Bye 1976, 1985). Most adults are familiar with these remedies, but if they

are not confident in their treatment, they ask help from others who are known for their broad knowledge of natural medicines.

People in Rejogochi also occasionally use commercial drugs they buy from Chabochis. They consider these medicines to be particularly appropriate for curing the personified illnesses known as *nawirí* (most of which they consider to be minor) because both the *nawirí* and the medicines come from the Devil. They also recognize the competence of Chabochi doctors, both folk practitioners and licensed M.D.s, in treating minor ailments and injuries. The residents of Rejogochi frequently carry their babies to several local Mestizo women to have the babies' fontanelles lifted, stating that these women are more adept at this procedure than are their Rarámuri counterparts.[6] They also take advantage of the medical services offered at nearby clinics and hospitals operated by the Jesuit missionaries and the Mexican government (Anzures y Bolaños 1978). However, the Rarámuri maintain that Chabochi doctors cannot cure illnesses caused by soul loss or sorcery and thus see no point in calling upon them for those illnesses, except perhaps as a last resort.

If people do not recover in a few days from a seemingly minor ailment that they believe to be caused by a *nawirí*, they may decide to give the *nawirí* food so that it will go away. If a man falls ill today, he waits three days and on the third night kills a chicken or goat. He puts a small wooden cross inside his house near the door and places a bowl containing a few bits of the meat in front of it. He repeats this procedure for three successive nights, and the *nawirí* consumes it (that is, its invisible parallel aspect) before the following morning. On the fourth day, the man buries the food and throws the cross away. If the diagnosis was correct, the *nawirí* then departs and the sick man begins to feel better; in three more days he will be fully recovered. If the affected person is a woman, she follows exactly the same procedure except in four-day segments.

When illnesses cannot be cured by these measures or the symptoms indicate that they are caused by soul loss, the patients or their families call in Rarámuri doctors. In most communities, several individuals profess curing abilities; in 1981 in Rejogochi, six men and one woman out of a total adult population of sixty were recognized as doctors. To claim to be a doctor a person must at least be able to perform the basic curing rite and be a competent dreamer. Some doctors maintain in addition one or more specialities, such as burning the *rumugá* from babies' heads, breaking up the mushrooms (*amaséware*) that grow inside peoples' stomachs, or sucking out worms and small stones (*sukí*) from their patients' bodies. The most respected and, at times, most feared doctors are the *bakánawi* and peyote specialists.[7]

Not everyone who claims to be a doctor is regarded as equally competent, and even among the specialists in more esoteric cures, some are considered incompetent. Since doctors are reimbursed for their services with food, maize beer, and sometimes money, people suspect that some people cure simply for the pay, particularly doctors who demand exorbitant fees rather than accepting what their patients consider appropriate. When selecting doctors to treat them, people first determine if their symptoms indicate the need for any special expertise and then choose among the available doctors on the basis of their reputations. All else being equal, people will select the practitioner who is most closely related to them.

After they have been called in, doctors first draw their own conclusions about the cause of the ailment and decide on treatment. If they decide the ailments are not serious, they may tell their patients to take certain medicines or they may use special techniques. For example, if a patient is diagnosed as having mushrooms growing inside the stomach, the doctor will roughly squeeze the abdomen to break up the mushrooms so they will pass out as waste.

To alleviate more serious illnesses, doctors usually rely on their advanced capacity to dream. Doctors do many things in their dreams, including removing objects that sorcerers have placed inside their patients' bodies and, more importantly, locating souls that have been captured by sorcerers and other beings. Finding lost souls is difficult because doctors never know where they might be; often the doctors' souls must travel great distances to locate the souls. The urgency with which doctors must recover kidnapped souls depends upon how dangerous the beings are who hold them. The water people, *bakánawi*, or peyote seldom harm the souls they capture, but hold them for ransom that the patients pay under the doctors' supervision in ceremonies held especially for this purpose. The sickness their victims experience is caused by the simple absence of their souls and will not be fatal if the souls can be recovered within a few weeks or months. In contrast, haste is essential if the patients' souls have been taken by sorcerers or their animal familiars because these evil beings will kill, cook, and eat the souls soon after they kidnap them.

In addition to dreaming and doctors' other activities to restore health, curing most serious illnesses requires the performance of special rituals. Different types of rituals for different kinds of ailments each have unique features and themes. When a person's soul has been captured by the water people, for example, the patient and doctor, sometimes joined by relatives of the patient and others, assemble on the edge of the body of water at the probable place of the kidnapping. The patient gives the doctor food and occasionally coins, which are dropped into the water as ransom for the lost soul. The doctor then tells the water people to return the soul and not to threaten people in the future. The group then returns to the patient's home where the cure concludes with the patient being rubbed with special medicines and placed in a pit over hot coals to sweat out the excess water that has caused his or her body to swell.[8] Similar but more complex rituals are designed to ransom souls from *bakánawi* and peyote and simpler ones to extract stones, worms, and other foreign objects from the body.

The Basic Curing Rite

Most Rarámuri curing rituals include as a central component the basic curing rite. The purpose of this rite, which also can be performed by itself, is to fortify a person's souls so they can defend themselves against harm and to make the souls content so they will not abandon the body. It is performed to keep healthy people well and to strengthen sick people so they can recover.

The basic curing rite usually is performed in public, typically during drinking get-togethers, because maize beer is required both to complete the ritual and to pay the doctor. It can take place either indoors or out and involves the doctor, often an assistant, the patient, and an informal audience of the other people in attendance, all or most of whom will be cured in turn.

Doctors do not perform the basic curing rite in exactly the same way on every occasion, but the general content remains the same. The doctor sits on a stone or wooden block with an assistant (usually his wife or child, who is learning to cure) beside him.[9] He wears one or more metal crucifixes on necklaces that are displayed on the outside of his garment. On the ground next to him is a cup containing bits of agave hearts cooked in water and a container of maize beer. The patient kneels in front of the doctor facing him and the curing begins.

The basic curing rite has five major components. In the first, the doctor administers the agave decoction and the maize beer separately to the patient. The agave decoction is considered "medicine" (*owáame*) and is said to protect people from lightning and from the dangers of consuming food or beer contaminated by the dead, the Devil, or other malevolent beings. Maize beer is considered a gift from God and is used in curing rituals to help people become or remain plump, a sign of good health, or, in the case of children, in small amounts to encourage their growth. The doctor dips his crucifix in these ritual liquids and then traces the outline of a cross on various parts of the patient's body where their souls principally reside: the chest, crown of head, back, shoulders, elbows, wrists, palms, knees, ankles, and feet. This act protects and strengthens the souls, and some people compare it to branding cattle: the crosses mark the people with God's brand so the Devil will be reluctant to harm them. Then the doctor gives the patient small portions of the liquids to drink in units of three for males, four for females.

The second component of the rite also involves the use of the crucifix but without the liquids. The doctor places the necklace to which his crucifix is attached around the patient's neck and presses the crucifix to the patient's chest and sometimes to either side of his lower rib cage. Then he replaces it around his own neck. The Rarámuri consider these crucifixes, which they purchase from Chabochis, to be an emblem of the status of doctor. Only those people who have received permission and knowledge from God to cure are supposed to wear them, although sorcerers also reportedly use them. When God gives people the ability to cure, he also assigns one of his sons, known as *sukrísto* (literally "Jesus Christ" but distinct from the biblical figure of Christ), to help them. This *sukrísto* is associated with the crucifix and endows his strength or toughness to the person to whom it is applied.

The third component, which does not invariably appear in all basic curing rites, can be characterized as massaging the patient. The patient stands and the doctor squeezes and rubs his legs from the knee to the ankle, repeating this procedure with the patient's arms. Sometimes he grasps the patient's shoulders and presses the patient's chest against his own. Doctors massage and embrace their patients to transfer their own strength to them and also to warm their limbs so that their souls will remain in their proper places. Because numbness in the hands and feet is attributed to the retreat of the souls from there to more central areas of the body, this treatment is felt to be especially appropriate for older people, who may suffer from poor circulation.

With the patient kneeling again, the doctor leans forward and blows several strong puffs of breath into his mouth and over the top of his head and upper torso. Sometimes the doctor holds his crucifix in front of his own mouth or inserts it into the patient's mouth before blowing. This act is the fourth component of the rite and is completed because the breath is soul substance that comes directly from the doctor's heart and partakes in his strength and toughness. One person told me that the soul conveyed by doctors to their patients is a small portion of the doctors' own souls. It enters the patients' hearts where it converses with their souls, encouraging them to have strength, before returning to the doctors' hearts. Another person, a doctor, told me that the souls he transfers to his patients are not his own souls but souls that God has given him in his dreams expressly for this purpose. When he blows into a patient's mouth, the soul does not subsequently return to him but remains inside the patient, fortifying his souls.

The fifth and final component is the verbal dimension of the rite. The doctor and patient often joke or chat for a few minutes at the beginning of the rite; if the person is ill, they will review the patient's symptoms and the possible causes of the ailment. At the end of the rite, the doctor usually takes the patient's right hand in his and, in a low voice, makes a short speech to him. The speech contains the doctor's advice, or "thinking" (*nátiri*), and is addressed primarily to the patient's souls, although he does not specifically mention the souls. He tells them to stay inside the patient's body and to think well so they will always act to the patient's benefit. When the speech is over, the patient and doctor shake hands, with the patient thanking the doctor for his help and the doctor responding in kind. The doctor, patient, and assistant exchange gourd dippers of maize beer, and then the procedure is repeated for the next person until all who so desire have been cured.

CURING PRACTICES AND THE CONCEPT OF SOUL

The Rarámuri's curing practices are crucial in the reproduction of the concept of soul within the society. The members of different households seldom discuss their ideas about souls except when diagnosing illnesses. Then the concept of soul emerges as a central topic of conversation, providing both the framework within which diagnoses are formulated and the vocabulary through which they are expressed. In addition, curing rituals are one of the few public contexts where the Rarámuri explicitly link the concept of soul to practical action. These rituals not only expose the members of many different households to ideas about souls but, because they are performed by specialists recognized for their knowledge of the universe, they endow the concept of soul with the sanction of cultural validity.

As discursive knowledge, ideas about souls are more readily conveyed by the discursive curing practices than by the nondiscursive ones. Discursive curing practices include most importantly diagnoses of illnesses, but curing rituals also have a verbal dimension. During curing rituals, doctors sometimes explain their diagnoses and frequently offer words of advice or encouragement to their patients, sing songs, chant, or say prayers. Following a ritual, the members of the community typically talk about whether it has worked and often discuss the significance of specific ritual elements and of the rituals as a whole. Like diagnoses, most of these other discursive forms derive at least a portion of their content from the concept of soul.

The information explicitly transmitted by discursive curing practices tends to be quite specific, restricted to analyses of the symptoms of particular individuals at given times and the illness's likely causes and cures. However, because Rarámuri etiology is based on the concept of soul and linked to more general social and cosmological concerns, these practices implicitly communicate much additional information. Diagnoses that attribute an illness to the loss or injury of a person's souls, for example, simultaneously reveal the contribution of the souls to a person's normal state. Because these illnesses usually are characterized by radical changes in a person's condition, such diagnoses lend credence to the idea that other alterations of a person's physical state, like sleeping and intoxication, can be explained by reference to the souls. On a more abstract level, by asserting that the souls have a direct impact on the body, these diagnoses imply that the spiritual and material dimensions of existence are intertwined, a basic premise of Rarámuri philosophy. In addition, because most serious illnesses are believed to be caused by other beings in the universe, discursive curing practices provide information about these beings and the Rarámuri relationships with them. By proposing that the irresponsibility of some people can bring harm not only to the offenders but also to their relatives and the whole community, these practices also convey the Rarámuri view that individual existence is inseparable from the life of the society and cosmos and that individual actions have far-ranging moral implications.

The information about souls communicated by these discursive practices exists on the same verbal-conceptual level as the concept of soul and can be interpreted almost automatically. Of course, to integrate this information, people must possess basic knowledge of the world, and the interpretation of complex statements, particularly those involving metaphors and other figures of speech, may require deliberate reflection and special knowledge and even then may remain only partial (Sperber 1975). Nonetheless, the presence of explicit information about souls in these discursive curing practices means that the members of many different households will be aware of it, even though some people may understand more than others.

The nonverbal components of the Rarámuri's curing practices are less important in the reproduction of the concept of soul because they cannot directly transmit discursive information. Although many of these practices are intended to prevent or cure soul-related illnesses, they are not simply externalizations of ideas about souls. The content of such nonverbal ritual practices is determined by the complex interaction of various social, historical, aesthetic, and intellectual factors, and even if actors report that they perform certain nonverbal acts to express specific ideas, these ideas seldom are unambiguously conveyed by the acts alone. In fact, the meaning of nonverbal ritual acts is never inherent in the acts themselves but can shift in response to changes in the circumstances within which they are performed.

On the other hand, nondiscursive ritual elements can communicate several kinds of messages, in some cases more effectively than words. As Rappaport (1979: 199) indicates, through participation in a ritual an individual acquires an understanding of it on the emotional and kinesic as well as conceptual levels, and certain kinds of ideas are best conveyed in this fashion; the notion of subordination, for example, is most effectively communicated when embodied in an act of subordination. Similarly, objects that are assigned symbolic significance can, through their appearance and manipulation in ritual contexts, transmit complex and abstract messages in a more condensed and evocative fashion than words (Rappaport 1979; Turner 1967, 1973).

Several scholars have suggested that rituals communicate such knowledge directly, without the intervention of discursive concepts. In his analysis of the "knowledge of the body" among the Kuranko of Sierra Leone, Jackson (1983: 328, 332) criticizes the anthropological "tendency to interpret embodied experience in terms of cognitive and linguistic models of meaning." He argues that the Kuranko do not need to formulate the meaning of a ritual in discursive form because their "ritual actions make sense to them at the level of immediate experience." Such knowledge need not be strictly nondiscursive "knowledge how" to perform the ritual but can include fundamental ontological knowledge. Robertson (1979: 404–5) proposes that philosophical tenets that are difficult to articulate are embedded in the *tayil* ritual of the Mapuche of Argentina and internalized by the participants experientially rather than conceptually. Similarly, Bourdieu (1977: 94, 218 n. 44; 1984: 466) asserts that fundamental cultural principles are embodied in dress, posture, manners, and ritual actions and are thereby "placed beyond the grasp of consciousness, and hence cannot be touched by voluntary, deliberate transformation, cannot even be made explicit."

These studies propose that nondiscursive practices can communicate extensive information but only to the nondiscursive consciousness and unconscious. If any of this information is to enter the discursive consciousness, it must be interpreted in words or concepts, which, as discursive forms of knowledge, must be conveyed separately from the nonverbal practices. These words and concepts are part of the discursive ground of interpretation of the nondiscursive, which individuals develop throughout their lives by observing practices and by assimilating discursive information about them provided by others.

Because nondiscursive acts and objects are more detached from the discursive grounds of their interpretation than verbal statements, their significance tends to be more ambiguous (cf. Jackson 1983: 338–39).[10] But the extent of their ambiguity varies somewhat depending on the relationship between the act or object in question and its intended or assumed message. In some cases this relationship can be purely conventional, as, for example, when a design like a circle is used to represent an abstract concept like completion. In other cases, the objects or acts may participate more directly in their referents, either by virtue of being caused by or part of them (e.g., the use of objects associated exclusively with women to represent women in a ritual) or sharing formal characteristics with them (e.g., religious icons or mimetic acts) (Peirce 1960; viz. Rappaport 1979 and Murray 1977). The possibility for diverse interpretations tends to be more limited when the relationship between the act or object and its message is not entirely arbitrary.

The interpretation of a nondiscursive practice also is constrained if the discursive information that indicates its intent or significance appears with it. In the rituals that the Rarámuri perform to cure specific ailments, the diagnosis of the illness usually is known to all present because it has been widely discussed in the community beforehand or is explicitly stated during the performance. Such diagnoses indicate the purpose of the ritual and thereby provide a general framework within which to interpret it. This interpretive framework serves as the basis for more complete exegeses of the ritual that people develop informally outside the ritual context.

The kinds of information that nondiscursive practices are capable of communicating can be determined more precisely by examining the Rarámuri's basic curing rite. The content of this rite tends to be context-insensitive: essentially the same acts are performed for everyone whether they are sick or well. Consequently, it lacks the direct link to diagnoses that guides the interpretation of curing procedures that are intended to relieve specific ailments.

The nondiscursive dimension of the basic curing rite consists of an arrangement of people and material objects in a particular physical setting and a sequence of actions involving the interaction of these people and their manipulation of these objects. This rite communicates symbolically several significant messages, perhaps the most important of which is that all individuals rely on society and its deities for their existence and well-being. This message is conveyed primarily through the use of objects and substances with specific symbolic values. Agave, the preeminent ritual medicine, stands for the protective and healing power of natural substances and by extension that of God, who endowed these substances with their efficacy and made them available for the Rarámuri's benefit. Beer brewed from maize, the basic element of Rarámuri diet, represents health and prosperity as well as God's beneficence, since he provided them with maize and taught them how to make beer with it. Because drinking maize beer is a central component of almost all social events and is regarded by the Rarámuri as the basis for social cooperation, it also symbolizes the society as a whole. The crucifixes with which these substances are applied represent the special powers that God provides doctors, who themselves stand for God by serving as intermediaries between him and the Rarámuri community. The application of these substances in the form of a cross indicates the Rarámuri's special relationship with God because the sign of the cross is identified with God. Finally, the breath that doctors blow over their patients and into their mouths is a symbol of vitality and life and ultimately of God, who is the source of breath and life.

This symbolic interpretation of the basic curing rite does not correspond entirely to the interpretations that the Rarámuri of Rejogochi themselves offer for it. For them, the rite is essentially a technical operation, designed to achieve certain material ends rather than to represent cosmological ideas.[11] From their perspective, the substances and objects are used not because they stand for something else but because their intrinsic properties benefit the patients. In any case, this interpretation is based on discursive knowledge that is not conveyed by the acts and objects themselves.

When examined apart from such discursive knowledge, the nonverbal acts in the basic curing rite communicate only nondiscursive information. Besides the practical knowledge of how the rite is to be performed, this information includes appropriate body postures, the proper ways to organize people and objects in space, and a culturally specific tempo of social interaction. In addition, because the rite is set apart from the activities of daily life, it indicates that certain substances and objects, like agave, maize beer, and crucifixes, are of special significance and that some body parts—the chest, head, and joints—are, as the focuses of ritual action, more important than others. This attribution of significance is reinforced by the appearance of these same objects and actions in other ritual contexts.

These nonverbal acts also convey information that approaches the discursive level. Such communication is possible where the relation between an idea and an action is sufficiently direct that the action can "enact" the idea. Distinctions in the way in which the ritual liquids are administered to males or females, for example, establishes in yet another context the gender distinction upon which Rarámuri society is based. The status of doctors within the society is also vividly depicted. To function as a doctor, an individual must possess special knowledge and abilities. The inequality of doctors and patients in this regard is portrayed through the asymmetry of ritual action: doctors act upon patients, manipulating their bodies and giving them advice, but not vice versa. In the process, particular individuals make their claim to the status of doctor or, in the case of apprentices, indicate their intention to become doctors. In addition, by performing the rite for everyone present, the doctors publicly establish their role as the community's protectors.

Most acts in the basic curing rite do not bear such an indexical or iconic relation to a set of ideas. To the extent that they can be said to convey discursive information, their messages tend to be ambiguous, leaving room for individual interpretation and variation. In fact, even when the enactment of an idea is possible, it usually can be communicated completely only if additional information is available. For example, to be able to conclude from their interaction that doctors and patients are unequal, one must first be aware that the people involved are doctors and patients. Of course, only small children and foreigners would ever witness a basic curing rite without the knowledge required for at least a minimal interpretation. The relevant point here, however, is that this knowledge is not provided in the acts themselves, but must come from elsewhere.

When considered strictly as a set of nonverbal acts performed in a particular physical and social setting, the basic curing rite conveys information primarily about spatial, temporal, and social distinctions and relations and nothing about souls. The possession of a little relevant discursive information, however, dramatically enhances the communicative potential of these nonverbal acts. For example, if people are aware of the equivalence of souls and breath, an equivalence established in the Rarámuri language, they can draw several conclusions about the nature of souls: that people can act directly on souls, that souls can be transferred from one person to another and thus alienated from the body, and that in some contexts it is desirable to do so. The communication of these ideas is possible because breath constitutes a tangible marker of souls. Actions that involve the special use of breath thus represent enactments of these ideas.

Except for the ideas associated with the blowing of breath, the basic curing rite contains no additional information about souls. Nonetheless, these nondiscursive practices lend an experiential dimension to the concept of soul that verbal transmission alone cannot provide, thereby enhancing the credibility of the concept by demonstrating in practice its applicability to basic concerns of existence. Combined with the more extensive information about souls conveyed in discursive curing practices, especially diagnoses, these nonverbal acts provide the basis upon which people can develop, through private contemplation and informal discussions with others, a more complete concept of soul. The public presentation of these ideas increases the likelihood that the views of different individuals will tend to coincide (Sperber 1975: 137). It gives an illusion of consensus, establishing what Bourdieu (1977) calls an "official view," which individuals must take into account in the private formulation of their own ideas, even if they should disagree with it. As a result, it places constraints on private speculation, constraints that are less compelling than those deriving from the logical relations among ideas but which incline people to agree on more ideas than these logical constraints alone would require.

DEATH
PRACTICES

Anthropologists have long recognized that the ways in which people think of and respond to death often reveal their most basic understandings of life (Hertz 1960; Weiner 1976; Huntington and Metcalf 1979; Bloch and Parry 1982). The death beliefs and practices of the Rarámuri of Rejogochi are no exception to this expectation, but they differ significantly from those found in many other societies. The frequently encountered symbolic association between death and fertility, for example, is entirely missing in the Rejogochi case (Bloch and Parry 1982).[1] From the perspective of the people there, the life substance in the universe is not a "limited good" (Bloch and Parry 1982: 7–9) but inexhaustible, with God (or in the case of Chabochis, the Devil) providing each embryo with a new set of intrinsically fecund souls.[2] Thus, the reincarnation of the souls of the dead is not required for the continuity of life nor are these souls incorporated into some collective font of life from which the fertility of humans, their crops and animals, or the natural world in general derives.

Also absent from Rarámuri death practices is concern with affirming in the face of death the continuity and integrity of the social order that is so prominent a feature of death rituals in many other parts of the world (Hertz 1960; Weiner 1976; Huntington and Metcalf 1979; Bloch and Parry 1982). In Rarámuri society, all formal positions of power and authority are achieved rather than inherited, and no one holds any office for more than a few years. A person's qualifications for these positions—primarily oratorical skill and an exemplary life—are sufficiently general that the positions can be held by many different people. Consequently, the death of an incumbent does not precipitate a crisis in the functioning of the society as a whole. The implications of death in Rarámuri society generally are limited to disruptions in the emotional and social lives of the deceased's relatives and close friends (cf. Woodburn 1982).

The principal themes expressed in the Rarámuri's death practices directly reflect the dual goals they intend to achieve through them: to give the dead food and other necessities for the afterlife and to protect the living from the dead. At the same time, these practices define relationships among the living, the dead, and other beings in the universe, provide an image of everyday life and the organization of society, and enact the relations of obligation that structure the society.

The concept of soul pervades the death-related thoughts and actions of the Rarámuri. Since they treat death, like health, as a public matter, their death-related practices are directly implicated in the reproduction of the concept of soul within the society. Here information about souls is transmitted primarily in two public settings: the rituals they sponsor for the dead that commence at death and conclude several years later; and the speeches addressed to the dead in these and other ritual contexts. These rituals and speeches share formal similarities to the curing rituals examined in the last chapter and the public speeches of political leaders analyzed in chapter 3, but an important difference is that because the dead are identified as souls, ideas about souls appear more frequently and explicitly in these death-related practices than in any other contexts.

IDEAS ABOUT DEATH AND THE DEAD

The Origin of Death

The Rarámuri of Rejogochi attribute the origin of death to the horned toad (*wikókere; Phrynosoma* sp.). Long ago the horned toad was a Rarámuri. He was very lazy, had a large belly, and walked very slowly. At that time, people never died, which concerned the horned toad. He reasoned that eventually there would be so many people in the world that they would begin trampling him because he moved so slowly and would be unable to get out of their way. He asked God to start taking people's souls so that they would die and leave more room for him. Later he changed from a human being into his present form, but he still walks slowly and has a big stomach.[3]

The Afterlife

From the Rarámuri perspective, death occurs when all of a person's souls permanently leave the body. This permanent alienation of body and souls terminates the temporary union established when God (or the Devil for Chabochis) implanted souls into the amorphous mixture of menstrual blood and semen that was to develop into human form inside the mother's womb. When this connection is broken, the body and souls can never be reunited. The body begins its gradual decomposition into inanimate clay while the souls embark upon a new existence in the afterlife.

The Rarámuri say that at the moment of death, the deceased looks about and exclaims, "Everybody died." This conclusion concisely expresses the entire spectrum of relations between the living and the dead. The dead believe themselves to be alive and the living to be dead, so they refer to the living as "souls" (*ariwá* or *iwigá*), "the dead" (*chuwí*), "ancestors" (*anayáwari*), and "shades" (*kálawi*), the same terms the living use for them.[4] For the dead, night is day, day is night, sunrise is sunset, and sunset, sunrise. They call the sun "moon" and the moon "sun," sleeping in the day and moving about at night when their "sun" lights up their world. Their seasons also are reversed. They plant their crops when the living harvest and harvest when the living plant, cultivating the mountainsides instead of the valleys because, for the dead, the mountains are valleys and the valleys, mountains.

These reversals theoretically could encompass most facets of Rarámuri life, but in some cases the opposition is not entirely symmetrical. For example, while most people maintain that the dead can see the living at all times, only those living individuals with special knowledge can see the dead in their human form whenever the dead are present. Ordinary people usually perceive them only in their dreams, although occasionally individuals will report having encountered the souls of the dead while they were awake. Such encounters invariably take place at night, the time at which the dead are most active, and usually while a person is walking alone near a cemetery. In addition, everyone reports having heard the dead pass in the night, the adults laughing and shouting as they return from their drinking parties, the children crying because they cannot find their parents.

These oppositions suggest that the Rarámuri conceive of the worlds of the living and the dead as separate realms, which are mirror images of one another. In fact, however, the Rarámuri attribute these reversals not so much to differences in the worlds themselves as to opposed perceptions that the living and dead maintain of the single world that they share. The Rarámuri's conclusion that souls perceive the world differently when they are detached from the body is based in part on their own dream experiences, which they understand to be the activities of a sleeping person's souls outside the body. Dream events often appear to occur during the daytime even though it is night for the living, and the activities in which the souls engage during dreams, such as planting and harvesting, frequently are "out of sync" with the schedules of the living.

Nonetheless, even though the souls of dead people are the same ones that animated their bodies while alive, the transition from life to death is envisioned to involve a basic transformation. While the souls of the living can interact among themselves with no danger to themselves or to the people in whose bodies they reside, contact with the souls of the dead or consumption of food or beer contaminated by them make the living sick. Such contact endangers the living, they say, because the dead "have a different kind of soul" (sinú ariwé).

Immediately upon death, the souls of the deceased are believed to undertake a journey across the surface of the earth. As discussed in chapter 4, people have different ideas about this journey, but all agree that it invariably takes place and requires three days for men to complete, and four days for women.[5] Although living people usually cannot see the dead as they travel, they often identify the small whirlwinds that speed across the countryside as the souls of the dead in transit and on other occasions suspect their presence. For example, in 1978 a woman was making tortillas in her rockshelter above the Rejogochi valley when she heard footsteps but could see no one. Suddenly a strong wind whipped through her shelter, dislodging from the shelf above her a radio, which struck her on the back. The woman later learned that a distant relative had died in an adjacent settlement about the same time as this unusual event occurred. She concluded that the wind had been his spirit on the first leg of his journey.

At the midpoint of their journeys, the souls of the dead return to their homes to consume the food and retrieve the clothing and other goods that their relatives have provided them for the afterlife. Then they begin their ascent to heaven. As they approach the world above, God meets them to decide whether to let them pass or punish them. For the most part, he concerns himself only with Rarámuri souls because Chabochis go directly at death to the Devil on the bottom level of the universe. However, the souls of Chabochis who have had sexual intercourse with Rarámuri are said to ascend to heaven at death while those of their Rarámuri partners go to live with the Devil, switching places as it were. The Devil does not punish Chabochis because any wrongs they might have done are in keeping with his thinking.

Sometimes God will punish people before they die, taking their children if they mistreat them, for example, or making them sick if they transgress. He may even call the largest souls of living people to heaven to reprimand them for misdeeds. Such was the fate of one man in Rejogochi, who was punished during a dream and then given the ability to cure.

> Many years ago, when I was a young man, I didn't think when I would get drunk. I would get crazy and chase after a lot of different women. I wanted many women and would go with one woman for awhile and then another. God doesn't want a man to do such things and he became angry with me. "Why doesn't he think?" he asked. So he sent one of his peons to kill me because I wouldn't change my ways, to punish me so I would think well.
>
> God took me for a short time halfway up to heaven where his peon was. This peon was a captain, a soldier, and very fat. He was standing at one end of a big pit, at the other end of which was a cross. A very large fire burned in the hole over which metal bars had been laid.
>
> The captain ordered me to walk across the pit. I hopped from bar to bar until I reached the other end where I crossed myself in front of the cross and then jumped from bar to bar back to where the peon was standing. When I got there he said, "one more time," so I did it again, but when I had finished he told me, "one more time," so I crossed the pit a third time. Then the peon asked me, "Now will you think well?" and said, "It is good. It is good. Now you will think well." He talked to me, giving me his thought, and then handed me a white paper. "Here, take this paper back down with you. From now on, have only one woman and this way other men will not become angry with you and come after you. Now you are a doctor. You will care well for everything, for the Rarámuri and their children and their cattle so they will not die." When I woke up, I thought very well, I had learned very much. This is what God did to me.

In the case of individuals who commit certain serious crimes, God may begin their punishment on their deathbeds. Such is supposed to have happened to a man who lived near Basíhuare and reportedly bewitched several people who failed to offer him food quickly enough when he visited in their homes. He had also shot and killed a man with a rifle and had liaisons with several women. When he was dying, he felt that a large stone had been placed upon his back and saw beside his bed a bucket full of the blood of the people he had killed, which God ordered him to drink. He told his wife about the stone and the bucket, but she could not see them.

Regardless of punishment received in this life, people who commit misdeeds are guaranteed punishment in the afterlife. The punishment varies with the severity of the offense. God punishes minor offenses, like using obscene or aggressive language or aborting a pregnancy, with a stern scolding. Barren couples, considered more serious offenders, are both scolded and loaded down with all manner of household goods, which they must carry until God feels that they have been sufficiently punished.

The most serious crimes—assault, murder, theft, and incest—all receive capital punishment in the afterlife. God commands the souls of people who have violently abused or killed others to drink a bucket of fetid blood, intended to represent the blood of their victims. He baits them saying, "Here, drink this. It is very tasty." When they can drink no more, he weighs them down with bundles containing implements used in fighting—sticks, rocks, knives, stones, and so forth—which they must bear until they collapse. Then God sends them to the Devil to be burned.

Thieves suffer a similar fate. God does not force them to drink blood, but they must carry all the items they stole until they can no longer walk. He then sends them to the Devil for destruction. The Devil tends a large fire inside a deep hole on his level of the universe in which he burns the souls of the Rarámuri God sends him. Although he encouraged these same people to commit the offenses for which they are being punished, the Devil does not help or console them but instead laughs at their predicament.

A special punishment is reserved for incest. Although people disagree on the details of this punishment, most versions revolve around the transformation of one or more souls of the incestuous person into a wild animal, usually a coyote or fox, which preys on the chickens, lambs, and baby goats of the living. One can distinguish these were-coyotes from regular coyotes because they can easily break into sheep and goat corrals, and dogs will not attack them. The other souls of the offender ascend to heaven where God scolds them and then sends them to the Devil, who burns them in his fire. When these souls have been destroyed, the animal also dies.

Transformation into a wild animal also is the presumed fate of one or more of the souls of people who die while lying on an animal skin or who eat peyote. The Rarámuri often cover their sleeping platforms with animal skins, usually goat skins, to make them more comfortable. If a person dies on top of these skins, he or she will transform not into a goat but into a wild animal, usually a coyote. This transformation can be prevented by removing the skins before the person dies or by throwing them into a stream immediately following death.

When people who have taken peyote die, the peyote people capture their largest souls while another of their souls transforms into a wild animal. The Rarámuri usually identify coyotes, foxes, or bears as the animals into which these souls transform, although one man told me that his paternal grandmother became a white turkey buzzard. But sometimes the identification is not entirely clear, as I learned in the following conversation.

A man in Rejogochi and I were discussing the implications for the fate of the souls in the afterlife of having taken peyote. I asked what he thought had happened to the souls of a recently deceased old man named Aparicio who had used peyote frequently. The man responded, "Aparicio's soul transformed into a big furry animal; that's what his widow said." I asked, "A big what?" but he said he didn't know. "It was very furry, furry like a bear. It was lying inside the house, the old woman said, lying right next to her. She was scared to death. It was like a coyote lying inside, where they sleep. She was very frightened." "Did she talk to it?" I asked. "No," he answered, "she didn't say anything. She only saw it. It left the house right away."

The Rarámuri consider being transformed into an animal an unpleasant fate, both for the deceased and, if the animal preys on their livestock, for the living. When peyote is involved, the relatives of the deceased must sponsor a ceremony in which they repay the peyote people for assisting the dead person during life. The peyote people then will release the person's largest soul to rise to heaven, and the animal dies. When the transformation is because the deceased died on an animal skin, the animal dies and the souls are freed after the fiestas for the dead person are completed.

Despite their elaborate ideas about the potentially unhappy fate of their souls in the afterlife, the Rarámuri almost invariably emphasize that people should act in conformance with God's teachings to ensure a contented and prosperous existence in *this* world. They do not rely on the threat of eternal damnation or the promise of heavenly reward to motivate proper behavior, nor do they expect life in heaven to provide a release from the pains of earthly existence, for they believe that heaven and earth are much the same. People do not fear punishment in the afterlife because such punishment, if warranted, is over quickly. Several people who thought that their souls would be excluded from heaven and ultimately destroyed because of acts they had committed spoke unemotionally to me of their expected fates, as if they were detached commentators describing the destinies of strangers.

Once established in the afterlife, the souls of the dead that are not punished with destruction can return to earth to visit and even to live. Most people say that the dead maintain several different residences, both in heaven and on earth. On earth they are associated most closely with the cemeteries where their bodies are buried and with the margins of the lands inhabited by the living, but they can be encountered anywhere. Some people think that the souls of a dead person live together all the time in a single body and move from one home to another, much as the living shift residences during the year. Others propose that the souls of a person split up at death to lead separate lives, some remaining near the grave site, others near the settlements of the living, and still others occupying one or more homes in heaven with all changing residences at will. Some people also believe that the souls of the dead remain on earth only until their death rituals are finished, then ascend to heaven where they remain for eternity, rarely if ever returning to earth.

Attitudes toward Death

The Rarámuri of Rejogochi accept death as an inevitable part of their existence and speak openly and naturally about it. People often state matter-of-factly that they or one of their close relatives will soon die even though they seem to be in robust health or only mildly ill. But being open to death does not mean they are unperturbed by it. Death troubles them and they especially dread the possibility of suffering from a long, debilitating illness before they can die. However, they do not express a fear of death itself and in certain circumstances consider death desirable. They say, for example, that when one is old, it is good to die, and they report cases of elderly people who, saddened by the loss of a lifelong mate or friend or simply tired of living, willed their own deaths.

The Rarámuri's acceptance and in a sense their embracing of death is motivated in part by their awareness that the possibility—indeed, the likelihood—of death is a constant feature in their lives. Life expectancy figures are not available for the Rarámuri but my impression is that few people survive beyond their sixties and many die much younger. The infant mortality rate also is high; in Rejogochi, all but the most recently married couples have lost at least one child and several six or more. The joys of conceiving and nurturing a new child are tempered always by the painful realization that its life may soon end. For many, the joys are not worth the sorrow. A young Rarámuri woman who had recently endured the deaths of two of her four children poignantly expressed to my wife her feelings: "I don't want to have any more children. They just live long enough for you to grow attached to them and then they die. You stay sad all the time."

While the Rarámuri do not regard death with great trepidation, they do have fearful and ambivalent feelings about the dead. On the one hand, their emotional involvement with people diminishes only gradually following their deaths; they feel compassion for them and are concerned for their welfare in the afterlife. The dead themselves are said to be reluctant to sever their ties with the relatives and friends who survive them. They frequently visit them in dreams, trying to convince their souls to join them in the afterlife or, in keeping with Rarámuri etiquette, to share their food and beer with them. They also are believed to bother the living while they sleep, tickling them or squeezing their throats so they are unable to talk. But by trying to perpetuate their relations with the living, the dead jeopardize the well-being of the living: unpropitious contact with the dead or their possessions can lead to sickness and death. For this reason, the Rarámuri fear the dead.

The Rarámuri are clear about what they must do to protect themselves against the dead. If the dead frequently appear in their dreams, they will prepare food offerings for them or hasten to complete the required death rituals. If the dreamers find these appearances particularly disconcerting, they may move to another home or dismantle their houses and rebuild them on new sites. Most importantly, people must overcome their feelings of sadness as soon as possible after the death of a loved one because if one's souls are sad they will want to leave the body to be with the deceased. Although people often cry for months in private or while drinking after one of their relatives dies, they try to be happy. During fiestas for the dead, for example, the living dispel the funereal air by getting drunk, dancing, laughing, and joking. Local Chabochis often characterize the Rarámuri as cold and unfeeling because they seem to mourn so little. The Rarámuri respond that Chabochis allow themselves to become dangerously sad when confronted by a death, often crying uncontrollably and reveling in their emotions. As a result, they say, Chabochis "do not endure" (*ke rehorá*) but often die soon after the passing of a relative or close acquaintance.

The living also must convince the dead that they no longer have any relationship with the living, whom they should now leave in peace. However, the separation of the dead from the living cannot be entirely accomplished until the former fulfill certain obligations to their dead, including primarily giving them food, clothing, and other necessities until the dead have had

time to begin supporting themselves in the afterlife. The living complete
these obligations in part to assure that their loved ones are provided for but,
equally important, to keep the dead from harming them or their children.

DEATH RITUALS

The Rarámuri of Rejogochi and other areas say that certain animals announce
an impending death. In Rejogochi, these animals are foxes and owls. The
owl's hoot is interpreted as *kurúsi mukúri, mukúri* meaning "died" and *kurúsi*
being an imitation of the sound with no additional significance. Lumholtz,
writing at the turn of the century, reported that the Rarámuri understood
owls to say, " 'Chu-i, chu-i, chu-i,'—'dead, dead, dead.' " They believed
that the owl was "very bad. Whenever it comes to a house and screeches,
somebody falls ill. If it calls three times, in three consecutive nights, the sick
person will die." These Rarámuri also believed that a grey fox whistling
three times outside the house of a sick person meant death (1902, I: 308–
9). Bennett and Zingg found that the cries of different animals foretold the
deaths of different categories of people: the fox that of females, the owl males,
and a bird called *okó* the death of children (1935: 269).

If a person has been suffering a long illness, death need not be fore-
warned. People assume that it is inevitable; they are prepared for it and often
are relieved when it comes. In fact, when a person lingers near death for
days, his or her relatives frequently attempt to hasten the end. Slow deaths
often are attributed to the dying person having sat on a stone implement—
a metate, a mano, a sharpening stone, or the rocks called *tichóni* upon which
cooking pots rest. To do so is said to prolong death because these stones
themselves never die. To free the remaining souls from the body, one of
these stones is placed against the dying person's body and bits of the stone
are ground up, mixed with water, and then sprinkled over the body or given
to the dying person to drink (cf. Kennedy 1978: 153; Mares Trías 1982: 31–
34; Schalkwijk, et al. 1985: 95).

Burial

Whenever people die from illness, their relatives and other members of the
community always discuss the circumstances that led to the death. However,
they do not have formal procedures like hearings to determine the cause of

the death or to assign responsibility for it, even when sorcery is suspected. The actions they perform with respect to the dead are essentially the same for all, regardless of how they died, including suicide.[6]

The living fulfill their obligations to the dead in a series of rituals organized by the deceased's parents, children, spouse, and sometimes siblings. These rituals are completed through the same division of labor found in most ritual contexts. The women are responsible for preparing the food while the men lead the ritual performances, intervening as always between the women and children on the one hand and outsiders to the society on the other, a category to which the dead are assigned.

The first obligation of the living is to bury the dead. Soon after death the body is laid on its back with the legs extended and the arms along the sides. It is covered with a blanket or sheet, and a portion of whatever food is on hand is placed next to the head. A fire is kindled near the body, and candles if available are arranged at the head, the feet, and next to the shoulders to prevent the Devil from capturing the dead person's souls.[7] To protect their children from the dead, the adults of the household mark a cross on their foreheads with ashes and send them to neighboring homes to sleep. They also often explain to the children that the dead person is gone forever so that the children will not grow sad awaiting his or her return.

People say that all the souls abandon the body at death, leaving the body as an inanimate shell, but a few ideas suggest that corpses retain some animacy. For example, if the person did not want to die, the body is said to swing and shake inside the blanket in which it is being carried to the cemetery, sometimes causing the carriers to fall. People also report feeling unusually sleepy when a corpse is nearby and they are reluctant to touch or come too close to a corpse. Between death and burial, the body often is left alone inside a house while the living stay outside or in a nearby house. If there are several adults in the household to encourage one another to have strength and not to be sad, they may remain next to the body and if the deceased is a child, the parents usually stay. During this period a doctor may come to the house to apply agave water to the corpse and also to the living, thereby consecrating the corpse and protecting the living from the dead.

In Rejogochi, the disposal of the dead is a matter of household, not community, concern. The community as a whole does not pay last respects to the deceased or participate in the funeral activities except at the request of the deceased's family. The responsibility for burying adults falls exclusively to the men of the household, sometimes assisted by other men in the neighborhood. Women do not participate in burials unless the deceased is a child. If so, often the parents alone will see to its burial, with the mother carrying the child in her arms to the cemetery.

The body is interred a day or so after death. The corpse is carried outside the house and wrapped in a blanket, which is then fastened with wooden skewers. A person with the requisite knowledge sprinkles agave water over the covered body while delivering a short speech to the deceased. He tells the departed that he or she is now dead and offers his wish for a pleasant journey. He also tells the dead person not to harm the living left behind.

At the conclusion of the speech, the men who will attend to the burial leave for the cemetery, led by two men carrying the body lashed to a corral pole between them.[8] As the burial party departs, the members of the household who remain behind throw ashes toward them to prevent the deceased from returning to molest them. The bearers enter the cemetery by completing a counterclockwise circuit around the large cross erected there, turning counterclockwise at each of the four sides. This series of movements, which the Rarámuri perform when they enter or leave a fiesta, signifies the arrival of the corpse in the domain of the dead. The body is then placed on the ground and the grave is dug.

Rarámuri graves tend to be rather shallow compared to those of Chabochis because, the Rarámuri explain, their souls go up to heaven while those of Chabochis go below. When the grave is ready, the body, still wrapped in the blanket, is untied from the corral pole and lowered into the grave, face up.[9] The feet are placed to the west so that the corpse faces away from the rising sun, in the opposite direction from the orientation of the living during most of their rituals. Placed with the corpse are extra articles of clothing and food of prescribed types and quantities: a spoonful of ground parched maize wrapped in a cloth, three pieces of a tortilla, three maize kernels, and three uncooked beans (or four of each of these if the deceased is female). This food will sustain the deceased for some time because, for the dead, each maize kernel and each bean is equivalent to an entire sack. Also enclosed in this bundle of food is a metal crucifix or small wooden cross together with three (four if female) large beads used in making the necklaces on which crucifixes are strung. These crosses and crucifixes are regarded as the signs of God and are included to identify the dead as belonging to God rather than the Devil.

For the same reason, there are several kinds of items that cannot be buried with the corpse. These include sandals with tire rubber soles and new articles of clothing, both of which are acquired from Chabochis and are associated with the Devil. Washing the clothing apparently eliminates this connection, for it can then be buried with the dead. Red articles also are said to belong to the Devil and cannot be placed in the grave. Should the Devil encounter the souls of the dead in new or red clothing or wearing rubber-soled sandals, he will identify them as his own and take them with him to the underworld.

After the body is placed in the ground, one of the men assisting in the burial approaches the grave and speaks to the deceased in the stereotyped speech style. He essentially repeats the earlier speech, emphasizing that the living have provided the deceased well for the proximate journey and will augment these supplies at intervals in the future. In return, he says, the deceased should leave the living in peace. When the speaker has finished, ground parched maize mixed with water—the preeminent trail food of the Rarámuri—sometimes is sprinkled over the corpse. Then each person at the grave site drops three (four if the deceased is female) pinches of dirt on top of the corpse and the grave is filled in. Rocks are piled on top to prevent animals from exhuming the body and a wooden cross is erected at the head.

In my experience, the men engaged in burying the dead, regardless of their relationship to the deceased, display no signs of sadness or bereavement but perform the task rather perfunctorily. This does not mean that they are not saddened by their loss but that they express their emotions in ways not immediately associated with mourning. During the burials I observed, I sensed a nervous tension in the air, and the men seem to be more excited or invigorated than normal. They also tended to joke a great deal, as they do whenever they work in groups. For the most part, their joking was about unrelated matters but sometimes included references to the dead. For example, at Calistro's funeral, his brother-in-law kidded me that I would be unable to walk by the cemetery at night because Calistro would grab me. I asked how he would be able to pass without danger and he laughed, saying he would put a cross in ashes on his forehead every time he approached the cemetery at night. Then another man joined in the joking, indicating that he planned to place spiny prickly pear pads along the edge of the road next to the cemetery so the dead could not come close to him. Such jokes are not considered disrespectful of the dead but rather helpful to people in avoiding the sadness that makes them vulnerable to the dead.

When the burial is completed, the men kindle a small fire near the grave on which they pile juniper or cedar boughs, bathing themselves and the implements used to inter the body in the billows of white, aromatic smoke that rise from the fire. This smoke protects them from any harm that could come from their contact with the dead. Sometimes they also bathe themselves in a nearby creek for the same reason. Then they gather up their tools and return to the home of the deceased, where they are given portions of the food that was placed near the corpse. This food must be heated before it is eaten to eliminate any contamination from the dead. The parents, children, siblings, and spouse of the deceased cannot eat any of this food. If they do, they could contract the same illness from which their relative died.

After a corpse is buried, it is never disturbed, except perhaps accidentally after many years when the exact location of the grave is forgotten and a new grave is dug in the same spot. Remains uncovered in this way are reburied but the Rarámuri do not practice intentional secondary burial. They also do not use the bones of their dead for any purposes, although sorcerers reportedly use the bones found in ancient burial caves to bewitch footracers. These bones are said to belong to the first inhabitants of the world, the Kapáche, whom God destroyed for their cannibalism and replaced with the ancestors of the Rarámuri.

The Rarámuri say that the corpse rots in the ground, gradually becoming clay, the substance from which God created the bodies of the first Rarámuri people. People do not return to the graves of their loved ones to mourn or maintain the grave. They do, however, send offerings to the cemetery during the death rituals sponsored for the dead, in their Easter ceremonies, and during the rituals they perform to cure their crops and livestock. In addition, when children die before having completed the series of rituals designed to burn away the *rumugá*, their parents join doctors at their graves to perform these rituals, using the crosses that mark the graves as substitutes for the children themselves.

Following a death, the relatives of the deceased are not expected to observe any prohibitions. If the deceased was married, the surviving spouse can remarry without stigma as soon as he or she desires (for regional variations on this, see Bennett and Zingg 1935: 248–49). In fact, the community often pressures a widow or widower to take a new spouse, in part to preclude the sadness that comes with loneliness, in part because some tasks of everyday existence are more competently performed by men and others by women. In addition, unless they are quite old, widows and widowers are considered to be likely sexual partners of their married neighbors and thus to constitute a threat to the order of the community.

Minor Death Rituals

The first formal offerings for the dead coincide with the conclusion of their journey across the face of the earth, three or four days after death. The women of the household, sometimes with the help of their close female relatives, prepare boiled meat (usually goat, mutton, or chicken), beans, and other dishes like mustard greens and parched maize kernels, the latter ground either wet to produce *kiorí* (in Spanish *esquiate*) or dry for *kobísi* (in Spanish *pinole*). They also make small thick tortillas called "offering tortillas" (*rimé nutewá*), which are only about three inches in diameter and are prepared especially for the dead.[10]

On the appropriate day they place this food in containers outside the house next to a small cross, along with those possessions of the deceased that were not buried and other things that they want the dead person to have, like money. Usually only the members of the deceased's household take part in this event, but at its end they pass the food through a juniper or cedar smudge and then distribute it among all the individuals who assisted in the burial except the deceased's parents, children, siblings, and spouse.

The living are supposed to give a dead person food and other items three times (four for deceased females) in the three (four) years after this initial ritual and before they complete their obligations in one final fiesta. There is, however, considerable regional variation among the Rarámuri in the scheduling of these rituals (Lumholtz 1894: 444; Lumholtz 1902, I: 384 ff.; Bennett and Zingg 1935: 236 ff.). People may also put out offerings for the deceased at other times, whenever they have a fiesta or are troubled by the appearance of the dead in their dreams.

Bennett and Zingg (1935: 240–50) and Kennedy (1970b: 41; 1978: 152, 174) report that people who maintain a special joking relationship with a person during life are responsible for major portions of these death fiestas. Bennett and Zingg mention only the deceased's siblings-in-law in this regard, while Kennedy includes both siblings-in-law and grandparents and grandchildren. He writes, "The general feeling seems to be that the joking relatives are the only ones who are not endangered by the power of the souls of the dead" (1970b: 41). In Rejogochi joking relations exist among these categories of kinsmen, but they have no unique duties to perform in death rituals. Instead the immediate family prepares the food and organizes the offerings and other events, although other relatives and friends may choose to give things to the dead. These rituals are community events and often occur in conjunction with the performance of other rituals or work projects. In addition to the food they prepare, the members of the sponsoring household brew maize beer to offer to the dead and to repay their guests for the assistance they provide in the completion of these tasks.

These small death rituals often are held for the benefit not only of the most recently deceased but of all close relatives who have died within the previous few years. Each dead person is represented in the rituals by a small wooden cross, called "cross of the dead" (*kúrasi anayáwari*). These crosses are placed together inside or adjacent to the homes where the rituals take place or, if a larger ceremony is being performed, on the dance patio near the crosses and offerings for God. Necklaces bearing crucifixes or carved crosses sometimes are hung from them. The dead are said to arrive at these crosses in the company of other relatives from the afterlife, who share the food and beer with them and help carry the goods back to their homes.

The offerings are arranged in front of these crosses, often on top of a blanket or plank but sometimes directly on the ground. A goat or sheep usually is slaughtered and its meat, after boiling for hours, is mashed with beans and mounded on top of the offering tortillas, which are then placed in baskets. These tortillas are supposed to be offered in multiples of three or four, depending on the gender of the deceased, but the number often varies because the Rarámuri are not particularly concerned with such details. With these tortillas are one or more bowls of meat stew, containers of liquid maize dishes (*kiorí* and *kobísi*), and, in season, ears of green maize. Sometimes cups of heavily sugared coffee also are included. The clothing and tools left behind by the deceased are placed next to these food offerings, together with other items the living want them to have. Containers of the ritual liquids so prominent in curing rituals—agave water and maize beer—also are present, as is a lighted candle if available.

A man who can communicate with the dead officiates at the formal presentation of the goods.[11] He kneels before the crosses, sometimes touching the small crosses hanging from them, and crosses himself. He then takes in turn (although not necessarily in this order) the agave water, the beer, and the liquid foods and sprinkles them over the crosses, crossing himself after each offering. The agave water is applied to the crosses to cure the dead and to protect the living from them. The beer also cures the dead and is given, along with the liquid foods, for the dead to consume. Next he stands and offers each basket of food, the clothing, and the tools to the dead by lifting them toward heaven. He begins facing the crosses, then turns in the opposite direction, continuing in this way around the crosses, lifting the objects, crossing himself, and turning counterclockwise at each of the four sides. He

Figure 18. Offerings for the dead. Rejogochi, June 1981. A basket of tortillas topped by goat meat mixed with beans, food offerings for the dead, is placed in front of a small cross bearing necklaces and a crucifix. An olla of maize beer, also for the dead, sits behind, a gourd dipper floating on top. On either end of the larger plank are matachine wands, headdress, and rattle. The basket in the center holds traditional foods to be presented to the sponsors of the following year's fiesta along with the white banner. The olla to the right of the central cross holds water, later tossed in the air around the crosses to remind Our Father to send rain. Containers of medicines for maize and livestock curing are lined up behind the crosses.

concludes at the front facing the crosses and replaces the offerings in their original locations. Kneeling again, he sometimes drinks a bit of beer, then crosses himself, and stands.

Music is usually a part of this ritual. Almost always someone will play a violin and a few people may dance the shuffling steps of the *paskóla*. If the death ritual is part of a more complex ceremony, a chanter (*wikaráame*) or matachine dancers will perform. People say that the music and dances are beautiful and are intended to entertain the dead and make them content; they assume that the dead themselves often join in.

At the conclusion of the offerings, the other people present kneel in turn before the crosses, dripping agave water and beer over them and sipping bits of these liquids. In so doing, they simultaneously make offerings of these liquids to the dead, cure the dead, and protect themselves from them. Then the person in charge returns to the crosses, kneels, crosses himself, and makes a speech to the dead. He repeats the now familiar admonitions that the dead should be contented in their new existence and, because their needs have been provided for, should leave the living in peace. He ends by crossing himself and then hands the containers of food to a few of the people standing or sitting nearby to eat then. As in the previous rituals, close family members never eat this food.

After a period of general drinking, the person officiating distributes the remaining offerings among some of the people present and, carrying the small crosses ahead of him, leads them in a procession for a short distance toward the cemetery. The purpose of these processions is to escort the dead away from the domain of the living and toward their resting place in the cemetery

Figure 19. Maize beer for the dead. Rejogochi, June 1981. The man in the right foreground fills a gourd dipper with beer to sprinkle over the cross before him as an offering to the dead before drinking the remainder himself. The host of the fiesta, holding a white banner, prepares to transfer sponsorship of the fiesta to the man and woman kneeling in front of him. A tutubúri chanter performs to the left of the crosses while matachines dance at the back of the patio, their musicians seated beside them.

Figure 20. A death procession. Rejogochi, June 1984. A doctor kneels and tosses bits of food into the air as offerings to the dead, the dog gobbling up the food as it hits the ground. The other people carry offerings of food, beer, and a blanket. Adult matachine dancers perform to one side, joined by boys from the local Jesuit school. The school appears in the left background.

and their final destination in heaven. Usually the participants first complete a circuit of the house and then wind their way around the homestead, to the accompaniment of musicians and sometimes dancers. Periodically they lift the items they are carrying heavenward and complete a tight counterclockwise turn to offer these goods to the dead. About thirty meters or so from the house, the leader stops, plants the crosses in the ground, and again offers the food and goods to the dead. He speaks a few words in parting to the dead and then tosses the crosses in the air toward the cemetery to send the dead on their way. The other members of the procession then drop what they are carrying to the ground, often collapsing themselves to signify that they too have died. Sometimes people will exaggerate their falls—for example, by turning somersaults—and everyone in the procession laughs. The processions, like the rituals of which they are a part, are not intended to be solemn.

After a few seconds the participants rise and gather around a bucket of maize beer that was carried in the procession, exchanging dippers among themselves until the supply is exhausted. Then they collect the items and return them to their owners, who use them as if they had never been offered to the dead. The rest of the fiesta is devoted to drinking and involves no special activities directed toward the deceased.

The general tone of these rituals is no different from that of other drinking get-togethers. People chat, dance, make jokes, and sometimes, when they are drunk, quarrel and fight. At the same time, the rituals provide the individuals closest to the deceased an opportunity to accept their grief and to enact their separation from the dead person in a context where they have the support of the larger community.

Occasionally the family members of the deceased express their emotions overtly during these rituals. I recall in particular a death ritual held in Rejogochi in September of 1978. The ritual was sponsored for two members of the Rejogochi community: a girl about five years old and her classificatory grandfather, who was about seventy years old. Both had died several months before in the Jesuit clinic in Creel—the man from a lingering illness apparently due to his advanced age, the girl from meningitis—and both had been buried in Creel. Because of the danger of contagion, the girl had been buried immediately, before her parents had time to get to Creel to view the body. They were not entirely convinced that she had died and had heard rumors that she had been taken to a Jesuit school in the mission center of Sisoguichi. In fact, one man from the Basíhuare area said he had seen her there.

The girl's parents and the man's widow jointly organized the ritual. Their emotional states during its performance were quite similar and perhaps best described as volatile. For most of the time they acted like the other people present, but sometimes they would begin to weep. After crying briefly, they would abruptly stop to start talking and joking with the people around them, shifting with little transition from subdued weeping to boisterous laughter. At these times, other people would bring them beer to drink and encourage them to have strength and not to become disheartened.

"When We Write with Ashes"

The final death fiesta is more elaborate than any of the previous ones and ideally should be given at least three years (four years for females) after death but not before the other, smaller fiestas have been performed. Although the smaller death rituals can be held at any time of the year, the final death rituals, like those for bakánawi and peyote, are never staged during the maize growing season. The only explanation the Rarámuri offer for this restriction is that holding these ceremonies before the maize is mature would anger God who would destroy their crops. Because of the expense, poorer households often delay sponsoring these fiestas for many years, despite the risks from the dead.

The dead present the greatest danger to the living in this interim period. They are said to remain near their living relatives until the completion of this ritual and will punish them by making them ill or taking the souls of their children if they feel forgotten. To avoid sad memories, people dispose of the possessions of the deceased during this time, selling them or giving or throwing them away. They also distribute the dead person's land, animals, and stores of maize among his or her children or grandchildren or, if none of these heirs survive, to his or her siblings and other collateral relations. A spouse inherits only if the deceased has no other relatives in the community. This distribution is supervised by the president of the section, the local representative of the national government, who is supposed to resolve conflicts over the inheritance.

The final death ritual includes all of the features found in the three (or four) rituals that precede it along with several unique elements. The purpose of all these rituals is to protect the living from the dead and to provide the dead with the food and other items they require. Unlike the simpler rituals, however, the final fiesta is intended to fulfill conclusively the obligations of the living to the dead and to effect a complete separation of the dead from the living. In it, elements from various domains—social, political, religious, and economic—are combined to create a representation of Rarámuri life, which is adapted on each occasion to reflect the gender or personal interests of the deceased. These rituals thereby provide the dead (and thus the living) with an image of their life and society and a final opportunity to participate in it before they are sent away to the afterlife.

The Rarámuri call these elaborate fiestas *napisó osiwáchi* (when we write with ashes) because near the end of the ritual everyone present gathers to cross their foreheads with ashes for protection from the dead. They also scatter ashes around the homestead to prevent the dead from returning to harm them or their animals. In addition, during these rituals and on other occasions, they draw lines or crosses with ashes on the outside of their beer ollas, often sprinkling ashes on the ground around the ollas. These measures are intended to keep the dead from breaking the ollas or drinking the beer (that is, its invisible parallel aspect, which is associated with its aroma and sometimes its potency). If people drink beer contaminated by the dead, they will fall ill, typically with upset stomachs, unless they have taken the precaution of sipping agave water or sprinkling it into the beer.

Ashes produced from the bark of a local juniper (*awarí*) are preferred for these purposes because they are of a lighter color than those derived from other materials. When I asked why the color of the ashes is significant, people responded only that whiter ashes were more attractive, and when I inquired why ashes in general are employed to protect the living from the dead, they replied simply that the dead are afraid of ashes. It is possible that ashes were selected to perform this role because they represent the ultimate remains of organic (that is, animate) things and thus maintain a structural correspondence with the dead. However, the ritual application of ashes in the *napisó* fiesta also bears a number of similarities to the Catholic ritual of Ash Wednesday, which marks the beginning of Lent, in which crosses are drawn on the foreheads of the members of the congregation.[12] These correspondences suggest that the Rarámuri derived this component of the *napisó* ritual and possibly the symbolic association between ashes and the dead as well directly from Catholic missionaries.

That the Rarámuri were exposed to the Ash Wednesday ritual and its significance early in the colonial period is documented in a 1676 account of the religious instruction provided to converts in two missions located in the eastern portions of Rarámuri territory:

> On Ash Wednesday, all the people from each of these two missions assembled where the priests lectured them, explaining what Easter was and the obligations they had as Christians.
>
> Because they are such barbarous people, they seemed to have concluded that putting ashes on them was something related to their drinking bouts. They are accustomed to paint themselves with earth in the manner of ashes, and perhaps because they usually paint some figures, they concluded that painting crosses on their faces was done for them to become intoxicated, for it is a sign of a fiesta to paint oneself with dirt. All of this appears to impede the fruit of penitence that is hoped from so sacred a ceremony. . . .
>
> The word of God overcame all of these challenges because it was explained to them with much distinction the significance of ashes. They were told as on other occasions of the body and the soul, that as they worked for the good of the body, suffering and wanting many things, so should they work for their souls, suffering and wanting for their sins. That the sign of the cross which was painted on their foreheads that day signified all that Our Lord suffered for us, even to dying on the cross.

And with the ashes it is signified that our bodies will return to ashes and
that all the desires of this life will be extinguished (Tardá and
Guadalaxara 1676: 378v).

I attended three *napisó* rituals in the Rejogochi area, one in November of
1977 and two in March of 1978. All three performances included the same
basic components, but rather than present a generalized summary of them,
I will recount the events of the one staged on March 7, 1978, for which I
have the most detailed description and explanation.

The ritual was sponsored for a man named San Pedro who died in his
early thirties about four years before, apparently from the tuberculosis that
is endemic among the Rarámuri. Although the Rarámuri encourage surviving
spouses to remarry as soon as possible after a death, San Pedro's widow,
Dolores, resisted attempts to provide her with a new husband.[13] After San
Pedro's death, she moved back to her natal rancho of Waéachi a few kilometers
away, and returned to Rejogochi for the *napisó* ritual.

The ritual was held at San Pedro's former home and was organized primarily by his mother and stepfather, with the assistance of San Pedro's
mother's sister, who was married to one of Dolores's cousins. San Pedro's
sister and her husband and San Pedro's half-siblings with their spouses also
helped. Together they supplied two goats, one sheep, four chickens, and the
maize from which about four hundred liters of beer and large quantities of
tortillas, tamales, and other maize dishes were prepared. Dolores in turn
provided a cow that had belonged to San Pedro, which she had kept especially
to be killed on this occasion.

Major preparations for the fiesta got under way on March 6. In the
morning four of Dolores's male relatives arrived from Waéachi to deliver the
cow to be sacrificed and to help the men of San Pedro's family slaughter it.
After it was butchered, Lorenzo, who was both Dolores's cousin and the
late San Pedro's uncle by marriage, distributed choice cuts among the men
who were helping. The men also cleared a patio and erected a wooden cross
about four feet tall in front of which they killed the goats and sheep and
later offered food to God. The meat and blood was turned over to the women,
who spent most of the day cooking the blood, grinding maize, making tortillas
and tamales, and seeing that the beer was fermenting properly.

That night, a metal oil drum, cut in half, was filled with meat and water
and set to simmer.[14] About the same time, a chanter (*wikaráame*) began shaking a gourd rattle and intoning the lines of the *tutubúri* ritual, moving back
and forth across the patio in front of two crosses where the goats and sheep

had been sacrificed. He continued all night long, stopping only briefly at intervals to rest, in preparation for the offering of food to God the next day.

Soon after dawn, San Pedro's family dispatched Mariano Sikóchi, a man about forty-five years old who could communicate with the dead, to the cemetery in Basíhuare where San Pedro was buried. His errand was to invite San Pedro and other deceased relatives of the people sponsoring the ritual to come to the fiesta. They gave him the names of nine people—four males and five females, and mostly children—so he could invite them specifically, but they assumed that the souls of other dead people would arrive as well. They gave him a small wooden cross to carry before him as he walked and a gallon jug of beer and some ground parched maize to share with the dead. A younger man, Mauricio González, went along to help him carry the beer on the twenty kilometer roundtrip.

By midmorning most people had arrived at the fiesta, over a hundred people in all. The women joined in preparing food while the men completed or watched the ritual performances. These ritual activities took place on two separate dance patios. On the first, prepared the day before, white muslin cloths were draped over two crosses, and a necklace made of Job's-tears seeds and bearing a small wooden cross was hung over the cloth on the taller of the two. These crosses, oriented toward the rising sun, were designated as God's; the chanter, whose function was to elicit God's goodwill, performed around them. A third cross, like the other two around four feet tall and similarly oriented, had been erected about two meters from them to the north. This was designated as the cross of the matachine dancers, and five small wooden crosses, representing the dead, stood around its base. A bench for the violinists and guitarist who would accompany the matachines was set up along the back edge of the patio in front of this cross.

A second patio was prepared about ten yards southeast of the main patio. Instead of crosses its central feature was a platform formed of planks resting about five feet above the ground on the near horizontal branches of two otherwise trimmed pine saplings. This raised platform, around which the major offerings for the dead were to be placed, is called *nutegátili* (offering place) and is built only for *napisó* rituals. I originally assumed that the offerings are elevated much higher in this ritual than in others because the purpose is to provision the dead for a journey to heaven. However, the Rarámuri I questioned never offered this interpretation, stating only that this sort of platform has always been used in these rituals.

The chanter continued his performance with short breaks until around 11:00 A.M. when containers of meat stew and ground parched maize mixed with water were placed in front of the crosses for God and the dead. A plastic bucket of maize beer stood next to the crosses for the dead. About this time, a man emerged from the trees above the house, where he had changed into his matachine costume. This elaborate costume consisted of a number of components, most of which are not used in everyday dress: a "crown" constructed of a metal box made from four mirrors with crepe paper streamers hanging down the back and a kerchief attached to the sides that concealed the dancer's chin; a white headband; a cape formed of two brightly colored strips of cloth attached at the shoulders to the dancer's long-sleeved shirt; white muslin pants extending just below the knees; a triangular "apron" consisting of a kerchief placed on top of a slightly larger piece of white muslin and held in place by a woven wool belt; knee socks; and work boots, each carrying a string of metal bells. The dancer also carried as part of his costume a wand made of a bent sapling decorated with red and blue crepe paper and a rattle made of wood shavings glued together around a wooden handle topped by a small wooden cross. While dancing he shook the rattle in his right hand while holding the wand in his left. He was joined by another dancer who did not wear a costume but had a rattle of the same type and some corn husks instead of the wand. The musicians who would accompany them assembled along the back of the patio and began tuning their instruments.

The matachines then started to perform in front of their cross in preparation for the offering of food to God. Because the fiesta was sponsored for a man, they danced in sets of three pieces each before taking a break; had the principal deceased been female, each set would have included four pieces. The chanter resumed his own dance beside them, and another man began playing a flute to an entirely different tune next to the matachines' musicians. The juxtaposition of *tutubúri* and matachine is typical during such fiestas, but flutes and their companion instruments, large snared drums, are used only during the Easter season. Drums and flutes accompany the dances of the Pharisees and Soldiers, the two groups responsible for the organization of the Easter activities, but representatives of these groups did not perform until later in the day.

Three men approached the crosses of God, and all the other men stood and removed their hats. The three lifted the containers of food up toward heaven in offering to God and then placed them at the opposite edge of the patio. San Pedro's stepfather called the men to eat, beginning with the performers and those who had helped prepare the fiesta and then the others.

When all had eaten, food and beer were offered to the dead. Lirio, a Rejogochi man who had been asked by San Pedro's family to lead the death ritual, knelt in front of the crosses of the dead, crossed himself, spoke a few words in a very low voice, and sprinkled small amounts of the food and beer over the crosses. Then he tossed beer to the four directions and ate some of the food, next calling the matachine group to eat. All the men gathered at the crosses to exchange gourd dippers of beer while the chanter and matachines resumed their dances. A woman left the other women to dance beside the chanter for a few pieces.[15]

About 2:00 P.M., Mariano and Mauricio came from the cemetery, Mariano in front carrying the small cross, Mauricio behind him with the empty beer jug, both men quite drunk. They went directly to the patio and walked clockwise twice around both sets of crosses. Mariano then placed the small cross among the others, and he and Mauricio completed three more clockwise circuits of the crosses before joining the other men in drinking.

Because people in Rejogochi usually circle the crosses counterclockwise, I later asked Mariano and others why he had moved clockwise here. Mariano explained that in his home pueblo of Samachique, many such movements are reversed in death rituals. Bennett and Zingg (1935: 251), who worked in Samachique around 1930, observed reversals in death rituals there, attributing them to the belief that the world of the dead is a reversal of that of the living. Natives of Rejogochi, however, rejected this explanation, characterizing Mariano's actions as drunken mistakes.

With the appearance of Mariano and Mauricio, the level of activity increased dramatically, for the dead were said to have arrived with them. The women completed the final food preparations for the major offerings to God and the dead. The food was placed in front of God's crosses and on the raised platform below rather than at the small crosses on the patio. By this time, other items to be given to the dead had been arranged on and around the platform. These goods are supposed to include all that the dead require to establish themselves in the afterlife. On this occasion they consisted of clothing, wool, cloth, blankets, some coins, necklaces, a hoe, a metal plow point, a chisel, an oxen yoke, an axe, a few ears of maize in a sack, and two wooden balls and two sets of sticks and hoops for men's and women's footraces. Two ollas of maize beer stood in the center underneath the platform with a candle next to each.

The Pharisees and Soldiers began dancing on the patio in front of the matachine cross, alternating with the matachines. Two men and two women retrieved the racing balls and sticks-and-hoops from underneath the raised platform and simulated racing by walking around the platform and the crosses on the patio before heading up the valley at full pace. Although such races were staged during all three *napisó* rituals I attended, I was told that they were held on this occasion because San Pedro had been an accomplished racer and that he and other of the dead ran along with the living during them.

As the racers were leaving, a man appeared at the patio from the nearby creek carrying a can of the Pharisees' white paint, a mixture of clay and water, with which he coated the legs, arms, and faces of several of the men, including the four who had been appointed as the leading Pharisees for the year. Moreno picked up the small crosses from the patio and led the matachines, Pharisees, Soldiers, and musicians, all performing, first to the platform, where he stuck the crosses into the ground underneath, and then inside the house where the application of ashes would later take place. The chanter resumed his dance on the patio as the racers passed on their way down the valley.

Soon after the racers completed their brief contest and returned their equipment to the platform, final food offerings to God were made. The two doctors who were directing the ritual—Lirio and Mariano—formed a line with their wives across the back of the patio, facing the matachine cross, while the matachines danced. The chanter stood a few feet below them in front of the crosses of God, shaking his rattle. Five men approached these crosses and circled them counterclockwise, with one of the men tossing out agave water to the four directions to protect the living from the dead. Lirio, together with his wife Rosario, Mariano, and Mariano's wife María Elena led the matachines around the patio and down by the platform where the Pharisees and Soldiers were dancing. Then the group moved on to the house.

Back at the patio, the five men offered the food to God while the chanter performed, and then each sipped some of the agave water before passing it on to the other men present. They drank this to avoid sickness that would result from consuming food and beer possibly contaminated by the dead. This food was then divided among the chanter and other performers and what remained was returned to the women for general distribution.

At the conclusion of these offerings, the focus of the ritual shifted from God to the dead. Drinking had begun from ollas inside the house where people were assembling for the ritual application of ashes. Three walls of this house were made of pine logs interlocked as for a log cabin, while the fourth, on the north side, was formed by hand-hewn pine planks leaned against the roof. Some of these planks had been removed from either end of this wall to create two entrances, one on the east for women, one on the west for men. Lirio and Mariano sat opposite the men's entrance, their wives,

Rosario and María Elena, opposite the women's. Next to each pair was arranged the articles to be used in the ritual: an olla of beer; a gourd dipper;
a bucket containing three (for males) or four (for females) dippersful of beer
for each of the dead for whom the fiesta had been sponsored; a small wooden
cross with a lighted candle next to it; a can of water with a pine needle brush
in it; and a dish of ashes. To protect the beer from contamination by the
dead, Lirio and Rosario drew crosses with ashes on the sides of the ollas
next to them, eight crosses on the men's olla, seven on the women's. Then
Lirio, Mariano, Rosario, and María Elena individually traced the outline of
a cross on their foreheads and splashed water with the pine needle brushes
on their partner's head, back, and chest.

The other people present began lining up for the ritual, the men entering
the house through the western opening, the women through the eastern.
They knelt in turn, crossed themselves, and made crosses on their foreheads
with the ashes. Lirio (for the males) or Rosario (for the females) then struck
them lightly at the appropriate spots of their bodies with the pine needle
brushes dipped in water, and Mariano (males) or María Elena (females) drew
out some beer from the ollas for them to drink. The ashes and water were
intended to repel the dead, and the beer was drunk to fortify the living against
the dangers of contact with the dead. After drinking the beer, they crossed
themselves again, and left. Some people took a pinch of ashes with them to
scatter outside the house to prevent the dead from entering. Throughout
this period, the matachines performed at the platform and inside the house
while a drum and two flutes played outside.

When everyone had completed this ritual, they continued drinking inside
the house. Then Mariano emerged from the men's entrance with a dish of
ashes and María Elena from the women's with a can of water and a pine
needle brush. Walking in opposite directions, they scattered ashes and water
around the house to create a barrier against the dead and then reentered
through the same openings from which they had exited. About the same
time, the matachines moved to the raised platform to dance and preparations
were begun for the procession that would conclude the ceremony.

San Pedro's stepfather and stepbrother entered the house and emerged
a minute or so later, carrying a white sheet between them. The two small
crosses that had been used in the ashes ritual rested inside. Following them
were Mariano with a dish of ashes, María Elena with a can of water and pine
needle brush, and another couple carrying the buckets of maize beer that
had been set apart for the dead during the ritual application of ashes. They
all moved to the platform, where Lirio and Rosario stood, the latter with a

basket of meat and tortillas she had taken from the platform. They lowered the sheet to the ground in front of the platform and placed the small crosses and candles there with the other crosses. Lirio took bits of meat and tortillas from the basket held by his wife and dropped them over the crosses inside the sheet. He then dipped out small amounts of maize beer from one of the buckets and the two ollas under the platform and sprinkled it over the crosses. Then the sheet was carried counterclockwise around to the back of the platform, where Lirio repeated the offerings.

The procession next moved up to the other patio. San Pedro's stepfather and stepbrother led the way with the sheet while his mother and widow walked to either side. Lirio followed the sheet, singing and talking to the crosses—that is, to the dead—telling them to return contentedly to their homes, that they would receive nothing else from the living, and to leave the living in peace. Rosario followed Lirio with the basket of food and was in turn followed by Mariano and María Elena with the ashes and water, then by the couple bearing the buckets of beer, the matachines, the Pharisees and Soldiers, and the musicians. The two pairs of racers circled the procession in opposite directions, as if they were competing.

When they arrived at the patio, the members of the procession halted first in front of the crosses designated as God's and again behind them, where Lirio sprinkled bits of food and drops of beer over the crosses inside the sheet. Then they returned to the raised platform where Lirio handed the items remaining there to other people, who joined the procession. San Pedro's stepfather removed the metal plow point and chisel from the platform and stored them inside his house so that they would not be lost. His wife took his place carrying the sheet.

To separate the dead from the domain of the living, the procession moved down the hill away from the house in the direction of the cemetery. At the bottom, they laid the sheet on the ground, Lirio spoke a few words of parting to the dead, and ordered the sheet to be lifted and the crosses tossed into the air to send the dead on their way. At the same time, people dropped the items to the ground, a few fell to the ground themselves, and Mariano exclaimed, "The dead are going home." Then everyone assembled around the buckets of beer to drink.

By now the sun had set and a fire had been lit next to the platform. A few drops of rain began to fall, unusual for this time of year. When they finished the beer from the buckets, the members of the procession hurriedly gathered the items they had carried and returned to the platform to continue drinking with the others for the rest of the night.

SPEECHES TO THE DEAD

A central element of all death rituals is words spoken to the dead. This discursive component ranges in complexity from a few brief phrases muttered by ritual specialists as they lead the dead away from the world of the living to fully developed and clearly enunciated speeches comparable in elaboration and formality to those delivered on other occasions to the living. Despite the differences among these discursive forms, the messages they convey are basically the same, not only within the Rejogochi community but across the Rarámuri region as a whole and over the last century as well.

On the basis of research conducted around 1930 in four separate areas of Rarámuri country, Bennett and Zingg concluded, "The content of these sermons of advice to the dead are similar in all regions. The principal theme is that the man is now dead, is living in another world, and should not interfere with those left behind" (1935: 248). They provided in paraphrase one example of this counsel, delivered beside the corpse by the family members of the deceased:

> The man was told that he was now dead and was going to live in another world. They said that he must not worry, for he would be given food for his journey, and three *fiestas* (four, in the case of a woman), so that he could travel well to heaven. They asked him to leave all his things on earth for his family and not to return to molest or frighten them. Above all, he was urged not to return in the form of an animal to do damage to the herds and crops (1935: 237).

These themes predominate in speeches to the dead recorded by Lumholtz in the last decade of the nineteenth century. In fact, the content of one speech he documented is almost identical to that of the speeches summarized by Bennett and Zingg:

> Now be off to the other world; we don't want you here any longer, now that you are dead. He who is above us will carry you off. What do you wish here, wandering around like a coyote? Go away from us. We don't want you. Therefore we give you provisions for the journey (Lumholtz 1894: 444).

This speech was given by each member of the deceased's family (excluding the children presumably) at the end of the ritual held for him one year after his death. Lumholtz also heard speeches addressed to corpses prior to burial that were essentially the same as those delivered in these rituals. He recorded one remarkable example in which the aged father-in-law of a man who had committed suicide sat at the feet of the corpse near the mouth of the cave that was to become his tomb and engaged him in an imaginary dialogue:

> Why are you there?—Because I am dead.—Why are you dead?—Because I died.—Why did you die?—Because I chose to.—That is not right. You have no shame. Did your mother, who gave you birth, tell you to do this? You are bad. Tell me, why did you kill yourself?—Because I chose to do it.—Now what did you get for it, lying there, as you are, with stones on top of you? Were you not just playing the violin in the house with us? Why did you hang yourself in the tree?
>
> Here I leave this tesvino [maize beer] and food for you, the meat and tortillas, that you may eat and not come back. We do not want you any more. You are a fool. Now I am going to leave you here. You are not going to drink tesvino in the house with us any more. Remain here! Do not come to the house, for it would do you no good; we would burn you. Good-bye, go now; we do not want you any more! (1902, I: 388–89)

Such sentiments were not reserved for deceased adults alone. Lumholtz also reports that

> a mother says to her dead infant: "Now go away! Don't come back any more, now that you are dead. Don't come at night to nurse at my breast. Go away, and do not come back!" And the father says to the child: "Don't come back to ask me to hold your hand, or to do things for you. I shall not know you any more. Don't come walking around here, but stay away" (1902, I: 382).

In Rejogochi, the most elaborate and formal speeches to the dead that I heard were delivered not in rituals devoted specifically to the dead but in annual curing ceremonies for the community's crops and livestock. Each year in June or July, various households pool their resources to sponsor a ceremony in which a doctor and several assistants meander through their fields and by their corrals to cure their maize and livestock. The assistants sprinkle medicines over the plants and animals to protect them from harm and to encourage their growth. The doctor performs several ritual acts to ward off hail, lightning, and the Devil and delivers speeches along the way, encouraging the plants and animals to have strength and to live according to what is proper for them. He also scans the fields and corrals searching for the *rumugá* of the plants and animals, which only he and other people with special knowledge can see. In its circuit of the valley, the curing procession always stops at the local cemetery so that the doctor can destroy the *rumugá* of the dead people there (which continue to grow from the crowns of their heads even after death), and to give the dead beer and advice. I recorded the curing of the dead and the accompanying speech at the Rejogochi cemetery on two occasions, once in 1981 and once in 1984. The following description is from June 27, 1981.

When the procession arrived at the cemetery, the doctor planted the cross he was carrying at the edge and his assistants sat down to watch. The doctor walked past a bucket of beer that had been placed at the foot of a grave in the middle of the row of graves and on to the large wooden cross in the middle of the cemetery. Standing in front, he crossed himself and then began staring fixedly at each side of the cross. Every few seconds he found a *rumugá* and either cut it with a knife or burned it with the tips of three smoldering corn cobs. Then he proceeded down the row of graves. In some cases, he passed the knife and corn cobs over the graves and around the crosses at their heads. When he saw no *rumugá* he passed to the next grave.

When he completed the survey of the graves, he placed the corn cobs around the cross of the central grave and stuck the knife in the ground next to them. Then he told an assistant to give beer to the dead. The assistant stood at the foot of the central grave and sprinkled small portions of beer over the grave and to the other directions. The doctor then joined him and delivered the following speech to the dead:

> Now this is what I say to you people who live here. May you have strength. We have brought you the beer that you have been awaiting. We do not always bring you food; we often eat it ourselves instead. But always have strength and live contentedly here. Do not let yourselves become disheartened or sad, I say to you. Fill yourselves with this beer in a beautiful fashion. Sit calmly talking to one another and thinking well so that you will talk straight.
>
> I have come here for a reason. Others have sent me; I could not come on my own. I am standing here saying this to you. I was sent to say these things.
>
> Each one of you, may you always have strength every day and every night as you go about.
>
> From the beginning of time, we all have had the same kind of soul, but now your bodies and souls have been split apart. But do not be disheartened or sad. Have a long, contented existence. We all must lose our souls [i.e., die]. Do not be sad or discouraged. When someone makes

beer they will feel compassion for you and will bring a bucketful here for you to drink. So drink your fill with strength and always sit contentedly talking among yourselves.

We all are the children of Our Father and the children of Our Mother. We have the same parents, not different ones. This is how it is for all of us.

You older people, give all the children here good advice. They still cannot think well. Help them as they learn gradually how to think well. Do not come to the houses of the living to cause them harm. Concern yourselves for your own well-being. We will bring you food and beer so you will not be hungry and thirsty. Be contented.

This is what I have to say to you. These are the words of Our Father. These words are all I have to say. Thank you.

Then the doctor extended his arms out to his sides and drew them to his chest, calling the dead together. At the same time a few of his assistants responded to his speech in the standard fashion, "Thank you. It is good," to which the doctor replied "It is good. Thank you. May you all have strength." Then the men gathered to drink the beer from the bucket that had been brought to the cemetery. When they finished it, the doctor told the dead that we were returning upstream to the house where the procession had begun, and we left.

The man who gave this speech was an accomplished orator who had developed his skills during several terms as a leading pueblo official. This experience is reflected in his adoption of the rapid speech style of sermons delivered in the pueblo center and his use of several standard phrases from these sermons, in particular the admonitions that the dead should have strength and avoid becoming disheartened and the instructions on how they should behave while drinking. In addition, he established the legitimacy of his words by portraying them as coming from God and describing a situation that had existed from the beginning of the world, rhetorical devices often used in formal speeches to the living.

This speech incorporates several themes, all of which relate ultimately to the relationship between the living and the dead. The doctor indicated the physical and social separation of the living and the dead by addressing the dead (that is, their souls) as the people who live at the cemetery and by identifying himself to them as the representative of the living. To encourage the dead not to harm the living, he emphasized their commonality of spirit and parentage and that they both would eventually share the fate of death. At the same time, while specifying the separation of the body and souls as the principal difference between the living and the dead, he minimized the significance of this distinction and its implications for the possibility of a contented existence in the afterlife.

In describing the interaction between the living and the dead, the speaker mentioned only offerings of food and drink that the living would bring to the cemetery. The hunger and thirst of the dead that these offerings are supposed to satisfy perhaps can be interpreted as standing for all the desires and emotions that the dead feel for the living. However, in my understanding of the speech, the image of offerings is not used like the exchanges of food and beer mentioned in the pueblo sermons to summarize a complex set of social interactions. Rather these offerings represent the only kind of interaction that should take place between the living and the dead. The dead are not expected to reciprocate these offerings but only to wait patiently for them and to refrain from going to the houses of the living. The promise of offerings is made not to establish a relation of balanced reciprocity with the dead but, as in the case of offerings to the Devil and "diseases," to neutralize a potential threat.

The dead are encouraged to create their own society, forgetting about the living and concerning themselves exclusively with their own well-being. They are asked to provide the children among them the guidance they require to develop the ability to think well, thereby fulfilling the social role that the living parents of these children no longer can. Here as in the speech as a whole, the intention is to convince the dead that their current situation is not unfortunate and that they should accept it and strive to be contented.

DEATH PRACTICES AND THE CONCEPT OF SOUL

The death practices of the Rarámuri allow the bereaved to acknowledge death and to define it in such a way that its unpleasant reality and their grief can be dealt with by practical action. At the same time, these practices communicate considerable information about souls and several other topics. Because they are both discursive and nondiscursive in nature, the way in which these practices contribute to the reproduction of the concept of soul within Rarámuri society is analogous to that of the health practices discussed in the last chapter.

The Rarámuri's health practices transmit a broad range of information, from the relationship between the souls and the body to that between the

Rarámuri and the whole universe. In contrast, the death practices focus only on the dead and their relationship to the living, but because the discursive component of death practices is more elaborate than that of health practices, they explicitly convey more information. In addition, all discourse about the dead and many of the nondiscursive practices directed toward them contain some information about souls because the dead are identified as souls. This identification is publicly established both by calling the dead *ariwá* and *iwigá* (soul[s]) and through a variety of practices that treat the dead as souls, that is, as the animate aspect of people that persists after death.

Death frequently is a topic of informal conversations within households and the larger community. Speculation on the cause of specific deaths always occurs, and accounts of encounters between the living and the dead circulate rapidly and widely among households, particularly if these happen while the people are awake. A family's failure to sponsor death rituals at the designated times also is the subject of much gossip, and any misfortunes they may experience, such as illnesses or the death of a child, often are attributed to the anger they have provoked in the dead.

The formal public presentation of discursive information about the dead takes places almost exclusively in the speeches delivered to them in ritual contexts. These speeches convey, explicitly and implicitly, a great deal of information about the Rarámuri concept of the dead and their relations with the living. The simple performance of the speeches asserts that the dead are a real although invisible audience. It also indicates that the dead can understand the spoken words of the living and thus are animate and sentient, and that communication between the living and dead is possible, especially through the mediation of specialists who are portrayed as the representatives of the community to the dead. By taking place at the cemetery or by directing the dead back to the cemetery from the sites of the rituals, the speeches define the proper location of the dead within the space of their everyday world and indicate that the living and dead share this world.

Occasionally souls are explicitly mentioned in these speeches. For example, the doctor who delivered the speech during the maize and animal curing ceremony characterized the separation of the body and souls as the cause of death and the basic feature distinguishing the living from the dead. Almost in the same breath, he stated that the living and the dead have the same kind of soul and that they derive ultimately from the same parents.

The idea that the dead are in many respects the same as the living pervades the speeches and other ritual acts directed toward them. The dead are portrayed as retaining individual identities and as forming social relations, both among the living and the dead. In fact, the dead pose a threat to the living because of these similarities. They try to perpetuate their relations with the living because of emotional attachment and because they have many of the same needs, which the living are obliged to help them meet. In the concluding speeches of the *napisó* ritual, the dead are told that the living have fulfilled all their obligations to them and that all relations between them should end. In the curing speech, the adults among the dead are told to assume responsibility for the proper upbringing of the dead children of the living, in other words, to establish their own separate society, the relations within which should replace those between the living and the dead.

Because the dead are souls, almost everything said about the dead can easily be rephrased to apply to all souls. Such messages include that souls are animate, that they can live apart from the bodies of the living, that they are social beings, and so on. Given the obvious inanimacy of corpses, it does not require a major speculative leap for the Rarámuri to conclude from such ideas that their own animacy derives from their souls. The only idea about the dead that is not extended to souls in general is that contact with them always endangers the living. The Rarámuri maintain that the souls of the living can interact with one another with impunity, as they frequently do in dreams.

Because these speeches are discursive, the information they explicitly convey can be assimilated more or less directly into the discursive consciousnesses of the people who hear them. In addition, these speeches enable discursive knowledge about souls to be communicated through the nondiscursive acts in these death rituals. They explain to the dead and thus to the living the general purpose of the rituals. They also indicate that the dead are the objects of the ritual actions and, perhaps more importantly, that the small crosses used in the rituals represent the dead.

As I argued in the last chapter, the principal means by which nondiscursive acts can convey discursive knowledge is through the process of enactment, which requires that this knowledge be represented in the acts by markers. In death rituals, the souls of the dead are regarded as human actors, albeit distinct from the living participants, and their presence is marked in part by the living acting as if they are there but more tangibly by the small crosses. These crosses are offered food and drink, moved from place to place, spoken to by the doctors who direct the activities, and eventually removed from the domain of the living. Since the identification of these crosses with the dead is explicit, all the actions taken with respect to them can be interpreted unambiguously by everyone present as interactions with the dead and thus with souls.

In addition to such information, these nondiscursive practices, like those associated with curing, convey considerable information about such things as the proper use of the body, the organization of space and time, the categories upon which Rarámuri life and society are based, and the nature of the relations among the various segments of society. Together with the discursive practices to which they are linked, they also communicate ideas that are basic to the concept of soul and to their understanding of death, including that souls exist and that death is caused by the permanent separation of the souls from the body. However, the ideas transmitted through these practices represent only a small portion of Rarámuri thought on such subjects. Among other things, the elaborate ideas they maintain about the causes of death and the activities of the dead in the afterlife are expressed in these rituals only rarely and then only briefly. In addition, more general ideas about the universe upon which a fuller interpretation of these death practices depends are transmitted outside these ritual contexts, for the most part in informal conversations.

The contexts within which such ideas are presented obviously affect the extent to which people will agree on them. The death practices convey information in public settings through ritual forms that are sanctioned by tradition and from which debate is excluded. Of course, there always is room for alternative interpretations of ritual acts and scepticism about the accuracy of the ideas they convey, but such doubts tend not to be raised during the rituals themselves. In addition, as discussed in the previous chapter, the enactment of ideas, despite its limitations as a form of communication, is an effective way of establishing their legitimacy. By enacting ideas, people simultaneously embody and participate in them. The ideas acquire an emotional and sensual as well as conceptual reality, especially in emotionally charged contexts like death rituals.

The public presentation of information does not necessarily guarantee that it will be understood by everyone present or that it will be diffused widely within the society. In the Rarámuri's death rituals, the specialists sometimes whisper or mumble the words they impart to the dead, and even when they speak clearly, the number of people who actually hear them at any time seldom exceeds fifteen or twenty. On the other hand, because the ideas conveyed by these words are presented redundantly in several different contexts, everyone is exposed to them eventually. Moreover, people from many different settlements attend the larger death rituals like the *napisó* and often rely on the same small group of doctors to perform them. As in the Rarámuri's curing practices, the performance of these rituals places constraints on the ways in which individuals develop their ideas about the dead and souls in general, increasing the likelihood that certain ideas will be widely shared within the society.

CONCLUSIONS

The emerging consensus among anthropologists that small-scale societies cannot be portrayed as ideologically homogeneous represents a major advance over the earlier dominant view that such homogeneity not only characterized these societies but was necessary for their existence (Durkheim 1933). Yet simply acknowledging the presence of ideological diversity or, as is done in many studies of intracultural variation, mapping it out across the divisions of society, is insufficient. Such approaches in effect deny the relationship between knowledge and practice and create a false image of knowledge as a static system of ideas rather than an unfinished, dynamic process.

In the preceding excursion through Rarámuri history, oratory, philosophy, and ritual, I have attempted to avoid this sort of reification by examining the processes by which the Rarámuri concept of soul is reproduced within the society. The Rarámuri convey information about souls in public primarily during the performance of their curing and death rituals. The topic of souls also emerges in informal conversations among the members of the same and neighboring households, particularly in their discussions of dreams and their diagnoses of illnesses. Only a small number of the ideas that make up the concept of soul are explicitly transmitted in these contexts, but this information provides common points of departure from which people develop their individual concepts of soul, establishing some constraints on the directions in which their thinking will proceed. People interpret the ideas to which they are exposed, evaluating them against their experiences, establishing connections to other ideas, and creating new ideas. That in the course of this mostly private process different individuals frequently should arrive at the same conclusions reflects the existence of additional constraints on their thinking that derive from the logical relations among the ideas in question.

In my investigation of the Rarámuri concept of soul, I discovered that people shared basic ideas about the relationship between the body and souls, the contributions of souls to human existence, and, at a general level at least, the explanations of most physiological states. They tended to disagree on the number of souls each person possesses, how the souls are organized within the body, the fate of souls in the afterlife, how to account for sleep, and in specific details of the explanations of other states. For the most part, consensus occurred on higher-level ideas within the concept but also on some lower-level ideas while variation was associated with other lower-level ideas. This pattern expresses the tendency for people to agree on ideas that either are conveyed in public contexts or are logically presupposed by these ideas and to disagree on ideas that are neither communicated in public settings nor contingent upon those that are. However, this generalization does not account for all the data, the most notable exception being the consensus found on the explanation of inebriation.

Neither logical constraints nor the information about souls presented publicly requires people to explain intoxication by the departure of one or more of a person's souls nor to reject the obvious alternative that attributes inebriation to the intoxication of the souls themselves. As I discussed in chapter 4, different people agree on how to explain inebriation because they establish similar connections between lower- and higher-level ideas from different domains of their knowledge. However, because they are not compelled to take such wider concerns into consideration in the process of creating their knowledge, consensus based on such connections is more likely to break down than that produced by constraints on variation deriving from the public presentation of information or the logical relationships among ideas. In fact, Mariano Sikóchi and Cornelio Rowhárare differed in their explanations of sleep precisely because Cornelio linked his explanation to more general cosmological ideas while Mariano did not.

The basic principles and conditions that determine how the concept of soul is reproduced within Rarámuri society apply not only to the reproduction of other segments of Rarámuri knowledge but to the reproduction of knowledge in all societies. The reproduction of all knowledge involves at a minimum two steps: the transmission of information through social practices, and the incorporation, organization, and elaboration of this information by individuals. As I argued in chapter 3, the reproduction of different kinds of knowledge requires different kinds of practices. Nondiscursive practices can partially communicate certain kinds of discursive knowledge, and they often endow the knowledge with an experiential dimension that transmission in words alone cannot provide. Similarly, discursive practices can set the stage for the reproduction of nondiscursive knowledge and supply the conceptual frameworks into which this knowledge is incorporated. Ultimately, however, discursive and nondiscursive forms of knowledge depend respectively on discursive and nondiscursive practices for their reproduction. Recognizing this basic condition for the reproduction of different kinds of knowledge is important to avoid assuming that practices of one kind are capable of conveying knowledge of the other, for example, that nonverbal ritual acts alone can reproduce complex cosmologies.

The transmission of information through social practices does not guarantee that knowledge will be reproduced automatically and immutably (Bourdieu 1977: 23; Williams 1977: 36). People often transform knowledge by applying it in practice and never explicitly spell out all the implications and interconnections of the ideas they present. As Hefner (1985: 269) notes, "even the most public and conventionalized of cultural media—myths, liturgies, ideological charters—are never conveyed as finished meanings, their significance specified from within." To be reproduced, the information transmitted in social practices must be interpreted by individuals who develop it in potentially idiosyncratic and innovative ways in the course of their thinking.

The cognitive operations by which people interpret and elaborate knowledge are determined in the last instance by the nature of the human brain, but several factors intervene to affect the process. The extent of people's mental development obviously affects how they incorporate information as does the relevance of the information to them, which in turn reflects their unique life histories and positions in the society at the time of the transmission. In addition, people seldom integrate new information without first evaluating the authority of its source and its plausibility in terms of the social and intellectual contexts within which they live.

The reproduction of knowledge thus depends on the reproduction of the grounds of interpretation and evaluation, of the social relations and institutions through which it is accomplished, and of the general social environments within which the knowledge is rendered both appropriate and compelling (Eickelman 1979; Hefner 1985). At the same time, because society is reproduced through the agency of its members acting on the basis of their knowledge of the world, this knowledge must be reproduced if action is to occur. In addition, such knowledge often performs an ideological function by portraying current social arrangements as part of the natural order of the universe, thereby motivating the practices that perpetuate these arrangements.

Conceived in this way, the reproduction of knowledge, while a social process, begins and ends with the individual. However, this reproduction also takes place on the level of the society as a whole, as reflected in the distribution of knowledge among its members. The social distribution of knowledge encompasses not only the possession of different kinds of knowledge by the members of different segments of a society but also the consensus and disagreement associated with all knowledge within a society, regardless if it is restricted in distribution or generally available. In this second sense, the social distribution of knowledge is the product of the dialectical relation between the creative potential of human thought and constraints on this creativity that derive from the social and logical contexts within which the thought takes place.

A particular segment of knowledge likely will be widely shared if it is presented to people from throughout the society, either during general public gatherings or in activities that are repeated in many different settings.[1] Whether a particular body of knowledge is transmitted in such contexts depends upon its relevance to the practices that take place within them. In some cases, knowledge provides the basic understandings and skills that enable actors to produce the practices. Such practical relevance contrasts with what might be termed "categorical relevance," in which the knowledge participates in the same conceptual fields as the practices but is not immediately involved in their actual production. Actors often draw upon such knowledge to define and pursue their interests and to interpret and rationalize practices.

Practices invariably display some of the nondiscursive practical knowledge that is required for their production. When people play musical instruments, for example, they demonstrate their techniques, providing the people who witness their performances the basis for reproducing this knowledge through imitation. In contrast, practices may not convey any of the discursive knowledge that is categorically or practically relevant to them, particularly if these practices are entirely nonverbal. Whether specific practices transmit such knowledge and, if so, the kinds of knowledge they convey, varies from practice to practice, determined in each case by the complex interplay of various historical, social, and ideological factors. Nonetheless, ideas that address basic concerns or are logically presupposed by many other ideas tend to be relevant to a range of practices and thus to appear implicitly or explicitly more frequently than ideas with more specific significance.

The contexts within which knowledge is communicated have a major impact on its distribution among the members of society, but this distribution also is influenced by factors that affect how people incorporate and elaborate the information they receive from others. In the case of discursive knowledge, the internal relations among ideas place important constraints on the ways in which different people develop the knowledge. These relations include the more compelling one of logical presupposition, which requires the acceptance of an idea upon which other accepted ideas are contingent, and the weaker one of suggestion, which inclines people to reach similar conclusions on the basis of shared ideas. In the construction of their knowledge, individuals also extend beyond sets of closely related ideas to establish connections among ideas in disparate domains. The result can be either agreement or disagreement in the knowledge held by different people as well as contradictions in the ideas of one person. Such diversity is possible because ideas in different domains tend not to be linked by relations of logical presupposition.

These social and cognitive factors affect the reproduction of all knowledge within a society, but the patterns of consensus and variation associated with different areas of knowledge seldom are identical. Since logical constraints on variation are intrinsic to the knowledge, they apply equally in all areas. Differences in the extent of variation in different domains of knowledge thus reflect differences in the relationship between the knowledge and public practices. In the case of Rarámuri theoretical knowledge, for example, there is widespread consensus in ideas directly relevant to the proper conduct of social life because these ideas are explicitly conveyed in both private households and public speeches and reinforced through application in social interaction. Similarly, certain elements of cosmological knowledge are widely shared because they are relevant to the performance of a diversity of practices and provide the ideological foundation for the authority of the pueblo officials, whose speeches ensure that this knowledge remains part of everyday life. In contrast, considerable variation is found in knowledge that tends to be transmitted only within households and to maintain few direct connections to public practices, for example, in folktales.

Given the processes by which knowledge is reproduced, the existence of some variation among the members of a society is inevitable. The extent of such individual variation presumably varies from society to society, but it cannot be assumed that it increases simply as a function of population size, that is, that ideological variation always is greater in larger societies than in smaller ones. The social integration of increasing numbers of people tends to be accompanied by the emergence of formal institutions intended to standardize their knowledge in order to facilitate the coordination of their activities. Such institutions either do not exist or are less elaborate in societies with smaller populations. In addition, societies with comparable populations can range from highly centralized to diffuse in political organization and residence patterns, which in turn affect patterns of social interaction, the relationship between knowledge and social process, and thus the ways in which knowledge is reproduced among their members. On the other hand, ideological variation potentially is of greater consequence in larger societies because they tend to be characterized by more extensive internal divisions and social inequality. In such contexts, differences in ideas can become the focus of conflict between the members of competing social segments. In smaller, more egalitarian societies, a diversity of ideas, especially in theoretical knowledge like the concept of soul, seldom is assigned political significance.

The presence of ideological variation in all societies indicates that knowledge is embedded in social process and is created and recreated by thinking individuals in the course of their lives. When this variation cuts across generational lines, as in the case of the Rarámuri concept of soul, it suggests that the members of the society are reproducing preexisting variation rather than transforming the knowledge, but the possibility for ideological change always exists. People modify their knowledge to eliminate logical inconsistencies, to accommodate new ideas, or to bring it more in line with the external conditions in the world around them. As Giddens (1979, 1984) and Sahlins (1981) have noted, the circumstances within which people act and the consequences of their actions do not inevitably conform to the actors' understandings of and anticipations for them. Discrepancies between conceptions and expectations on the one hand and circumstances and consequences on the other can encourage individuals to make changes in their knowledge and in the practices enabled by it.

Some changes in the Rarámuri concept of soul possibly could occur in those areas where the opportunity for choice or elaboration exists, through minor shifts in emphasis or the creation of different connections between the concept and more general ideas. A wholesale reformulation on strictly internal intellectual grounds alone is improbable, however, since the concept is largely nonfalsifiable. Should extensive change take place, it most likely will result from challenges to Rarámuri thought emanating from the larger Mexican society in which they increasingly participate.

Rarámuri medical theory is the area of the concept of soul most vulnerable to change because the Rarámuri can evaluate the efficacy of their curing practices against that of the procedures of Western medicine. Although explanations for failure are always possible in both systems, the Rarámuri have already modified their thinking in this area, as evidenced in their conclusion that Western doctors can cure certain kinds of illnesses, although not those resulting from soul loss or sorcery (see chapter 5). In effect, while continuing to rely on the concept of soul to understand and address most health-related matters, they have created a niche for Western medicine in their scheme of things. This niche potentially will expand in response to pressures to accept Western medicine being brought to bear on them by government representatives and missionaries.

Should the Rarámuri conclude that Western doctors are more effective than their own in treating *all* kinds of illnesses, the social role of doctor in Rarámuri society will be undermined along with the etiology these specialists apply in their practice. Such a transformation would have a major impact on the concept of soul. The Rarámuri's curing practices, together with those associated with death, sustain the concept of soul. By presenting ideas about souls in public contexts, the curing practices provide the basis for the reproduction of the concept within the society as a whole. In addition, considerable revision in the realm of cosmology would likely result since the majority of beings who populate the Rarámuri's universe are relevant to human affairs only because they they impinge on people's health. Perhaps most significantly, the adoption of Western medicine would shift the relations of dependence between the Rarámuri and their doctors from within Rarámuri society to the outside, increasing their subordination within the regional economy and society.

Given the compartmentalization of ideas within the concept of soul, however, changes in the beliefs and practices related to matters of health would not necessarily result in pervasive modifications in other areas nor the rejection of the concept as a whole. To the contrary, the persistence of this knowledge in some form seems assured, for it is crucial to Rarámuri life. While in content it is abstract and metaphysical, it is linked to the most basic concerns of human existence and perpetuated through the concrete social practices that address these concerns. For the immediate future, the most likely prospect is the continued reproduction of the concept of soul as a dynamic body of thought central to the practical consciousness through which the Rarámuri understand and experience their world.

ACKNOWLEDGMENTS

The completion of this study was possible because many people generously provided their assistance and encouragement. My greatest debt is to my wife Cecilia Troop who, in the decade since we arrived in Rejogochi, has been an unfailing source of intellectual stimulation and moral support. While living in Rejogochi, she has been an enthusiastic fieldworker, providing invaluable insights into Rarámuri culture and, through her contacts with the women of Rejogochi, collecting information to which I otherwise would have had no access. During the writing of this book, she also has assumed much more than her share of the responsibilities for running our household and raising our children. For her help, understanding, and love, I will always be grateful.

I also am deeply indebted to the residents of the *ejido* of Basíhuare and particularly to the members of the Rejogochi community for their goodwill throughout the time we have lived among them. The contributions of a number of these people have been crucial to the success of our research but, to protect their privacy, I am unable to mention them by name. To all I am grateful for their assistance and consideration and for so profoundly enriching our lives by allowing us to share in theirs.

A special thanks must be extended to the staff of the Tarahumara Mission in Creel, Chihuahua, and especially to Father Luis Verplancken, who has helped us in innumerable ways over the years. I also am very grateful to Cecilia's parents, Harry and Ana Luisa Troop, for their hospitality during my research in the archives of Mexico City, and to my own parents for their continual encouragement and support.

For their invaluable assistance during my investigation of Rarámuri history, I would like to express my appreciation to Luis González Rodríguez, Liborio Villagomez Guzmán, Manuel Pérez Alonso, David Marley, José Luis

Mirafuentes Galván, Susan Poniatowski, Phyllis Gron, Félix Zubillaga, Roberto Beristáin, Paul Vanderwood, and Christon Archer. I am especially indebted to Luis González Rodríguez for his guidance in the initial stages of this project and for his careful research on this topic, which has greatly facilitated the work of those of us who follow him.

The initial version of this book served as my doctoral dissertation at the University of Michigan. I would like to thank Gary Witherspoon, Dick Ford, Ray Kelly, Skip Rappaport, Vern Carroll, and Jack Meiland for their guidance and support during its completion.

For her assistance in preparing the manuscript for publication, I am especially grateful to my editor, Michelle Smith, whose intelligence, insight, and considerable editorial skill contributed immeasurably to shaping its final form.

I also benefited enormously from the critical readings of a number of other friends and colleagues. Mary Jo Arnoldi, Michael Brown, Don Burgess, Bob Bye, George Carlson, Claus Deimel, Daniel Goodwin, Martha Graham, Bob Hefner, Ivan Karp, John Kennedy, Henry Selby, Cecilia Troop, and Luis Verplancken generously took time to comment on earlier drafts of the book, and Kris Hardin, Jake Homiak, and Sergei Kan provided crucial advice on specific sections.

Bob Bye, Richard Vari, and Ronald Hodges kindly assisted me in making botanical and zoological identifications, and Don Burgess, Ives Goddard, Eva Berinstein, and John Ahala provided much-needed guidance in linguistic matters. I also would like to thank Darla Hawkins for her help in preparing the manuscript and Julie Perlmutter and Victor Krantz for their care in producing the illustrations.

Permission to use excerpts from published works or unpublished manuscripts was kindly granted by the following institutions: American Philosophical Society Library, Archivo General de la Nación (Mexico City), Archivum Romanum Societatis Iesu, Bancroft Library, Farrar, Straus and Giroux, Harlan Davidson, and University of Pennsylvania Press.

Finally, I am grateful to the University of Michigan, the National Institute of Mental Health, and the Smithsonian Institution for providing the financial and logistical support that has made my research and writing possible.

NOTES

CHAPTER 1. RARÁMURI KNOWLEDGE

1. Deimel (1980: 12) points out that the term "Rarámuri" does not appear in the literature as a designation for these people until the early nineteenth century (Tellechea 1826), "Tarahumara" and related terms ("Tarahumar," "Tarahumare," "Tarahumari," etc.) being the only names employed for them in documents of the Spanish colonial period. Whether the Rarámuri referred to themselves as "Rarámuri" in the seventeenth and eighteenth centuries is unknown, as is the historical relationship between "Rarámuri" and "Tarahumara."

2. To protect the privacy of the people of Rejogochi, I use fictitious names throughout.

CHAPTER 2. THE RARÁMURI

1. Rarámuri settlements in the adjacent states of Durango, Sinaloa, and Sonora have been noted by Passin (1943: 361), in Durango and Sinaloa by Pennington (1963: map 2), and in Sinaloa by Eugene Boudreau (1981: personal communication). Françoise Brouzés (1981: personal communication) also reports the seasonal migration of Rarámuri agricultural laborers into Sinaloa and Durango, and Rarámuri people have entered the United States since at least the 1940s, both legally (David Challinor 1987: personal communication) and illegally. According to the 1980 Mexican census (Secretaría de Programación y Presupuesto 1982–84), there are Rarámuri people living in every state of the Mexican Republic. Of the 62, 419 recorded speakers of the Rarámuri language over five years of age, 56,400 reside in Chihuahua, 2, 124 in Sinaloa, and 1, 074 in Sonora. The Rarámuri speakers in the remaining twenty-nine states number less than a thousand per state, ranging from the 718 in Durango to the one speaker found in Tabasco.

2. Several writers have reported a tendency or even a requirement that postmarital residence begin with the wife's family (Neumann 1682; Lumholtz 1902, I: 270; Bennett and Zingg 1935: 226–27; Passin 1943: 485), but in Rejogochi the economic circumstances of the families involved seems to be the principal determining factor (cf. Passin 1943: 485–86; Kennedy 1978: 176–79).

3. This document appears in English translation in Sheridan and Naylor (1979: 73–78), where the location of Estrada is incorrectly given as "Tomochi" rather than "Themeichi," as it appears in the original document.

4. This and all other translations of quoted material in the text are mine unless noted otherwise.

5. The Jesuit mission system among the Rarámuri was divided into a number of mission units called *partidos*. Each *partido* consisted of a principal settlement, or *cabecera*, in which one or more priests resided, and one to several subordinate settlements, called *visitas*, which the missionaries visited as circumstances permitted.

6. Census data on which this figure is based indicated only Rarámuri speakers five years of age and older. I define the boundaries of the "Sierra" on the basis of the list of *municipios* in which Rarámuri people lived in 1945 (Plancarte 1954: 101–2).

7. Pennington (1963: 51) reports that Rarámuri from the Guagueybo area formerly used bat guano to fertilize their corn. Today some Rarámuri in Rejogochi have begun using commercial fertilizers, but because goat, sheep, and cow manures are cheaper and more readily available, they continue to be their principal forms of fertilizer.

8. In his translation of Ratkay's report, González Rodríguez (1982: 187) renders the Rarámuri name for this paradise as *osomachigüi*. I have been unable to determine the meaning of this term.

CHAPTER 3. RARÁMURI SERMONS AND THE REPRODUCTION OF KNOWLEDGE

1. In their book *Reproduction in Education, Society and Culture*, Bourdieu and Passeron (1977) focus not so much on the reproduction of knowledge per se but on the reproduction of society, especially asymmetrical power relations, through the processes and institutions of pedagogy.

2. My distinction between nondiscursive and unconscious knowledge differs slightly from the classification of knowledge offered by Sperber (1975: x), who combines the two into the single category of unconscious knowledge.

3. Of course, while nondiscursive practices are by definition nonverbal, discursive practices, because they are speech acts, always have a nondiscursive dimension.

4. This phrase literally means "they are good baptized people," *pagótame* meaning "one(s) who is (are) baptized," but whether people have received the sacrament of baptism is regarded as irrelevant to their being "good people."

5. The Rarámuri have several different names for these deities. In addition to "Our Father" (*tamuhé onorá* or *kéte onó*), they refer to the male deity as "The One Who is Father" (*onorúame*) and "The One Who Lives Above" (*mi paní bitéame*). Another name, *táta riósi* or simply *riósi*, derives from the Spanish *dios* (god) combined with the Rarámuri term *táta* (father) to mean "God the Father." The Rarámuri of Rejogochi employ the terms *táta riósi* and *riósi* to refer not only to God the Father but to other beings who are associated with him, including his wife, the offspring of their sexual union, and the envoys he dispatches to earth, who are known as God's "captains" (*kapitáne*) or "soldiers" (*sontárasi*). They call the female deity "Our Mother" (*tamuhé yéra* or *kéte ye*), "The One Who Is Mother" (*iyerúame*), and "God's wife," formed by combining any of the names for God and *upíra* (wife). They also refer to her as *chíchi*, which means both "mother" and "breast." Some people in Rejogochi identify these deities as the Sun (*rayénare*) and Moon (*michá*), but others conceive of these celestial bodies as these deities' houses, which move across the sky like airplanes. Still others regard them as torches carried by the peons of God and his wife, or mirrors, flashlights, or light bulbs that traverse the sky at the bidding of these deities.

6. Rarámuri orators give their speeches at a rate of approximately five hundred syllables per minute compared to the pace of around three hundred syllables per minute characteristic of ordinary conversation. The speed of utterance of Rarámuri speakers in normal conversation falls at about midpoint in the range of speech rates determined by Chiba (1935: 115–23) for nine different languages (expressed in syllables per minute rounded to the nearest whole number): Japanese 476; Russian 348; Korean 345; Hindustani 314; French 269; German 265; Mongolian 259; Chinese 256; and English 232. Fónagy and Magdics (1960) report an average speech rate for Hungarian (both read material and spontaneous conversation) of 681 syllables (or "sounds") per minute, which far exceeds that of any of the languages analyzed by Chiba.

7. In some pueblos, where the influence of the Jesuit missionaries is particularly strong, the sermons of the Rarámuri political officials often incorporate some of the ideas presented by the priests in Mass (Velasco Rivero 1983: 129–30).

8. The division of sermons into separate sections for men and women is a standard feature of Basíhuare sermons but seems not to characterize speeches from other areas (Lumholtz 1902, I: 348–49; Bennett 1931).

9. The Rarámuri of the Basíhuare area assume that the Devil is married, but they seldom mention the Devil's wife. She figures in cosmological accounts only as the mother of non-Indians, playing no other role in the operation of the universe.

10. The Rarámuri of Basíhuare see the robes in which saints invariably are portrayed as dresses and consequently identify saints as female.

11. The term *sukurúame* is employed as both an adjective and a noun to convey several distinct meanings of differing specificity. Most generally, it means "strange, unusual, unfamiliar, foreign, or mysterious" and can describe anything or anyone that appears out of the ordinary. More specifically, it describes individuals and objects capable of influencing the behavior or well-being of others by means that are not generally available and therefore are mysterious. Included here are "magical" stones as well as people who possess special knowledge acquired from God or the Devil that allows them to cause or alleviate illnesses. Catholic priests sometimes are described as *sukurúame* in this sense because the Rarámuri assume that their relation with God is particularly close. Most specifically, *sukurúame* designates sorcerers and contrasts with several terms the Rarámuri use for "doctor": *rimérike* (possibly from Spanish *remedio*, "remedy"), *rotóri* (from Spanish *doctor*), and *owirúame*, "one who cures." It also is applied to the animals and objects that sorcerers employ in their sorcery. In this sense, *sukurúame* has clearly evil connotations.

12. In other Rarámuri pueblos, gentiles are mentioned for precisely this reason, as, for example, in a sermon recorded by Wendell Bennett (1931) in the Samachique pueblo:

> If you were heathern [*sic*] you could stay out on your ranchos because you would not have a pueblo. We have a pueblo to which to come to pray every Sunday, all must come to see each other, and to give pleasure to the maestro. Also the Gob[ernador] wishes to see you all. When you do not come they are all sad. When you come they are happy.

This sermon, entitled "Gobernadors Sermon (As given in Spanish by Lorenzo V)," is filed with the papers of Jules Henry.

13. The etymology of "Rarámuri" has been the subject of much speculation but little agreement. The translation most frequently encountered is "footrunners" in reference to the Rarámuri's endurance in footracing and analyzed as *rará* (sole of the foot) plus *-mu-* from *ma* (to run) and the formative suffix *-ri* (Brambila [1980]: 451). However, Thord-Gray (1955: 436) does not discount the possibility that "Rarámuri" may have originally meant "tortoise foot (feet)" from *rara* (foot [feet]) and *múri* (tortoise) or to have been derived from *raramúri* (lightning or struck by lightning), a word phonetically identical to "Rarámuri" except for the shift in stress. Burgess (1984: 54) doubts the translation as "footrunners" and suggests

instead "that *ra* comes from *rayéna* 'sun' and that the word possibly means something like 'children of the sun-god.' "

14. There is one Native American group whose proper classification is problematical for the Rarámuri: the Apaches. In contemporary Rarámuri thought, the Apaches were ferocious killers who raided Rarámuri settlements until they were rounded up by soldiers and taken to the United States. The Apaches, they say, lived in caves in the forests and mountains surrounding the Rarámuri settlements and subsisted on wild foods except when they could plunder the Rarámuri's storehouses. Today the Rarámuri regard the Apaches as comparable to other monsters of the past, and the confusion associated with their classification derives primarily from the Rarámuri's lack of information about them. Their supposed habitation of the *kawichí* (wilds) and their failure to cultivate crops incline the Rarámuri to think of them more as wild animals than as human beings. In fact, soon after my arrival in Rejogochi, men began interrogating me about the Apaches in the United States, inquiring if they also killed *gringos* and if they were like human beings or animals. One man told me he had encountered some Apaches in Mexico City where he had been sent as a young man to study. From his description of these "Apaches," it became clear that he was referring to a cageful of monkeys he had seen at the zoo. If the Rarámuri came in contact with Apaches today, I suspect they would classify them as Rarámuri on the basis of their physical features. In the absence of such contacts, the Apaches remain apart, neither Rarámuri nor Chabochi and neither clearly human nor clearly animal.

15. Rarámuri oratory is not restricted to these sermons nor performed exclusively by political officials. As mentioned above, speeches that resemble them in both form and content are delivered during drinking parties and on various ritual occasions. Less formal examples of oratory emerge in group discussions as well as, fleetingly, when people argue and scold one another. Of the range of Rarámuri speech forms, however, the sermons are the most formalized and elaborate.

16. Speeches in other Rarámuri pueblos sometimes include more detailed information on a wider range of topics than those of Basíhuare, but none presents more than a small portion of Rarámuri theoretical knowledge (Velasco Rivero 1983: 123–31; Bennett 1931).

CHAPTER 4. THE CONCEPT OF SOUL

1. In the case of these as well as most other Rarámuri nouns, singular and plural forms are identical so that *ariwá* and *iwigá* denote both "soul" and "souls." Don Burgess (1986: personal communication) informs me that *ariwá* is rendered in the western dialect of Rarámuri as *alawá*. He suggests that both *ariwá* and *alawá* may derive ultimately from the Spanish word for "soul," *alma*.

2. This terminology, of course, reflects the sibling relations among the souls as viewed by a speaker outside the system; from the perspective of the souls themselves, the application of the terms "older sibling" and "younger sibling" depends on the position of a particular soul within the hierarchy.

3. According to some people, the largest soul of an individual is married to the largest soul of that individual's spouse so that the "soul spouses" live in separate bodies.

4. The identification of a person's largest soul as the husband and the next largest as the wife is from a male perspective. I do not know if Rarámuri women similarly classify their souls.

5. Of course, in the single soul view, the body is united with only one soul rather than a whole complement of souls.

6. Despite their associations with souls and life, some of these derived terms can describe inanimate objects. For example, a boulder that is difficult to dislodge or move is described as *we iwéame*. In this context, *iwéame* means "unyielding" rather than "strong," "forceful," or similar adjectives that, in English, have connotations of animacy.

7. Pastron (1977: 102–3) reports that the Rarámuri of the neighboring pueblo of Samachique believe that doctors "possess from birth a rare and innate ability" that enables them to cure, rather than receiving this ability from God at some point after birth.

8. Three terms mean "crazy" or "insane." *Uchuwátiri* (also pronounced *uchugátiri* and *wichuwátiri*) describes people whose behavior is strange, particularly if they are emotionally unstable. Brambila ([1980]: 599) indicates that the form *wichulátiri* is applied to females and *wichuwátiri* to males, but I did not encounter this gender distinction in Rejogochi. The term *ke richóti* is composed of a negative *ke* and the adjective *richóti*. In some Rarámuri communities, *richóti* (or *rechóti*) means "intelligent," "sensible," or "wise" (Brambila [1980]: 459), but in Rejogochi it is used only in conjunction with the negative to indicate the absence of good or intelligent thought. The related term *richarúame* is employed to indicate someone who thinks well. The adjective *lowíame* has connotations of the loss of bodily as well as mental control; rabid animals and people who are prone to excessive violence or exaggerated emotional displays are characterized as *lowíame*. Despite their reference to psychological disorders, however, all three terms are applied to people who act improperly but who, from a Western perspective, otherwise appear sane.

9. One man suggested that individuals who are particularly bad are not shamed by

such lectures. During them, they hang their heads not in shame but in conversation with the Devil from whom they derive their evil thought.

10. Burgess (1981: 13) notes that in other Rarámuri communities, this requirement extends to words, blood, tears, and fingernails.

11. The model of a hierarchy of propositions has been widely used to represent knowledge (see, for example, Kluckhohn and Leighton 1946; Albert 1956; Goodenough 1963; Werner 1970; Blackburn 1975; Witherspoon 1977; Rappaport 1979). Obviously this model cannot be appropriately applied to knowledge that is nonpropositional in form. However, the recognition that different kinds of knowledge exist does not require that they all be represented within a single framework. The fact that some knowledge is propositional in character and composed of ideas linked through logical relations has an important bearing on its reproduction. Such is the case with bodies of theoretical knowledge like the Rarámuri concept of soul.

CHAPTER 5. CURING PRACTICES

1. This discussion of Rarámuri medical practices applies only to the Rarámuri of the Basíhuare area. For information on these practices in other communities, see Lumholtz 1902, Basauri 1927 and 1929, Bennett and Zingg 1935, Passin 1942, Plancarte 1954, Pennington 1963, García Manzanedo 1963, Bye 1976 and 1985, Palma and Irigoyen R. 1977, Pastron 1977, Kennedy 1978, and Anzures y Bolaños 1978.

2. Not all ailments called *nawirí* are personified or believed to be sent directly from the Devil. Venereal disease (*bikarí*), for example, is considered *nawirí* but is said to be caused by the intermingling of body fluids that occurs during sexual intercourse with a Chabochi or with a Rarámuri contaminated by a Chabochi.

3. In contrast, Kennedy (1970b: 47) writes that in the area where he conducted his research, "A common direction of witchcraft accusation is toward a wife or husband," and in a later publication (1978: 137) he relates the case of a woman who reportedly had killed four of her husbands by sorcery.

4. Lumholtz (1902, I: 315), Bennett and Zingg (1935: 158), and Kennedy (1978: 136–37) all report that sorcerers can harm their victims simply by thinking ill of them. The residents of Rejogochi did not share this view entirely. For them, evil thoughts always precede acts of sorcery but it is the acts motivated by these thoughts and not the thoughts themselves that injure the victim.

5. Such control over lightning usually is associated exclusively with those individuals who have peyote as their ally.

6. Apparently the notion that the fontanelle can fall and cause a baby to become ill has been introduced to the Rarámuri by their Mestizo neighbors, which would explain why they feel Mestizos are better able to cure this malady than their own doctors.

7. The Rarámuri of Rejogochi never say that a person is taught to be a doctor by other human beings; they consider the possession of special knowledge from God to be sufficient as well as necessary. However, they also recognize that some doctors train assistants, often their spouses and children, in the curing arts and teach them certain special techniques, like how to suck foreign objects out of their patients. In addition, there is some indication that they think the ability to bewitch can be transmitted among humans. When a suspected sorcerer died in Rejogochi in 1978, several people suggested that his wife inherited his *oromá* —the birds, identified with shooting stars, which sorcerers dispatch to steal the souls of their victims—which she would then use for her own purposes.

8. These medicines include agave water and decoctions prepared from *aposí* (*Erythrina flabelliformis*) and *wasálowi* (possibly *Buddleja cordata* [Robert Bye 1986: personal communication]).

9. I phrase this description as if both doctor and patient are male. Most curers are men but some women also cure; obviously patients are both male and female.

10. A number of obvious exceptions exist to "prove" this generalization. A sharp slap to the face usually is less ambiguous than the statement "I hate you," which can be made passionately, playfully, ironically, or sarcastically and which requires nondiscursive, metacommunicational information for its proper interpretation. However, the generalization does hold when the entire range of discursive and nondiscursive phenomena is considered.

11. See Brown 1986 for a discussion of the relevance of the instrumental-versus-expressive distinction for the interpretation of such social forms.

CHAPTER 6. DEATH PRACTICES

1. In some Rarámuri communities, sexuality but not fertility emerges as a theme in death rituals. Bennett and Zingg (1935: 246) report that in rituals sponsored for a deceased female, men don women's clothing "as a regular part of the ceremony" (in Panalachi and Nararachi) or while running a ritual footrace (in Samachique). Kennedy describes the same symbolic gender reversals in comparable footraces staged in the gentile area of Inápuchi. He also indicates that the relatives with whom the deceased maintained joking relationships "dress in the clothing of the opposite sex and dance up to his belongings, kicking at them and making obscene

jokes and remarks. . . . To end the death fiesta, the male and female joking relatives carry on a mock combat with machetes or knives. The clashing of the blades is said to prevent the ghost from returning" (1978: 152–53). Except for this combat, these authors do not provide the Rarámuri's explanations for these acts nor an analysis of their more general significance. Symbolic reversals of this sort do not appear in the death rituals performed in Rejogochi.

2. Some people suggest that God occasionally reuses the souls of babies who die soon after birth, sending them to animate fetuses in areas distant from where the first babies lived. However, most maintain that such reincarnation does not occur.

3. Bennett and Zingg (1935: 127) provide an almost identical account of the origin of death, collected fifty years earlier in another area of Rarámuri country.

4. *Kálawi* derives from the root *ka-* (shadows or shade). Despite the connection between souls and shadows that this term suggests, the Rarámuri of Rejogochi do not identify the shadows of living people in any way with their souls.

5. The mother of one woman in Rejogochi told her that she would not be able to complete her journey in four days because she had traveled so widely during her life. Nonetheless, food offerings were placed for her four days after she died.

6. For descriptions of the death beliefs and practices of other Rarámuri communities, see Lumholtz 1902, I: 380–90; Basauri 1929: 45–47; Bennett and Zingg 1935: 236–51; Plancarte 1954: 55–59; Kennedy 1978: 149–53; and Velasco Rivero 1983: 90–116.

7. While the use of fire in these contexts appears to be indigenous, the appearance of candles and their particular arrangement around the corpse corresponds to practices of local Mestizos.

8. The cemetery in Rejogochi was first consecrated by a Catholic priest in 1978, although people report that the same plot of land had served as a burial ground many years before. Prior to 1978, almost everyone who died in Rejogochi was carried the arduous ten kilometers to Basíhuare to be interred in the cemetery there or, in "ancient" times, under the church floor. The exception are babies who die unbaptized and are sometimes buried in the woods and hills near their homes.

9. Recently people in Rejogochi have begun burying some of their dead in coffins constructed from pine planks cut at the local sawmill. Calistro was buried in such a box, made from boards he had used to build his sleeping platform.

10. Lumholtz (1902, I: 385) reports that the size of the tortillas used in these rituals is determined by the age of the deceased at death: children receive small

tortillas, young people medium-sized one, and adults the ordinary size. In Rejogochi these small tortillas are offered to the dead of all ages.

11. People in Rejogochi do not say that only men can specialize in performing these death rituals, but I never saw a woman in this role.

12. In addition to the application of ashes in both, the *napisó* and Catholic Ash Wednesday rituals are similar because both are staged inside a structure (house or church), people stand in line for the ritual treatment, the ritual is supervised by specialists, and plain water is used instead of agave water, which, because it is employed to protect the living from the dead in other settings, would appear to be more appropriate in this context.

13. Dolores finally remarried in 1984, the marriage being arranged by the special marriage officials called *mayóli*. In the years between San Pedro's death and her remarriage, her supposed liaisons with various men in the area were the subject of much gossip.

14. Most of these drums are discarded by crews working on the main road through this portion of the Sierra Tarahumara. The Rarámuri retrieve them from the roadsides, cut them in half, and then burn away the petroleum residue to convert them into cooking vessels.

15. In another of the *napisó* fiestas I attended, which was sponsored primarily for a woman, several of the women joined the chanter on the patio and around the crosses in a special dance characterized by movements in sinuous lines.

CHAPTER 7. CONCLUSIONS

1. Here I ignore the transmission of knowledge through the mass media, which have enormous impact on the standardization of knowledge.

REFERENCES CITED

Aguirre Beltrán, Gonzalo
  1953   Formas de Gobierno Indígena. Mexico City: Imprenta Universitaria.

Albert, Ethel M.
  1956   The Classification of Values: A Method and Illustration. American
          Anthropologist 58: 221–48.

Alcocer, José Antonio
  1958   Bosquejo de la Historia del Colegio de Nuestra Señora de Guadalupe
          y sus Misiones, Año de 1788. ed. Rafael Cervantes. Mexico City:
          Porrúa.

Aldasoro, V.A.
  1941   La Región Minera de Batopilas. Boletín de Minas y Petróleo [Mexico
          City] 13(3): 19–22.

Almada, Francisco R.
  1955   Resumen de Historia del Estado de Chihuahua. Mexico City: Libros
          Mexicanos.

  1968   Diccionario de Historia, Geografía y Biografía Chihuahuenses. 2d ed.
          Chihuahua: Universidad de Chihuahua, Departamento de
          Investigaciones Sociales, Sección de Historia.

Andonaegui, Roque de
  1744   Letter to Lorenzo Gera, December 5, 1744, Themeychic. trans.
          Marion L. Reynolds. Bolton Papers, Bancroft Library, University of
          California, Berkeley.

Anonymous
  1754   Map associated with "Testimonio a la Letra, de la Entrega de las
          onze Missiones de la Topia, Pianola y Sierra de S. Andrés hecha
          porla Sagrada Religión de la Compañía de Jesús a la Sagrada Mitra

de dha. Cur.d de Durango, Reino de la Nueva Vizcaya, Año de 1754." Archivo General de la Nación, Misiones 13, exp. 1. Mexico City. Map located at folio 22.

Anzures y Bolaños, Carmen
1978   Medicina Tradicional entre los Tarahumares. Medicina Tradicional [Mexico City] 1(4): 39–47.

Arlegui, José
1851   Crónica de la Provincia de N.S.P.S. Francisco de Zacatecas. 2d ed. Mexico City: Cumplido.

Artaud, Antonin
1976   The Peyote Dance. trans. Helen Weaver. New York: Farrar, Straus and Giroux.

Ascher, Robert, and Francis J. Clune, Jr.
1960   Waterfall Cave, Southern Chihuahua, Mexico. American Antiquity 26: 270–74.

Bargas, Gregorio Xavier
1762   Letter to Nicolás de Calatayud, June 13, 1762, San Borja. Archivo General de la Nación, Jesuitas 2–27, n.p. Mexico City.

Basauri, Carlos
1927   Creencias y Prácticas de los Tarahumaras (Beliefs and Practices of the Tarahumaras). Mexican Folkways 3: 218–34.

1929   Monografía de los Tarahumaras. Mexico City: Talleres Gráficos de la Nación.

Benedict, H. Bradley
1972   El Saqueo de las Misiones de Chihuahua, 1767–1777. Historia Mexicana [Mexico City] 22: 24–33.

Benítez, Fernando
1967   Los Indios de México. Vol. I. Mexico City: Ediciones ERA.

Bennett, Wendell C.
1931   Tarahumara texts. Franz Boas Collection of American Indian Linguistics, American Philosophical Society, Philadelphia. [Some of these materials are filed with the Tarahumara notes of Jules Henry, 1940, in the same collection].

Bennett, Wendell C., and Robert M. Zingg
1935   The Tarahumara: An Indian Tribe of Northern Mexico. Chicago: University of Chicago Press.

Berger, Peter L., and Thomas Luckmann
   1966   The Social Construction of Reality: A Treatise in the Sociology of
           Knowledge. Garden City, N.Y.: Doubleday.

Blackburn, Thomas C.
   1975   December's Child: A Book of Chumash Oral Narratives. Berkeley,
           Los Angeles, and London: University of California Press.

Bloch, Maurice
   1975   Political Language and Oratory in Traditional Society. London, New
           York, and San Francisco: Academic Press.

Bloch, Maurice, and Jonathan Parry, eds.
   1982   Death and the Regeneration of Life. Cambridge, London, New
           York, New Rochelle, Melbourne, and Sydney: Cambridge University
           Press.

Boster, James S.
   1986   Exchange of Varieties and Information Between Aguaruna Manioc
           Cultivators. American Anthropologist 88: 428–36.

Boudreau, Eugene
   1975   Move Over, Don Porfirio: Tales from the Sierra Madre. Sebastopol,
           Cal.: Pleasant Hill Press.

   1986   Tarahumara Uprising, 1918. Password 31: 175–83.

Bourdieu, Pierre
   1977   Outline of a Theory of Practice. trans. Richard Nice. Cambridge,
           London, New York, and Melbourne: Cambridge University Press.

   1984   Distinction: A Social Critique of the Judgement of Taste. trans.
           Richard Nice. Cambridge: Harvard University Press.

Bourdieu, Pierre, and Jean-Claude Passeron
   1977   Reproduction in Education, Society and Culture. trans. Richard
           Nice. London and Beverly Hills: Sage Publications.

Bourke, John G.
   1891   On the Border with Crook. New York: Charles Scribner's Sons.

Brambila, David
   [1980]   Diccionario Rarámuri-Castellano (Tarahumar). Mexico City: Buena
           Prensa.

Braun, Bartholomé
   1764   Carta del P. Bartholomé Braun Visitador de la Provincia Tarahumara
           a los PP. Superiores de Esta Provincia de Nueva España Sobre la
           Apostólica Vida, Virtudes, y Santa Muerte del P. Francisco
           Hermano Glandorff. Mexico City: Colegio de San Ildefonso.

Brodie, Walter M.
    1905   Letter to W.V. Safford, May 23, 1905, Chihuahua, Mexico.
            In the Edward Palmer Papers, National Anthropological Archives,
            Department of Anthropology, Smithsonian Institution, Washington,
            D.C.

Brown, Michael F.
    1986   Tsewa's Gift: Magic and Meaning in an Amazonian Society.
            Washington and London: Smithsonian Institution Press.

Burgess, Don
    1970   Anayábari Raʔicháriara Jipe Nerúgame Raʔíchari (Cuentos de Antes
            y Hoy). Mexico City: Instituto Lingüístico de Verano.

    1978   Rabbit Steals Coyote's Bladder (Western Tarahumara). In Coyote
            Stories, ed. William Bright, 178–83. International Journal of
            American Linguistics, Native American Texts Series, Monograph
            No. 1. Chicago: University of Chicago Press.

    1981   Tarahumara Folklore: A Study in Cultural Secrecy. Southwest
            Folklore 5: 11–22.

    1984   Western Tarahumara. In Southern Uto-Aztecan Grammatical
            Sketches, vol. 4 of Studies in Uto-Aztecan Grammar, ed. Ronald W.
            Langacker, 1–149. Summer Institute of Linguistics, Publications in
            Linguistics, No. 56, Vol. 4. Arlington: Summer Institute of
            Linguistics and University of Texas at Arlington.

Burke, Kenneth
    1969   A Grammar of Motives. Berkeley, Los Angeles, and London:
            University of California Press.

Burrus, Ernest J., ed.
    1963   Misiones Norteñas Mexicanas de la Compañía de Jesús, 1751–1757.
            Mexico City: Porrúa.

Burton, Michael, and Lorraine Kirk
    1979   Sex Differences in Maasai Cognition of Personality and Social
            Identity. American Anthropologist 81: 841–73.

Bye, Robert A., Jr.
    1976   The Ethnoecology of the Tarahumara of Chihuahua, Mexico. Ph. D.
            diss., Harvard University.

    1979a   Hallucinogenic Plants of the Tarahumara. Journal of
            Ethnopharmacology 1: 23–48.

    1979b   Incipient Domestication of Mustards in Northwest Mexico. The
            Kiva 44: 237–56.

1985 Medicinal Plants of the Tarahumara Indians of Chihuahua, Mexico. In Two Mummies from Chihuahua, Mexico: A Multidisciplinary Study, eds. Rose A. Tyson and Daniel V. Elerick, 77–104. San Diego Museum Papers, No. 19, San Diego Museum of Man.

Campo, Francisco Javier del
1773 Letter to "Señor Comisionado de Temporalidades," August 20, 1773, Villa de San Phelipe el Real [Chihuahua]. Archivo General de la Nación, Temporalidades 8, 264–65v. Mexico City.

Carr, Barry
1973 Las Peculiaridades del Norte Mexicano, 1880–1927: Ensayo de Interpretación. Historia Mexicana [Mexico City] 22: 320–46.

Carrillo, Francisco Antonio
1773 Letter to Fernando José Manguino, February 5, 1773, Chihuahua. Archivo Histórico de Hacienda 304, exp. 6, n.p. Mexico City.

Champion, Jean R.
1955 Acculturation among the Tarahumara of Northwest Mexico since 1890. Transactions of the New York Academy of Sciences 17: 560–66.

1962 A Study in Culture Persistence: The Tarahumaras of Northwestern Mexico. Ph.D. diss., Columbia University.

Chiba, Tsutomu
1935 A Study of Accent: Research into its Nature and Scope in the Light of Experimental Phonetics. Tokyo: Fuzanbo Publishing Company.

Clune, Dorris
1960 Textiles and Matting from Waterfall Cave, Chihuahua. American Antiquity 26: 274–77.

Comitas, Lambros, and Janet Dolgin
1978 On Anthropology and Education: Retrospect and Prospect. Anthropology & Education Quarterly 9: 165–80.

Contreras, Gaspar de
1638 Letter to Andrés Pérez [de Ribas], August 9, 1638, Santiago Papasquiaro. Archivo General de la Nación, Misiones 25, 284–85v. Mexico City. [English translation in Sheridan and Naylor 1979: 11–13]

Crocker, J. Christopher
1977 The Social Functions of Rhetorical Forms. In The Social Use of Metaphor: Essays on the Anthropology of Rhetoric, eds. J. David Sapir and J. Christopher Crocker, 33–66. Philadelphia: University of Pennsylvania Press.

Croix, Caballero de
  1857   Carta del Caballero de Croix al Exmo. Sr. Virey [sic] de México, 27
          de Septiembre de 1777, Durango. In Documentos para la Historia de
          México, 4th series, vol. 4, 87–91. Mexico City: Imprenta de Vicente
          García Torres.

Crumrine, N. Ross
  1983   Mayo. In Southwest, ed. Alfonso Ortiz, 264–75, vol. 10 of
          Handbook of North American Indians, ed. William C. Sturtevant.
          Washington: Smithsonian Institution.

Deimel, Claus
  1980   Tarahumara: Indianer im Norden Mexikos. Frankfurt, West
          Germany: Syndikat.

  1985   Die Peyoteheilung der Tarahumara. Schreibheft, Zeitschrift für
          Literatur [Essen, West Germany] 25: 155–63.

Diario Oficial
  1930   Resolución en el Expediente de Dotación de Tierras al Pueblo de
          Basihuárachic, Estado de Chihuahua. Mexico City, Diario Oficial de
          la Federación, February 4, 1930: 5–7.

Di Peso, Charles C.
  1979   Prehistory: Southern Periphery. In Southwest, ed. Alfonso Ortiz,
          152–61, vol. 9 of Handbook of North American Indians, ed. William
          C. Sturtevant. Washington: Smithsonian Institution.

Dougherty, Janet W.D., and James W. Fernandez
  1981   Introduction. Special Issue on Symbolism and Cognition. American
          Ethnologist 8: 413–21.

  1982   Afterword. Special Issue on Symbolism and Cognition II. American
          Ethnologist 9: 820–32.

Douglas, Mary
  1975   Implicit Meanings: Essays in Anthropology. London and Boston:
          Routledge & Kegan Paul.

Dunne, Peter M.
  1937   The Expulsion of the Jesuits from New Spain, 1767. Mid-America
          19: 3–30.

  1948   Early Jesuit Missions in Tarahumara. Berkeley and Los Angeles:
          University of California Press.

Durkheim, Emile
  1933   The Division of Labor in Society. New York: Macmillan.

Eickelman, Dale F.
1979   The Political Economy of Meaning. American Ethnologist 6: 386–93.

Escalona, Joseph de
1744   Carta Annua, June 7, 1744, El Santissimo Nombre de María
         [Sisoguichi]. trans. Marion L. Reynolds. Bolton Papers, Bancroft
         Library, University of California, Berkeley.

Escudero, J.A. de
1834   Noticias Estadísticas del Estado de Chihuahua. Mexico City: Juan
         Ojeda.

Esparza Sánchez, Cuauhtémoc
1974   Compendio Histórico del Colegio Apostólico de Propaganda Fide de
         Nuestra Señora de Guadalupe de Zacatecas. Serie Historia, No. 1,
         Departamento de Investigaciones Históricas de la Universidad
         Autónoma de Zacatecas.

Estrada, Ignacio Xavier de
1730   Letter to Juan Antonio de Oviedo, November 23, 1730, Themeichi.
         Archivo Histórico de Hacienda 278, exp. 7, n.p. Mexico City.
         [English translation in Sheridan and Naylor 1979: 73–78]

Fernández de Cordova, Juan
1704   Letter to Don Gregorio Alvarez Tuñón y Quirez, November 18,
         1704, Parral. Biblioteca Nacional de México, Archivo Franciscano
         12/200 bis, 100–101v. Mexico City.

Florescano, Enrique, and Isabel Gil Sánchez
1976   La Época de las Reformas Borbónicas y el Crecimiento Económico,
         1750–1808. In Historia General de México, vol. 1, 471–589. Mexico
         City: Colegio de México.

Fónagy, I., and K. Magdics
1960   Speed of Utterance in Phrases of Different Lengths. Language and
         Speech 3: 179–92.

Font, Juan
1611   Carta Annua. Archivo General de la Nación, Jesuitas 3–29, n.p.
         Mexico City.

Fried, Jacob
1969   The Tarahumara. In Ethnology, pt. 2, ed. Evon Z. Vogt, 846–70,
         vol. 8 of Handbook of Middle American Indians, ed. Robert
         Wauchope. Austin: University of Texas Press.

1977   Two Orders of Authority and Power in Tarahumara Society. In The
        Anthropology of Power: Ethnographic Studies from Asia, Oceania,
        and the New World, eds. Raymond D. Fogelson and Richard N.
        Adams, 263–69. New York, San Francisco, and London: Academic
        Press.

García Manzanedo, Héctor
    1963   Notas sobre la Medicina Tradicional en una Zona de la Sierra
            Tarahumara. América Indígena 23: 61–70.

Gerhard, Peter
    1982   The North Frontier of New Spain. Princeton: Princeton University
            Press.

Giddens, Anthony
    1976   New Rules of Sociological Method: A Positive Critique of
            Interpretative Sociologies. London: Hutchinson.

    1979   Central Problems in Social Theory: Action, Structure and
            Contradiction in Social Analysis. Berkeley and Los Angeles:
            University of California Press.

    1984   The Constitution of Society: Outline of the Theory of Structuration.
            Berkeley and Los Angeles: University of California Press.

González Rodríguez, Luis
    1982   Tarahumara: La Sierra y el Hombre. Mexico City: Fondo de Cultura
            Económica.

Goodenough, Ward
    1963   Cooperation in Change: An Anthropological Approach to Community
            Development. New York: Russell Sage Foundation.

Green, Judith S.
    1971   Archeological Chihuahuan Textiles and Modern Tarahumara
            Weaving. Ethnos 36: 115–30.

Guadalajara, Tomás de, and José Tardá
    1857   Letter to Jesuit Provincial Francisco Jiménez, February 2, 1676, San
            Joaquín y Santa Ana. In Documentos para la Historia de México,
            4th series, vol. 3, 272–94. Mexico City: Imprenta de Vicente García
            Torres.

Hallowell, A. Irving
    1955   Culture and Experience. Philadelphia: University of Pennsylvania
            Press.

Hansen, Judith F.
    1979   Sociocultural Perspectives on Human Learning: An Introduction to
            Educational Anthropology. Englewood Cliffs, N.J.: Prentice-Hall.

Harris, Marvin
1968   The Rise of Anthropological Theory: A History of Theories of
         Culture. New York: Thomas Y. Crowell.

Hayman, Ronald
1977   Artaud and After. Oxford, London, and New York: Oxford
         University Press.

Hefner, Robert W.
1983   Ritual and Cultural Reproduction in Non-Islamic Java. American
         Ethnologist 10: 665–83.

1985   Hindu Javanese: Tengger Tradition and Islam. Princeton: Princeton
         University Press.

Hertz, Robert
1960   Death and The Right Hand. trans. Rodney and Claudia Needham.
         Glencoe, Ill.: Free Press.

Hilton, K. Simon
1969   Relatos Tarahumaras. Tlalocan [Mexico City] 6: 76–88.

Honigmann, John J.
1967   Personality in Culture. New York, Evanston, and London: Harper &
         Row.

Hountondji, Paulin J.
1983   African Philosophy: Myth and Reality. Bloomington: Indiana
         University Press.

Huntington, Richard, and Peter Metcalf
1979   Celebrations of Death: The Anthropology of Mortuary Ritual.
         Cambridge, London, New York, and Melbourne: Cambridge
         University Press.

Irigoyen Rascón, Fructuoso, and Jesús Manuel Palma Batista
1985   Rarajípari: The Kick-ball Race of the Tarahumara Indians. Annals of
         Sports Medicine 2: 79–94.

Jackson, Michael
1983   Knowledge of the Body. Man 18: 327–45.

Karp, Ivan
1986   Agency and Social Theory: A Review of Anthony Giddens. American
         Ethnologist 13: 131–37.

Karp, Ivan, and Kent Maynard
1983   Reading *The Nuer*. Current Anthropology 24: 481–503.

Kennedy, John G.
1963   Tesguino Complex: The Role of Beer in Tarahumara Culture.
        American Anthropologist 65. 620–40.

1969   La Carrera de Bola Tarahumara y su Significación. América Indígena
        29: 17–42.

1970a   Inápuchi: Una Comunidad Tarahumara Gentil. Mexico City:
        Instituto Indigenista Interamericano.

1970b   Bonds of Laughter among the Tarahumara Indians: Toward a
        Rethinking of Joking Relationship Theory. In The Social
        Anthropology of Latin America: Essays in Honor of Ralph Leon
        Beals, eds. Walter Goldschmidt and Harry Hoijer, 36–68. Los
        Angeles: University of California, Latin American Center.

1978   Tarahumara of the Sierra Madre: Beer, Ecology, and Social
        Organization. Arlington Heights, Ill.: AHM Publishing Corporation.

Kenny, Michael
1985   Review of African Philosophy: Myth and Reality, by Paulin J.
        Hountondji. American Anthropologist 87: 421–22.

Kluckhohn, Clyde, and Dorothea Leighton
1946   The Navaho. Cambridge: Harvard University Press.

Lartigue, François
1983   Indios y Bosques: Políticas Forestales y Comunales en la Sierra
        Tarahumara. Ediciones de la Casa Chata, No. 19. Mexico City:
        Centro de Investigaciones y Estudios Superiores en Antropología
        Social.

Lévi-Strauss, Claude
1972   Tristes Tropiques. trans. John Russell. New York: Atheneum.

Lionnet, Andrés
1972   Los Elementos de la Lengua Tarahumara. Mexico City: Universidad
        Nacional Autónoma de México.

Lister, Florence C., and Robert H. Lister
1966   Chihuahua: Storehouse of Storms. Albuquerque: University of New
        Mexico Press.

Lizassoain, Ignacio
1763   Informe del Padre Lizasoain [sic] Sobre las Provincias de Sonora y
        Nueva Vizcaya. Biblioteca Nacional de México, Archivo Franciscano
        15/280, 1–30v. Mexico City.

López Batista, Ramón
1980   Qui?yá Irétaca Nahuisárami (Relatos de los Tarahumaras). Mexico
        City: Instituto Nacional Indigenista.

Lumholtz, Carl
  1894   Tarahumari Dances and Plant-Worship. Scribner's Magazine 16:
          438–56.

  1902   Unknown Mexico. 2 vols. New York: Charles Scribner's Sons.

Mares Trías, Albino
  1975   Jena Ra?icha Ralámuli Alué ?Ya Muchígame Chiquime Níliga (Aquí
          Relata la Gente De Antes lo Que Pasaba en su Tiempo). Mexico
          City: Instituto Lingüístico de Verano.

  1982   Ralámuli Nu?tugala Go?ame (Comida de los Tarahumaras).
          Chihuahua, Mexico: Don Burgess McGuire.

Merrill, William
  1978   Thinking and Drinking: A Rarámuri Interpretation. In The Nature
          and Status of Ethnobotany, ed. Richard I. Ford, 101–17.
          Anthropological Papers, No. 67, Museum of Anthropology,
          University of Michigan, Ann Arbor.

  1981   The Concept of Soul Among the Rarámuri of Chihuahua, Mexico: A
          Study in World View. Ph.D. diss., University of Michigan, Ann
          Arbor.

  1983   Tarahumara Social Organization, Political Organization, and
          Religion. In Southwest, ed. Alfonso Ortiz, 290–305, vol. 10 of
          Handbook of North American Indians, ed. William C. Sturtevant.
          Washington: Smithsonian Institution.

  1987   The Rarámuri Stereotype of Dreams. In Dreaming: Anthropological
          and Psychological Interpretations, ed. Barbara Tedlock, 194–219.
          Cambridge: Cambridge University Press.

Miller, Wick
  1983   Uto-Aztecan Languages. In Southwest, ed. Alfonso Ortiz, 113–24,
          vol. 10 of Handbook of North American Indians, ed. William C.
          Sturtevant. Washington: Smithsonian Institution.

Ministro de Fomento
  1890   Carta General de la República Mexicana. Archivo General de la
          Nación, Archivo Rul, Illustration No. 5206. Mexico City.

Minnis, Paul
  1984   Peeking Under the Tortilla Curtain: Regional Interaction and
          Integration on the Northeastern Periphery of Casas Grandes.
          American Archeology 4: 181–93.

Miqueo, José María
  1745   Letter to Christóbal de Escobar, March 7, 1745, Yoquibo. Archivo
          General de la Nación, Jesuitas 1–16, 19–24v. Mexico City.

Mirafuentes Galván, José Luis
1975   Movimientos de Resistencia y Rebeliones Indígenas en el Norte de
        México (1600 1821). Colección Documental, No. 3. Mexico City:
        Archivo General de la Nación and Archivo Histórico de Hacienda.

Murray, David W.
1977   Ritual Communication: Some Considerations Regarding Meaning in
        Navajo Ceremonials. In Symbolic Anthropology: A Reader in the
        Study of Symbols and Meanings, eds. Janet L. Dolgin, David S.
        Kemnitzer, and David M. Schneider, 195–220. New York:
        Columbia University Press.

Nava, Pedro de
1794   Letter to Juan Ysidro Campos, February 7, 1794, Chihuahua.
        Archivo General de la Nación, Temporalidades 50, 27–28v. Mexico
        City.

Navarro García, Luis
1965   Las Provincias Internas en el Siglo XIX. Sevilla: Escuela de Estudios
        Hispano-Americanos.

Neumann, Joseph
1682   Letter to an unknown Father in the Province of Bohemia, February
        20, 1682, Sisoguichi. In Letters of Father Joseph Neumann S.J.,
        Missionary to the Heathen Tarahumaras; Together with his 'Historia
        Seditionum'. Collected by Herbert E. Bolton; Translated by M.L.
        Reynolds; Edited and with an introduction by Allan Christelow.
        Berkeley, 1936. Unpublished manuscript in the Bolton Papers,
        Bancroft Library, University of California, Berkeley.

1969   Révoltes des Indiens Tarahumars (1626–1724). trans. and ed. Luis
        González R. Paris: Institut de Hautes Études de l'Amérique Latine
        de l'Université de Paris.

Ocampo, Manuel
1966   Historia de la Misión de la Tarahumara (1900–1965). 2d ed. Mexico
        City: Editorial Jus.

O'Neale, Lila M.
1948   Textiles of Pre-Columbian Chihuahua. Contributions to American
        Anthropology and History, No. 45, Publication No. 574, Carnegie
        Institution of Washington, Washington, D.C.

Ortiz Zapata, Juan
1857   Relación de las Misiones . . . 1678. In Documentos para la Historia
        de México, 4th series, vol. 3, 301–419. Mexico City: Imprenta de
        Vicente García Torres.

Ortner, Sherry B.
1984   Theory in Anthropology since the Sixties. Comparative Studies in
          Society and History 26: 126–66.

Paine, Robert, ed.
1981   Politically Speaking: Cross-Cultural Studies of Rhetoric.
          Philadelphia: Institute for the Study of Human Issues.

Palma, Erasmo, and Fructuoso Irigoyen R.
1977   Cha Okó! (¡Me Duele Mucho!): Manual de Propedeútica en
          Rarámuri, Rarámuri Nayúame Tibúma. Mexico City: Buena Prensa.

Parrilla, Luis
1794   Letter to Conde de Revilla Gigedo, April 10, 1794, Mexico City.
          Archivo General de la Nación, Provincias Internas 15, exp. 4, 4–4v.
          Mexico City.

Pascual, Joseph
1651   Carta Annua, Misión de San Felipe y sus Visitas. Archivo General de
          la Nación, Jesuitas 3–15, exp. 2, n.p. Mexico City. [English
          translation in Sheridan and Naylor 1979: 17–30].

Passin, Herbert
1942   Sorcery as a Phase of Tarahumara Economic Relations. Man 42: 11–
          15.

1943   The Place of Kinship in Tarahumara Social Organization. Acta
          Americana 34: 360–83, 471–95.

Pastron, Allen G.
1977   Aspects of Witchcraft and Shamanism in a Tarahumara Indian
          Community of Northern Mexico. Ph.D. diss., University of
          California, Berkeley.

Peirce, Charles S.
1960   Collected Papers of Charles Sanders Peirce, vol. 2, Elements of
          Logic. eds. Charles Hartshorne and Paul Weiss. Cambridge: Harvard
          University Press.

Pennington, Campbell W.
1963   The Tarahumar of Mexico: Their Environment and Material
          Culture. Salt Lake City: University of Utah Press.

1983   Tarahumara. In Southwest, ed. Alfonso Ortiz, 276–89, vol. 10 of
          Handbook of North American Indians, ed. William C. Sturtevant.
          Washington: Smithsonian Institution.

224 RARÁMURI SOULS

Piñán, Manuel
1900 Ligeras Nociones de la Misión Tarahumara [unpublished reports and letters]. Archivo Histórico de la Provincia de México [Jesuit Provincial Archives]. Mexico City.

Plancarte, Francisco
1954 El Problema Indígena Tarahumara. Memorias del Instituto Nacional Indigenista, Vol. 5. Mexico City.

Pollnac, Richard B.
1975 Intra-Cultural Variability in the Structure of the Subjective Color Lexicon in Buganda. American Ethnologist 2: 89–109.

Porras Muñoz, Guillermo
1980 Iglesia y Estado en Nueva Vizcaya (1562–1821). Mexico City: Universidad Nacional Autónoma de México.

Provincia de Zacatecas
1854 Tabla Capitular [list of personnel affiliated with the Franciscan Provincia de Zacatecas in 1854]. Museo Nacional de Antropología e Historia, Fondo Franciscano 182, 204–208v. Mexico City.

Queipo de Llanos, Pedro Antonio
1773 Letter to Antonio Bucareli y Ursúa, March 30, 1773, Chihuahua. Archivo General de la Nación, Provincias Internas 42, exp. 3, 398–408v. Mexico City.

Quine, W.V., and J.S. Ullian
1978 The Web of Belief. 2d ed. New York: Random House.

Radin, Paul
1927 Primitive Man as Philosopher. New York and London: D. Appleton.

Ramírez, Santiago
1884 Noticia Histórica de la Riqueza Minera de México. Mexico City: Secretaría de Fomento.

Rappaport, Roy A.
1979 Ecology, Meaning, and Religion. Richmond, Cal.: North Atlantic Books.

Ratkay, Juan María
1683 An Account of the Tarahumara Missions, Carichic, March 20, 1683. trans. Marion L. Reynolds. Bolton Papers, Bancroft Library, University of California, Berkeley.

Revilla Gigedo, Conde de
 1966   Informe sobre las Misiones—1793—e Instrucción Reservada al
         Marqués de Branciforte—1794—. ed. José Bravo Ugarte. Mexico
         City: Editorial Jus.

Robertson, Carol E.
 1979   "Pulling the Ancestors": Performance Practice and Praxis in
         Mapuche Ordering. Ethnomusicology 23: 395–416.

Rubio Mañé, J. Ignacio
 1959   El Teniente Coronel Don Hugo O'Conor y la Situación en
         Chihuahua, Año de 1771. Boletín del Archivo General de la Nación
         [Mexico City] 30: 353–91.

Sahlins, Marshall
 1981   Historical Metaphors and Mythical Realities: Structure in the Early
         History of the Sandwich Islands Kingdom. Ann Arbor: University of
         Michigan Press.

Salmón, Roberto Mario
 1977   Tarahumara Resistance to Mission Congregation in Northern New
         Spain, 1580–1710. Ethnohistory 24: 379–93.

San Vicente, Juan de
 1773   Letter to Antonio Bucareli y Ursúa, March 30, 1773, Chihuahua.
         Archivo General de la Nación, Provincias Internas 41, 379–379v,
         381. Mexico City.

Sapir, J. David
 1977   The Anatomy of Metaphor. In The Social Use of Metaphor: Essays
         on the Anthropology of Rhetoric, eds. J. David Sapir and J.
         Christopher Crocker, 3–32. Philadelphia: University of Pennsylvania
         Press.

Sapir, J. David, and J. Christopher Crocker, eds.
 1977   The Social Use of Metaphor: Essays on the Anthropology of
         Rhetoric. Philadelphia: University of Pennsylvania Press.

Schalkwijk, Bob, Luis González Rodríguez, and Don Burgess
 1985   Tarahumara. Mexico City: Chrysler de México.

Schmidt, Robert H., Jr.
 1973   A Geographical Survey of Chihuahua. Southwestern Studies,
         Monograph No. 37, University of Texas at El Paso. El Paso: Texas
         Western Press.

Schneider, Luis M.
1984   Artaud y México. In Antonin Artaud, Mexico y Viaje al País de los
        Tarahumaras, ed. Luis M. Schneider, 7–97. Mexico City: Fondo de
        Cultura Económica.

Secretaría de Educación Pública
1983   Resumen Censal de Basíhuare, 1982–1983. Secretaría de Educación
        Pública, Dirección General de Educación Indígena, Subdirección de
        Educación Básica Bilingüe, Departamento de Supervisión.
        [Photocopy in author's possession].

Secretaría de Programación y Presupuesto
1982–84 X Censo General de Población y Vivenda, 1980. Mexico City:
         Secretaría de Programación y Presupuesto.

1983   X Censo General de Población y Vivienda, 1980, Estado de
        Chihuahua. Mexico City: Secretaría de Programación y Presupuesto,
        Instituto Nacional de Estadística, Geografía e Informática.

Shepherd, Grant
1938   The Silver Magnet: Fifty Years in a Mexican Silver Mine. New
        York: E.P. Dutton.

1966   Batopilas (Entraña de Plata). trans. Concepción Montilla de Camú.
        Ciudad Juárez, Chih.: Impresora Tipográfica.

Sheridan, Thomas E., and Thomas H. Naylor, eds.
1979   Rarámuri: A Tarahumara Colonial Chronicle, 1607–1791. Flagstaff,
        Ariz.: Northland Press.

Silva Herzog, Jesús, ed.
1984   De la Historia de México 1810–1938: Documentos Fundamentales,
        Ensayos y Opiniones. 2d ed. Mexico City: Siglo Veintiuno.

Sperber, Dan
1975   Rethinking Symbolism. trans. Alice L. Morton. Cambridge,
        London, New York, and Melbourne: Cambridge University Press.

1982   Apparently Irrational Beliefs. In Rationality and Relativism, eds.
        Martin Hollis and Steven Lukes, 149–80. Cambridge: MIT Press.

Spicer, Edward H.
1961   Types of Contact and Processes of Change. In Perspectives in
        American Indian Culture Change, ed. Edward H. Spicer, 517–44.
        Chicago: University of Chicago Press.

1962   Cycles of Conquest: The Impact of Spain, Mexico, and the United
        States on the Indians of the Southwest, 1533–1960. Tucson:
        University of Arizona Press.

1980   The Yaquis: A Cultural History. Tucson: University of Arizona
        Press.

Tamarón y Romeral, Pedro
    1937   Demonstración del Vastísimo Obispado de la Nueva Vizcaya—1765:
            Durango, Sinaloa, Sonora, Arizona, Nuevo México, Chihuahua, y
            Porciones de Texas, Coahuila y Zacatecas. ed. Vito Alessio Robles.
            Mexico City: Porrúa.

Tardá, Joseph
    1674   Untitled [history of the Tarahumara mission system from its
            founding to 1674], San Joaquín y Santa Ana, February 24, 1674.
            Archivo General de la Nación, Jesuitas 3–29, n.p. Mexico City.

Tardá, Joseph, and Tomás de Guadalaxara
    1676   Letter to Francisco Ximénez, August 15, 1676, n.p. Archivum
            Romanum Societatis Iesu, Mexicana 17, 355–392. Rome.

Tellechea, Miguel
    1826   Compendio Gramatical para la Inteligencia del Idioma Tarahumar.
            Mexico City: Imprenta de la Federación en Palacio.

Thord-Gray, Ivan
    1955   Tarahumara-English, English-Tarahumara Dictionary and an
            Introduction to Tarahumara Grammar. Coral Gables, Fla.:
            University of Miami Press.

    1960   Gringo Rebel (Mexico 1913–1914). Coral Gables, Fla.: University of
            Miami Press.

Tristán, Estevan Lorenzo de
    1791   Letter to "Guardián del Colegio App.co de Guadalupe de
            Zacatecas," February 8, 1791, Durango. Biblioteca Nacional de
            México, Archivo Franciscano 17/368, 5v–7. Mexico City.

Turner, Victor
    1967   The Forest of Symbols: Aspects of Ndembu Ritual. Ithaca and
            London: Cornell University Press.

    1973   Symbols in African Ritual. Science 179: 1100–05.

Ugarte y Loyola, Jacobo de
    1788   Letter to Manuel Antonio Flores, June 30, 1788, Mexico City.
            Archivo General de la Nación, Provincias Internas 168, 82–82v.
            Mexico City.

Velasco Rivero, Pedro de
    1983   Danzar o Morir: Religión y Resistencia a la Dominación en la
            Cultura Tarahumar. Mexico City: Centro de Reflexión Teológica.

228   RARÁMURI SOULS

Vicariato Apostólico de Tarahumara
    1980   Planeación 1980. Sisoguichi, Chihuahua.

Wasserman, Mark
    1973   Oligarquía e Intereses Extranjeros en Chihuahua Durante el
            Porfiriato. Historia Mexicana [Mexico City] 22: 279–319.

Weiner, Annette B.
    1976   Women of Value, Men of Renown: New Perspectives in Trobriand
            Exchange. Austin and London: University of Texas Press.

Werner, Oswald
    1970   Cultural Knowledge, Language, and World View. In Cognition: A
            Multiple View, ed. Paul L. Garvin, 155–75. New York and
            Washington: Spartan Books.

West, Robert C.
    1949   The Mining Community in Northern New Spain: The Parral Mining
            District. Ibero-Americana 30. Berkeley and Los Angeles: University
            of California Press.

Williams, Raymond
    1977   Marxism and Literature. Oxford and New York: Oxford University
            Press.

Witherspoon, Gary
    1977   Language and Art in the Navajo Universe. Ann Arbor: University of
            Michigan Press.

Woodburn, James
    1982   Social Dimensions of Death in Four African Hunting and Gathering
            Societies. In Death and the Regeneration of Life, eds. Maurice Bloch
            and Jonathan Parry, 187–210. Cambridge, London, New York, New
            Rochelle, Melbourne, and Sydney: Cambridge University Press.

Zingg, Robert M.
    1937   The Philistine Spirit of Tarahumara Culture. University of Kansas
            City, The University Review 4: 12–16.

    1940   Report on Archaeology of Southern Chihuahua. University of
            Denver Contributions, No. 3, Center of Latin American Studies,
            No. 1.

    1942   The Genuine and Spurious Values in Tarahumara Culture. American
            Anthropologist 44: 78–92.

INDEX

Advice, 110, 184; giving and receiving, 63, 99–100
Afterlife, 178, 182, 189; aspects of, 112–14, 119, 155–60, 187–88
Agave water: ceremonial use of, 125, 138–39, 143–44, 149; use in death rituals, 163–64, 169–70, 174, 179
Age: and behavior of souls, 97–98; and strength of souls, 96–97
Agriculture, 18, 19, 20, 34, 38, 40, 44, 51, 72; during colonial period, 32–33, 35; at contact, 30–31; in mission system, 32–33; subsistence, 41, 42. *See also* Crops; Maize
Alakánte (mayor), 24, 64
Alawási (sheriffs), 24, 25
Animals, 113, 114, 154, 162; souls in, 90–91, 92; transformation into, 98–99, 158–59. *See also* Livestock
Apaches, 35, 38–39
Apostates, 48–49
Archaeology, 31
Army: Mexican, 38–39
Artaud, Antonin, 1–2
Ashes: in death ritual, 173, 174, 179, 180–81
Ash Wednesday, 174–75
Assimilation, 2, 34, 41, 47
Authority, 88–89, 153

Bakánawi, 130, 138, 141; ceremonies for, 123, 124–27; threats by, 75, 92, 121–22, 131, 135–36
Baptism, 3, 77
Basauri, Charles, 3
Basíhuare, 24–26, 34, 64; access to, 28–30, 39–40; Catholic church in, 37, 38, 43, 50–51; culture change in, 49–50; employment in, 41–42; school in, 51–52
Batopilas, 39, 40, 41
Batopilas Mining Company, 39
Bautizados, 3
Beer, 23, 24, 100, 138; in curing ceremonies, 124, 125, 143–44, 145, 149, 184; in death ritual, 168, 169–70, 173–74, 177–78, 180; souls' reaction to, 106, 108–109. *See also* Drinking parties; Inebriation
Behavior, 73; advice and thought in, 63, 98–99, 100; and attitude toward life, 70–71, 67–68; and attitude toward work, 98–99; while drunk, 109, 110–11, 119; inappropriate, 100–102, 110; role of souls in, 97–98
Bennett, Wendell, 2, 90, 102, 135, 162, 167
Bourdieu, Pierre, 12, 147; on structure and human agency, 54–55

Bourke, John, 38
Breath, 95, 106; and souls, 87, 90, 91, 96, 144–45, 150
Burgess, Don, 4
Burial rituals, 162, 166; offerings in, 164–65; responsibility for, 163–64. *See also* Death rituals

Captains. *See Kapitáne*
Catholic church, 37, 43. *See also* Catholicism; Franciscans; Jesuits; Mission system; Religion
Catholicism, 24, 30; concept of soul in, 46–47; conversion to, 3, 43, 46; in cosmology, 79–84; exposure to, 47, 48, 49; impact of, 2, 38, 46–47, 50–51, 80, 174–75; spread of, 47, 48
Cattle, 19, 44; use of in rituals, 126, 127
Ceremonies, 61, 79, 81, 82, 169; *bakánawi*, 123, 124–27; peyote, 123, 159. *See also* Burial rituals; Curing rituals; Death rituals; Fiestas; Rituals
Chabochis, 94, 129, 132, 133, 141; afterlife of, 113, 114, 156; defining groups of, 77–78
Chapió, 26, 29(fig.)
Chihuahua, 38, 39
Chinatú, 38
Chínipa, 31
Chiricahuas. *See* Apaches
Choguita, 132
Christianity. *See* Catholicism
Cimarrones. See Gentiles
Colegio Apostólico, 36–37
Colonial period, 30; labor force during, 33–34; mission system during, 32–33, 36; Rarámuri raids during, 35–36; settlement during, 31–32
Communication: with the dead, 164, 168–69, 176. *See also* Knowledge, transmission of; Sermons; Speeches
Community officials. *See* Public officials

Concho, 31
Corn. *See* Maize
Cosmology, 3, 4, 60, 61, 87, 164, 187; Catholic influences on, 46, 79–84; concepts of, 1–2, 14, 113, 119; and good thought, 63–64; in speeches, 65–66, 71–79, 80, 81. *See also* Deities; World view
Creation, 93–94
Creel, 28, 29, 40, 43
Crime: punishment for, 157–58
Crocker, J. Christopher, 82
Crops: ceremonies for, 183–86. *See also* Agriculture; Maize
Crosses, 163; in death ritual, 168–69, 170, 175–76, 177–79, 181, 188–89; ritual use of, 125, 126, 137–38, 141, 143–44, 164. *See also* Crucifixes
Crucifixes, 143–44, 149, 164. *See also* Crosses
Cultivation. *See* Agriculture
Cultural reproduction: and human action, 55–56; to individual, 53–54. *See also* Knowledge, reproduction of
Cultural transmission. *See* Cultural reproduction
Culture, 12, 50, 118; educational influence on, 51–52. *See also* Cultural reproduction; Culture change
Culture change, 47, 49–50, 51; selective integration in, 48–49, 52
Curers. *See* Doctors
Curing rituals, 61, 123, 141; *bakánawi*, 123, 124–26; components of 142–45; for crops and livestock, 183–86; nonverbal communication in, 149–50; to prevent illness, 138–40
Cusárare, 36, 37, 38

Dancers. *See* Matachines
Datura. *See Rikúhuri*
Death, 14, 87, 119, 187; attitudes toward, 160–62; causes of, 111, 189; defining, 88, 92–93, 112, 155; origin of, 154; and society, 153–54. *See*

Wool, 44
Work, 19(fig.), 27, 100; attitudes toward, 98–99; types of, 20–22
World view, 6–7, 8, 10, 13–14, 71–73,
85; approach to life and, 95–96; of
the dead, 155–56; diversity in, 12,
119–20. *See also* Cosmology

Yaqui, 31, 34, 40

Zacatecas, Provincia de, 37
Zingg, Robert, 2–3, 31, 90, 102, 135,
162, 167, 182